UNIQUE BUT NOT DIFFERENT

UNIQUE BUT NOT DIFFERENT

LATTER-DAY SAINTS IN JAPAN

Shinji Takagi, Conan P. Grames,
and Meagan R. Rainock

日本の末日聖徒を理解する

日本語要旨付

GREG KOFFORD BOOKS
SALT LAKE CITY, 2023

ISBN: 978-1-58958-791-5
Also available in ebook.

Greg Kofford Books
P.O. Box 1362
Draper, UT 84020
www.gregkofford.com
facebook.com/gkbooks
twitter.com/gkbooks

Library of Congress Control Number: 2023952730

Contents

Tables

Figures

PREFACE

Unique But Not Different seeks to elucidate how Japanese Latter-day Saints practice their faith as members of a minority religion in a country of 126 million people—a country where Christians constitute less than 2 percent of the population—and to identify the challenges and opportunities that current and prospective members will face in a society undergoing profound demographic, cultural, and other societal changes. While this work is specifically about Japan, the findings are widely applicable to any society in which Latter-day Saints must make personal acculturations as they adopt a new religious identity. We provide a general analytical tool for approaching minority religious practices. By applying a social-scientific perspective, we aim to advance our understanding of how members of The Church of Jesus Christ Latter-day Saints outside the United States, and especially in a non-Christian country, come to embrace Latter-day Saint identity and manage their conflicts with the host society.

According to the information provided to the authors, The Church of Jesus Christ of Latter-day Saints, at the end of 2022, maintained three temples,[1] six missions, twenty-two stakes and eleven districts, and 230 congregations (143 wards and 87 branches) in Japan. The latest reported membership of 129,912 constitutes less than 0.1 percent of the population, but it makes the Church one of the largest Christian denominations in Japan. While most major Christian denominations have experienced declines in membership, The Church of Jesus Christ of Latter-day Saints has registered a continuous, albeit modest, growth in recent years. Even so, the Church, too, faces the challenges of rising religious apathy in the country and an adverse demographic trend (Japan's population peaked in 2008 and has since been declining), as the membership growth has decelerated. The activity rate (the proportion of regular church attendees in total membership) remains low, perhaps in the neighborhood of an estimated 20 percent. This is the context that situates this study.

Yet, this work does not directly address the question of why the Church, much less Christianity, appeals to such a small segment of

---

1. A fourth temple, in Okinawa, was dedicated in 2023.

Japanese society. Nor do we address, at least directly, the question of why some converts find it difficult to remain active in the Church. Rather, we take an indirect approach to tackling these and other questions. Instead of focusing on investigators who choose not to convert, or on members who choose to drop out of activity, we place the focus of this study on active practitioners of the Latter-day Saint faith. By understanding how they successfully navigate the conflicting demands of church membership, we hope to understand—paradoxically—why others may find it difficult to do so.

This book grew out of the work we prepared for a volume of essays edited by Melissa Inouye and Laurie Maffly-Kipp, who had asked us to write a chapter on how Japanese Latter-day Saints practice their religion. In order to conduct an objective, data-driven analysis, we decided to administer an anonymous survey to practicing Latter-day Saints. As we were preparing the survey, it became obvious that doing justice to the data would require not a chapter but a book. We also recognized that, realistically, we had only one chance to administer a survey, given its time- and labor-intensive nature. Hence our decision to make the survey much more comprehensive than was necessary to complete our assigned task, even though this carried a risk of deterring potential survey takers. This book is an outcome of that decision.

The survey data were collected from October 22 through November 16, 2021, by Meagan Rainock. A link to the survey was sent electronically to about 300 individuals with known email addresses, with a request to forward it to additional people by email or through social media. In addition, the link was posted on several Facebook groups consisting primarily of active Latter-day Saints in Japan. Contrary to our expectations that few would start, much less complete, a survey of fifty-six questions, we were pleasantly surprised to receive between 440 and 530 responses, depending on the question. As is expected from the way the survey was administered, the sample consists almost entirely of religiously active Latter-day Saints.[2] Although the survey does not fully meet the standard of random sampling, these are precisely the type of individuals we had

---

2. We define activity status strictly in terms of church attendance throughout this work. Those who reported never attending church constituted only 1.6 percent (or eight individuals) of the 498 respondents who reported their church attendance. Because even these individuals responded to the survey as introduced by their church friends, and they identified as Latter-day Saints in the survey, we maintain that they, too, are "active" Latter-day Saints in an identity-theoretic sense.

aimed to reach. If there is any bias in the sample, it is toward those with active social networks within Japan's Latter-day Saint community. There is no reason not to believe that they accurately represent the population of church members one might expect to meet when attending Latter-day Saint services in Japan.

The title *Unique But Not Different* is meant to capture the sense of what we discovered. Religiously active Latter-day Saints in Japan represent a wide spectrum of Japanese society in terms of political and social views. The overwhelming majority of them have fully embraced the LDS identity and have prioritized this identity in the organization of their lives. The incidence of identity conflict occurs only rarely even in the workplace. By establishing long-term relationships and making conflict-avoiding career choices, Latter-day Saints have found a niche for their particular lifestyle. The survey thus provides prima facie evidence that it is possible to be both a Latter-day Saint and Japanese. Culture, while expecting a certain behavioral pattern from individuals, allows choice and variation. Japanese society is sufficiently tolerant of a range of behavior, allowing Latter-day Saints to be unique in their beliefs and practices but not different from other Japanese people in terms of how they relate to many aspects of Japanese culture.

We hope that this study offers something to each of several groups of stakeholders of the Church. Scholars may find in it a contribution to the literature on the growth of Christianity in a non-Christian culture. Latter-day Saint missionaries may find this work helpful in enhancing their understanding of the cultural background of the members and friends they meet. Latter-day Saint leaders may find particularly useful the statistical profiles of Japanese Latter-day Saints, including why they joined the Church, what they think, and how they practice their beliefs. Japanese Latter-day Saints, for the first time, will discover the political and ideological inclinations of their fellow Saints. These are just a few examples of possible takeaways from the study. The concluding chapter summarizes what different stakeholders may learn from the survey findings. The reader may want to start with the concluding chapter before embarking on the main body of the book.

This work could not have been completed without the help of many. While they are too numerous to mention all by name, we express special thanks to the following friends for helping to disseminate the survey in Japan (in alphabetical order): Akira Amano, Ryuichi Inoue, Yuji Mizuno, Takanori Mochizuki, Kanji Moriya, Haruyoshi Nakamura, Jiro Numano,

Akiko Orito, Hiromi Sakata, Akiko Takaiwa, Koji Tanaka, Takashi Yamada, and Ayumi Watakabe. We also gratefully acknowledge the feedback on preliminary survey findings we received in a virtual focus group meeting organized by Ryuichi Inoue, as well as the helpful responses to our inquiries from Takuji Nagano and Osamu Sekiguchi. Last but not least, we thank Jana Riess and Benjamin Knoll for giving us access to subsample data from the Next Mormons Survey.

Our survey was coded and executed under the responsibility of Rainock, who maintains exclusive access to the raw data. We felt that, given Takagi's and Grames's existing social networks in Japan, this arrangement would give an extra layer of assurance to the protection of anonymity already embodied in the survey. This work is based on the de-identified summary Rainock has provided. Takagi was principally responsible for drafting chapters 1–2 and 4–6, while Grames drafted chapter 3. The chapters subsequently went through several iterations so that everyone's views were fully reflected. We assume collective responsibility for the content of the survey, the views, opinions, and interpretations expressed, and any errors that may remain.

The book is organized as follows. Chapter 1 explains the context for the Church in Japan, the theoretical approach that we take, and the demographic and other characteristics of survey respondents. Chapter 2 describes the personal and social profiles of Latter-day Saints in Japan, including their social and political views. Chapter 3 discusses the personal conversion experiences of survey respondents, especially regarding what they found was particularly meaningful to the formation of their Latter-day Saint identity. Chapter 4 turns to investigating their religious beliefs and adherence to religious practices. Chapter 5 then examines the issue of identity conflict; that is, how survey respondents mitigate any conflicts they may experience between Japanese culture and their religious practices. Chapter 6, the last of the six main chapters, discusses the broader challenges and opportunities faced by the Church amidst Japan's changing cultural institutions.

For the benefit of those who want a quick review of the findings of the book, we have prepared a concluding chapter (chapter 7), which provides key findings in summary form addressed to various stakeholders or audiences: researchers and scholars of the Latter-Day Saint movement; missionaries and mission leaders assigned to Japan by The Church of Jesus-Christ of Latter-day Saints; Church leadership more broadly; Japanese members; and the general public. As assistance to Japanese readers, moreover, we have attached to the end of this volume an executive summary, with the titles and legends of tables and figures, and an afterword prepared in the Japanese language. We offer these as a small token of gratitude for the generosity of nearly 600 Japanese Latter-day Saints who have made this study a reality.

January 2023

Shinji Takagi
Conan Grames
Meagan Rainock

Chapter 1

An Approach to Understanding Minority Religious Practices

1-1. Introduction

This book, based on a representative dataset of religious participation collected in late fall of 2021, applies a social-scientific method to advance our understanding of the religious beliefs and practices, as well as the social identities, of Japanese members of The Church of Jesus Christ of Latter-day Saints. According to Japan's official government statistics,[1] the Church had a membership of 130,192 at the end of 2021 (Bunkachō 2022). Even though this makes the Church one of Japan's largest Christian denominations (Figure 1-1), Latter-day Saints remain a distinct minority group in a country of 126 million people where Christians constitute less than 2 percent of the population,[2] and they often face cultural obstacles to the full exercise of their religion.[3] We attempt to understand what they believe, how they practice their faith, and how they manage the conflicts they may encounter as members of a minority religion in Japan. We further seek to

---

1. The Church of Jesus Christ of Latter-day Saints is incorporated in Japan as a religious corporation under the Religious Corporation Law (*Shūkyō Hōjin Hō*). The Church voluntarily complies with the government's request to provide the Agency for Cultural Affairs (*Bunkachō*) with basic activity data annually, including the numbers of members, foreign and domestic missionaries, and places of worship.

2. According to official government statistics (Bunkachō 2022), Christians constituted 1.6 percent of the population in 2021, but this number was an underestimation of the true share of Christians. Some large Christian groups (notably the Unification Church and Jehovah's Witnesses) do not share their membership data with the government. Latter-day Saints constituted about 0.1 percent of the population.

3. Any obstacles Latter-day Saints may face in Japan are not legal but cultural. Freedom of religion is guaranteed by Article 20 of the Constitution of Japan, which reads: "Freedom of religion is guaranteed to all. No religious organization shall receive any privileges from the State, nor exercise any political authority. No person shall be compelled to take part in any religious act, celebration, rite or practice. The State and its organs shall refrain from religious education or any other religious activity." Official translation from the Prime Minister's office.

Figure 1-1. Membership in Japan's Largest Christian Denominations, 2021 (In thousands)

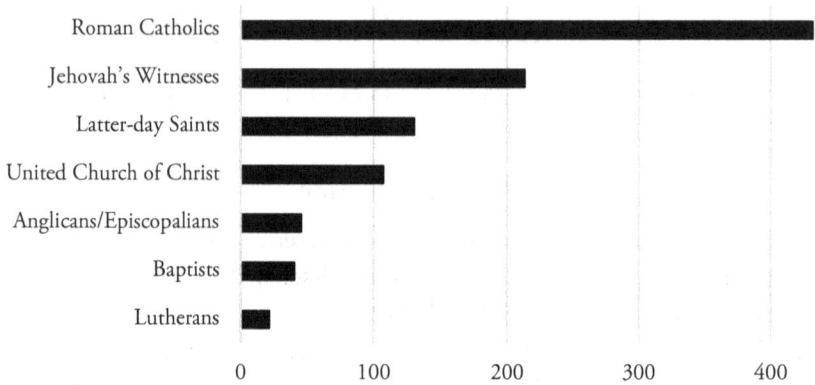

Denomination	Membership
Roman Catholics	(bar to ~440)
Jehovah's Witnesses	(bar to ~215)
Latter-day Saints	(bar to ~130)
United Church of Christ	(bar to ~110)
Anglicans/Episcopalians	(bar to ~45)
Baptists	(bar to ~40)
Lutherans	(bar to ~20)

Axis: 0   100   200   300   400

Note: end of 2021 (peak number during 2021 for Jehovah's Witnesses only).
Sources: Bunkachō, *Shūkyō Nenkan* (Tokyo: Bunkachō, 2022); for Jehovah's Witnesses only, Watch Tower Bible and Tract Society of Pennsylvania (2021).

explore the challenges and opportunities current and prospective members face in a country that is undergoing profound demographic, cultural, and other societal changes.

To understand the religious beliefs and practices of Latter-day Saints in Japan and to uncover any conflicts and challenges they may experience as they practice their religion, we utilize the de-identified summary of an anonymous survey (the "Japan LDS Survey") of more than 500 individuals administered by Meagan Rainock in late 2021. Cyril Figuerres, a former manager of the Church's research division who presided over a mission in Japan, discusses how difficult it is to retain, let alone convert, Japanese people as practicing Latter-day Saints (Figuerres 1999). Based on proprietary information made available by Church leaders, we estimate the share of Japanese Latter-day Saints who attend church at least once a month to be, at most, 20 percent of those on the official membership records. This is somewhat lower than but not too far from the average weekly attendance rate of about 25 percent in Asia and Latin America observed in the early 1980s (Heaton 1998a). In this book, however, we do not directly address the question of why it is difficult for a Japanese person to accept and practice the Latter-day Saint faith. Rather, our primary concern is to understand how the Latter-day Saint identity is embraced, and how the Latter-day Saint faith is lived, by those individuals who have found a way of successfully navigating the conflicting demands of church membership in the host society.

The rest of this introductory chapter is organized as follows. Section 1-2 presents a brief historical and contemporary context for The Church of Jesus Christ of Latter-day Saints in Japan, with a particular focus on the rapid growth of church membership during the post-World War II period through the early 1980s and the subsequent deceleration of growth in active membership in recent years. Section 1-3 presents the analytical framework ("identity theory") we use to frame the discussion and provides our operational definitions for culture and identity. Section 1-4 explains how the survey was administered as well as the broad demographic characteristics of those who responded to the survey, such as their gender, age, geographical profile, and marital status. Section 1-5 provides the respondents' religious and socioeconomic characteristics, including their employment, church activity, and membership status (i.e., converts vs. second- and third-generation members). Finally, section 1-6 presents a conclusion.

1-2. Historical and Contemporary Background

The beginnings of The Church of Jesus Christ of Latter-day Saints in Japan are traced to the turn of the twentieth century, when in 1901 the Church dispatched apostle Heber J. Grant and his three companions to this then-emerging nation, making it Asia's first country in which Latter-day Saint missionary work was carried out on a sustained basis. Compared to its investment in European countries at that time, the Church's general lack of commitment to prewar Japan is evident in the number of missionaries assigned to labor in the field: for a country of 45–55 million people (about half the population of the United States at the time), the number averaged 12.5 and never exceeded 20 at any given time. The small number of converts (174 men and women from 1901 to 1924) was in large part a reflection of this. Yet, the Church was not quite prepared to increase its missionary force. It instead closed the Japan Mission in 1924, and missionary work did not resume until 1948 when a modest number of missionaries returned to restart the work following the end of World War II. However, it was only in 1968 that the Church's geographical expansion began in earnest, with a division of Japan's single mission (the "Northern Far East Mission"). The Church has since doubled and then tripled the number of missions (and missionaries) and penetrated virtually every corner of Japan.

The Church has seen a sixfold increase in its membership since the early 1970s, with most of the growth taking place through the mid-1990s

Figure 1-2. Membership and Missions of The Church of Jesus Christ
of Latter-day Saints in Japan, 1973–2021

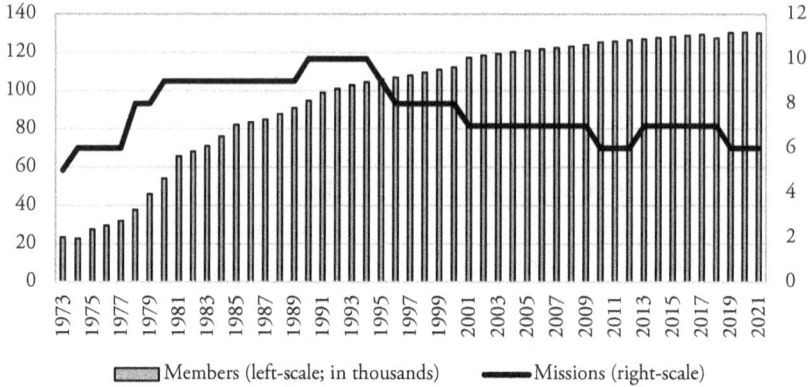

Members (left-scale; in thousands) ——— Missions (right-scale)

Sources for membership: Bunkachō, *Shūkyō Nenkan*, annual issues, supplemented
by official church data and Deseret News (1995–2001); for the number of
missions: various Church publications and authors' personal knowledge.

(Figure 1-2). Along with membership growth, the numbers of congregations (wards and branches) and of stakes (umbrella organizations compris-
ing wards and branches) have correspondingly increased as well (Figure
1-3). At the end of 2021, the Church operated 232 congregations and
25 stakes throughout Japan. It should be noted that, following the initial
growth spurred by the split of the mission in 1968, the number of congregations has not changed much since the early 1980s. The peak was
in 1982 at more than 300, and the number has since declined through
consolidation of smaller units into larger ones. Likewise, the number of
stakes increased rapidly during the 1970s (following the establishment of
the first stake in Tokyo in 1970), but the peak was reached in 2000 at 31.
The variations in the number of units in recent years (when membership
did not change very much) largely reflect the Church leadership's changing views on optimal organizational size.[4]

The Church now maintains congregations located in various munici-
palities across the country. It is not far from the truth to state that anyone living in or near a city of more than 150,000 can find a Latter-day

---

4. In June 2021, for example, eight stakes around Tokyo were consolidated
into five stakes, according to the official statement, in order to enhance
member experience by allowing more members to attend larger units. Further
consolidations took place during 2022 in Hokkaido and the Kinki region,
reducing the number of stakes in Japan to 22 currently.

**Figure 1-3. Congregations and Stakes of The Church of Jesus Christ
of Latter-day Saints in Japan, 1973–2021**

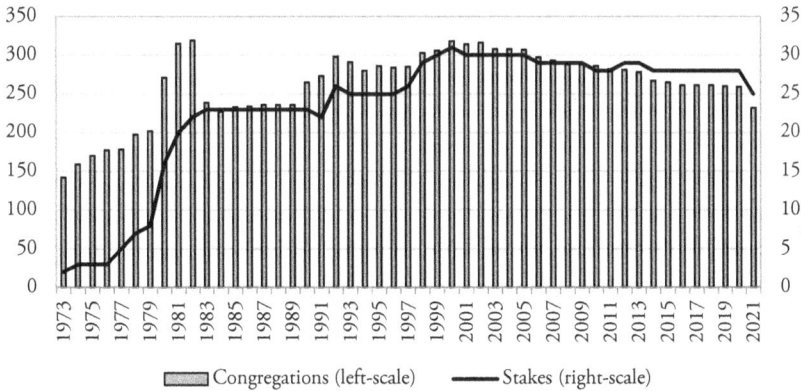

Congregations (left-scale) ——— Stakes (right-scale)

Sources for the number of congregations: Bunkachō, *Shūkyō Nenkan*, annual
issues; for the number of stakes: various Church publications and authors'
personal knowledge.

Saint meetinghouse within an hour's driving distance. The stronghold of
the Church is in the region around Tokyo, which accounted for about
a quarter of all congregations and stakes at the end of 2021. The region
around Osaka, another population center, accounted for more than 15
percent of congregations and stakes. Yet the geographical distribution of
the units does not fully reflect the distribution of Japan's general population. Relative to the population, the most successful area of the Church is
Hokkaido, where there is a unit for approximately every 200,000 persons.
The corresponding number for the Tokyo area is more than 700,000, and
the average for Japan is about 470,000 persons per unit.

The Church of Jesus Christ of Latter-day Saints has established its
presence among the Christian denominations in Japan through years
of sustained membership growth. Its membership growth exceeded 15
percent per year during 1970–80 and maintained momentum (at more
than 5 percent per year) through the early 1990s. As noted, however, the
growth decelerated sharply in the 1990s and virtually ceased in the early
2000s. Despite continued baptisms, the numbers remained flat due to a
declining birthrate, elderly deaths, and emigration. Yet, this "stagnation"
contrasts with the experience of most other religious groups. Not only did
those religious groups begin to experience stagnation earlier, but they have
also more recently seen absolute declines in membership (Figure 1-4). For
example, nontraditional religions (that is, "non-Shinto, non-Buddhist,"

Figure 1-4. Membership in Japan's Nontraditional Religions, 1971–2021
(In thousands)

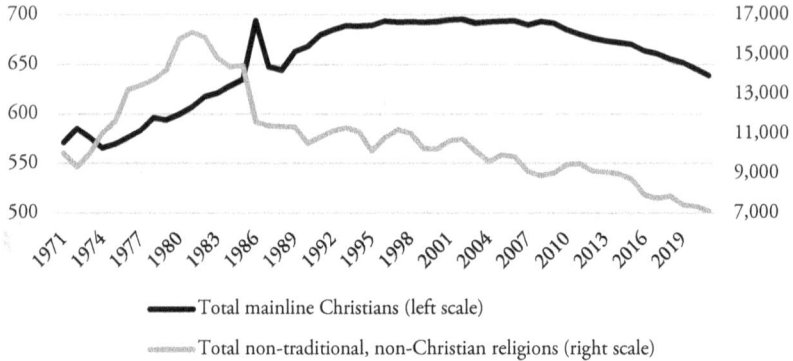

——— Total mainline Christians (left scale)

········ Total non-traditional, non-Christian religions (right scale)

Notes: "nontraditional" refers to non-Shinto, non-Buddhist religions (classified as *shokyō* in *Shūkyō Nenkan*). Mainline Christians refer to those who belong to Christian churches with historical roots in prewar Japan, which include Catholic Bishops' Conference of Japan; Anglican Church in Japan; United Church of Christ in Japan; Japan Evangelical Lutheran Church; and Japan Baptist Convention. Source: Bunkachō, *Shūkyō Nenkan*, annual issues.

but excluding Christian, religions) began to suffer membership declines in the 1980s. The membership growth of mainline Christian churches ceased in the 1990s, and a sharp decline in membership has been observed since the end of the first decade of this century.

The stagnant or negative growth of Christian and other nontraditional religions in Japan has occurred against the background of the general population's decelerating growth during the past few decades. Japan's population peaked in 2008 at 128 million and has been declining since. A statistical analysis of growth dynamics suggests that the stagnation of the growth of The Church of Jesus Christ of Latter-day Saints in recent years has been largely driven by the adverse demographic trend, but, unlike many other religious groups, the relative success of its missionary work has, to a considerable extent, offset the negative demographic impact by adding new members (Rainock and Takagi 2020). In this interpretation, church membership in Japan grew rapidly when Japan's general population was increasing, but growth began to stagnate when the population growth decelerated. This process may have begun in the 1980s, when Figuerres (1999) observed no "real growth" in active, faithful members. New converts, averaging around 700 per year, have been just enough to make up for the attrition of active membership.

1-3. Analytical Framework

We maintain the perspective of "identity theory" throughout the book to motivate and frame our discussion. Identity theory is a sociological framework that aims to understand how individuals align their behavior with the roles expected from membership in a particular group. As such, it is ideally suited to investigating the transplantation of The Church of Jesus Christ of Latter-day Saints in a foreign cultural setting. The Church, as a highly centralized organization, does not lend itself to a significant cultural adaptation in the mode of religious worship or practice. The *General Handbook* of instructions, prepared in Salt Lake City and translated word for word into Japanese, governs church administration. Thus, acculturation in the sense of cultural adaptation, if any, must take place primarily at the level of individuals, who must translate the meanings associated with their Japanese and Latter-day Saint identities into individual religious practice. Further, identity theory captures the reality of complex modern societies where individuals, having multiple identities, decide on a course of action when faced with competing expectations from the various social groups to which they belong. In this framework, individuals are seen as "agentic" (that is, actively choosing their behavior) in interaction with the bounds of norms accepted by the respective groups. Our focus is on how individual Latter-day Saints navigate the expectations of church membership against the competing demands of their memberships in various groups within the larger society.

What Is Culture?

Culture defies a simple definition (Minkov 2013; Hammersley 2019). In fact, there is no universally accepted scholarly definition of culture. Here, we take the view that the idea of culture is "a tool by which we reach understanding" (Morris 2012), a theoretical construct that offers an "interpretive framework" (Vivanco 2018). Accordingly, we broadly operationalize the concept of culture as referring to the set of beliefs, worldviews, values, meanings, institutions, and behavioral patterns, which are widely shared by a group of people. Three aspects of culture bear emphasis. First, elements of culture are often learned through the process known as "socialization" and are transmitted across and within generations. Second, as a result, culture has an element of inertia or persistence, which manifests itself as customs, traditions, and norms. Change is often resisted by those who belong to an older generation or have otherwise spent significant time and effort investing in what Pierre Bourdieu (1986) calls cultural capital.[5] Third, given this persistence, it is often difficult to trace the origin of a particular element of culture, especially when it has existed for a long time.

This book takes a broad view of culture. We make no distinction, for example, between centuries-old practices and what could be relatively recent ones, the origin of which may not be what we normally think of as "cultural." A foreign observer, upon arriving in Japan, may notice the long hours typical Japanese workers put in at their places of employment. Likewise, Japanese workers frequently spend their evening hours with their work associates at drinking establishments before going home. The foreign observer may ascribe these phenomena to Japan's centuries-old Confucius work ethic (Lipset 1992) or "group" culture (Nakane 1970; Lebra 1976). More likely, they are the outcomes, respectively, of restrictive labor laws that make it nearly impossible to dismiss workers once employed,[6] and of the labor practices that tie the worker to the firm in a long-term relationship.[7] Irrespective of their origin, Japanese people, when they accept membership in The Church of Jesus Christ of Latter-day Saints, must navigate the conflicting demands of membership in the larger society as they practice their religion. These demands—the roles one is expected to play—are part of what we broadly call Japanese culture.

Culture is not monolithic. That culture expects a certain behavioral pattern from individuals does not mean that everyone behaves the same way. Culture allows choice and variation, depending on the individual's tastes and preferences, though the range of variation may be more limited in some cultures with greater ethnic or religious homogeneity (e.g., Japan) compared to others (e.g., the United States). In cultural sociology, there is an approach originally associated with the work of Ann Swidler (1986) that views culture as a set of "complex rule-like structures that constitute resources that can be put to strategic use" (DiMaggio 1997, p. 265) or

---

5. Cultural capital is the intangible assets possessed by those who have absorbed the dominant culture in terms of knowledge, ways of speaking, manners, and the like.

6. Given the difficulty to lay off, let alone dismiss, workers once employed, except in the case of bankruptcy, firms in Japan (1) are not willing to hire additional workers during booms but instead require the existing employees to work longer hours and (2) tend to be perennially understaffed (Ikezoe 2018).

7. Given the expected long tenure of its employees, the Japanese firm typically has a strong personnel department that rotates them to different assignments across the firm every few years (Aoki 1990). Networking and building intra-firm relationships, facilitated by social drinking, becomes important.

"a toolbox that people use" consciously or unconsciously "to decide on actions . . . in particular situations" (Hammersley 2019, p. 39). In this approach culture defines the bounds of socially acceptable behavior: not as a single choice, but as a range of possible actions in a given situation. Individuals navigate their lives in such a way as to achieve their desired objectives by selecting from a menu of socially acceptable choices, piecing together fragments of cultural "scripts" in their micro-level interactions dictated by macro-level societal structures. We find such an approach particularly attractive for our purpose because it conceptualizes how the high-level meanings and demands of culture translate into individual behavior. Further, it theoretically accounts for how individuals select from often-conflicting cultural scripts, which are precisely the types of choices individual Latter-day Saints must be making every day as they confront the conflicting demands of membership in Japanese society.

What Is Identity?

Acculturation is a term typically applied to the process by which an individual or a group of individuals (such as immigrants)—following contact with a new culture—adopts or adapts to the norms of the host society (Sam 2006; Schwartz et al. 2010). If we apply the term to a religion, we may analogously think of acculturation as the process by which a foreign religion makes cultural adaptations in such a way as to make it widely acceptable to the host society. Without a *substantial* degree of acculturation (either on the part of the religion or the host population), no foreign religion can expect to become a majority religion. Conversely, even with little acculturation, a foreign religion may be embraced by a small minority of the population, to the extent that culture allows a range of beliefs and religious practices. This is consistent with the membership growth dynamics of the Church, as observed by Heaton (1998a), whereby conversion tends to be higher where "the LDS presence is relatively recent than in areas with more extended contact." While church membership may initially grow quickly, stagnation is likely to occur after a time as it does not appeal to the broad population, though the point at which this occurs may reflect the degree to which church practices and beliefs align or conflict with the culture of the host society. In Japanese religious history, the acculturation of Buddhism took the form of incorporating elements of Shinto, an indigenous belief system, thus creating Shinto–Buddhist syncretism (*shinbutsu shūgō*).[8] In discussing the transplantation of The Church of Jesus Christ of Latter-day Saints in Japan, however, acculturation is an ill-suited concept. The Church, based on the belief that it is founded on revelation from God, operates a highly centralized (and hierarchical) organization (with the prophet at the head) and guards its doctrines and rituals meticulously to maintain uniformity throughout the world. If anything, we must consider that acculturation of the Latter-day Saint faith takes place at the level of individuals in the sense that each person forms a new self by adapting themselves to the culture of the worldwide church.

An analytical framework that is ideally suited to discussing the transplantation of a foreign religion under such conditions is the theory of "identity salience" developed by Sheldon Stryker (Stryker and Burke 2000). Stryker's identity theory, in explaining social behavior in a particular cultural context, posits that individuals possess several identities associated with simultaneous memberships in various social groups. Identities are defined by the meanings individuals attach to the multiple roles they are expected to play. Such a framework captures the reality of complex modern societies, where individuals participate in multiple cultural traditions, which may well contain inconsistent elements (DiMaggio 1997). For example, we are simultaneously family members, employees or employers, students or teachers, or perhaps members of a church who play different roles under different circumstances, not always in a consistent manner. Identity salience determines the likelihood that a particular identity is invoked over another in a given situation (Stryker and Burke 2000). The higher an identity's salience is, the greater the likelihood that the individual will select a behavior consistent with the expectations attached to that identity.[9]

The concept of identity salience provides a far more attractive framework for looking at the choices individuals make when living a foreign religion than simply viewing the community of practitioners of the foreign religion as a subculture of the larger society. Unlike the Amish in the United States, for example, Latter-day Saints do not form a separate subculture in Japanese society (to be further elaborated in this book). Identity salience as an analytical framework is also complementary to Swidler's

---

8. See, for example, Takagi (2016), 90–92.

9. Hoffmann (2007) also appeals to identity theory to provide a framework for his discussion of Japanese Latter-day Saints. His work, however, is limited in scope (based on interviews with twenty-two Latter-day Saints in a small branch in Hokkaido), and it focuses on how Latter-day Saint identity is formed or how its salience is enhanced relative to Japanese identity.

cultural sociology approach to viewing culture as a resource ("a tool kit" or "a menu of choices") for individuals. Each identity carries a range of acceptable behavior, and one is allowed to choose one identity over another in a given situation.

As the term is used in social psychology, identity *salience* is a behavioral concept. When we say a particular identity is salient, we mean that that identity is acted upon in preference over other identities (Serpe 1987). In contrast, the term used to describe the subjective value one attaches to a particular identity is called identity *prominence*. While it can be assumed that prominence likely drives salience (Brenner, Serpe, and Stryker 2014), those who strongly identify themselves as Latter-day Saints may not choose to act on those beliefs if the conflict proves overwhelming. Alternatively, such individuals may find ways of minimizing or avoiding the conflict through judicious choices. For example, Japanese Latter-day Saints may choose an occupation that would allow them to go to church on Sundays, or would not place them in frequent situations of social drinking or of politely refusing green tea, a substance prohibited by their church. This process of negotiating what it means to be a Latter-day Saint and what it means to be Japanese requires embracing particular aspects of the religion over cultural norms and applying religious beliefs into a Japanese context. The Japan LDS survey was designed precisely to elucidate such conflicts and to infer any mitigating behavior from the data, as explained below.

1-4. The Japan LDS Survey

We base our study on the de-identified summary of an anonymous survey administered by Meagan Rainock, who collected the data from October 22 through November 16, 2021, using the Survey Monkey platform. The link to the survey was sent to about 300 known email addresses, with a request to forward it to additional people by email or through social media. In addition, the link, along with an introduction to the survey, was posted on several Facebook groups consisting primarily of active Latter-day Saints in Japan.[10] A total of fifty-six questions were asked, includ-

---

10. We define activity status strictly in terms of church attendance throughout this work. Those who reported attending church less frequently than "once or twice a month" constituted only 6 percent of the 498 respondents who reported their church attendance (only 1.6 percent, or eight individuals, reported never attending church). This does not mean that these individuals were not "active" Latter-day Saints in other ways; for example, in the observance of the Word of Wisdom. Because they responded to the survey as introduced by their church

**Figure 1-5. Gender Composition of Survey Respondents
(Percent of all respondents who identified their gender)**

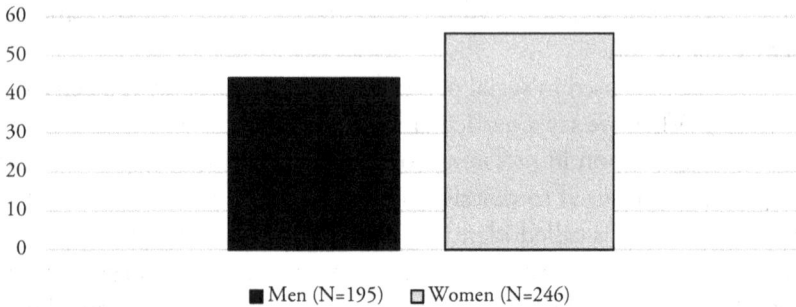

■ Men (N=195)   □ Women (N=246)

Source: Japan LDS Survey.

ing those related to religious beliefs and practices (Part 1), experiences as members of various social groups (Part 2), and socio-political views and general demographic backgrounds (Part 3). These included several optional open-ended questions in which the respondent was free to express his or her own views, and a surprisingly large number of individuals responded to each. We utilize these responses as qualitative data from time to time throughout the book, and especially in the penultimate chapter where we explore the future of The Church of Jesus Christ of Latter-day Saints in Japan. The sample reasonably represents the population of active Japanese Latter-day Saints, with a 4 to 5 percent margin of error when the full sample is used.[11]

All in all, 582 individuals started the survey, but 34 of them were screened out for being nonmembers, being non-Japanese, or living outside Japan, leaving 558 individuals who were eligible to continue. A dozen or so of these people did not continue the survey of their own choice after passing the initial screening questions. Some respondents also stopped partway through the survey. The effective sample size was thus between

---

friends, we maintain that all in our sample are "active" Latter-day Saints in an identity-theoretic sense, regardless of the frequency of church attendance. Frequency of church attendance had no noticeable impact on the various metrics of religious beliefs and practices that we examined. The survey results are therefore not disaggregated by attendance status.

11. This, of course, assumes that sampling was random, which it was not. It is possible that the sample is biased toward a segment of the religiously active Latter-day Saint population with more extensive human networks, but it is not clear how this might introduce a systematic bias into the responses to most of the survey questions. Our position is that it should not.

Figure 1-6. Age Distribution of Survey Respondents
(Percent of respondents in each group)

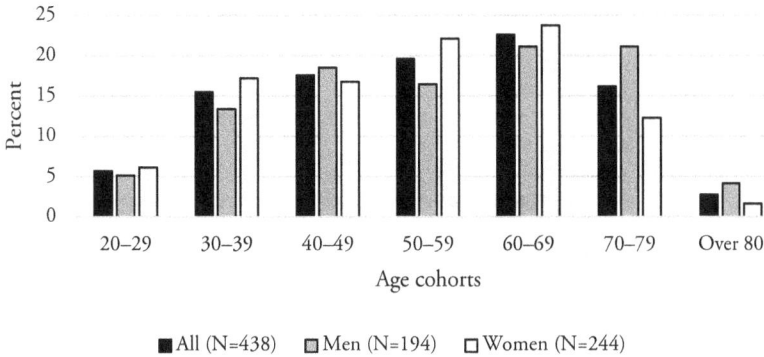

Source: Japan LDS Survey.

440 and 530, depending on the question. Of the 441 respondents who identified their gender, women constituted 55.8 percent and men 44.2 percent (Figure 1-5). This gender imbalance may call for caution in interpreting some of the survey results. A common practice in such cases is to correct for the gender bias by using the known shares of men and women in the population, as done, for example, in the Next Mormons Survey (NMS) of American Latter-day Saints conducted in 2016.[12] We chose not to do so because we are persuaded that, as women typically outnumber men among convert baptisms and remain more active (Heaton 1998a), the greater share of women in our sample is close to the true share in the active Latter-day Saint population. In order to avoid any gender bias, however, we compare men to men, and women to women, each time we report comparative statistics for Japanese and American Latter-day Saints, after controlling for church activity status (all comparisons involve Latter-day Saints who attend church at least weekly).

The survey targeted the adult population. Except for the youngest adult cohort (those aged 20–29, which accounts for only 5.7 percent when the sample is divided into seven age groups), all cohorts are well represented in the sample, albeit with a bias toward older generations (Figure 1-6). Those over the age of 60 constitute 41.6 percent of the whole sample, though the

---

12. The NMS was administered in 2016 by Jana Riess and Benjamin Knoll (Riess 2019), who have kindly given us access to their unpublished subsample data. The NMS not only is a gender-balanced survey but also includes a sample of religiously non-active Latter-day Saints.

**Figure 1-7. Geographical Distribution of Survey Respondents
(Percent of all respondents)**

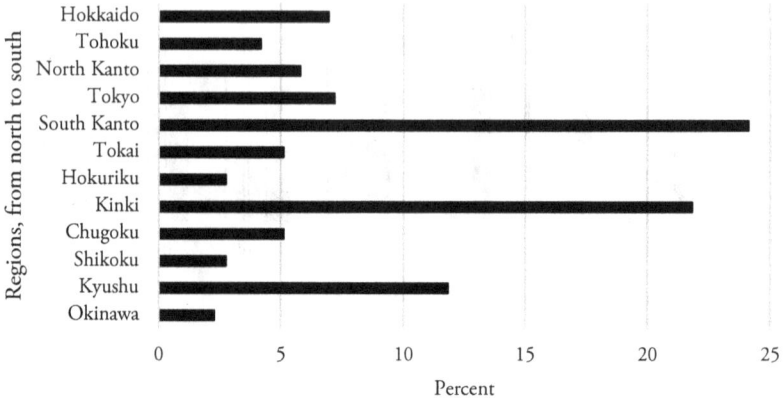

Note: sample size (N)=431.
Source: Japan LDS Survey.

distribution of the female respondents appears somewhat more balanced (with those over 60 accounting for 37.7 percent). While we acknowledge that the survey may not have reached younger generations as effectively, it must also be kept in mind that the relatively large share of the elderly reflects, to a large extent, Japan's demographic reality, where those over 60 years of age constituted 34.7 percent of the total population in 2021 (31.8 percent for men and 37.6 percent for women).[13] The figure for women in the general population is nearly identical to the share in our survey. Japan's aging society means that members of the Church are also aging.

All regions of Japan are represented, with 31.3 percent for South Kanto (centered in Tokyo, with Tokyo proper accounting for 7.2 percent) and 21.8 percent for Kinki (centered in Osaka); the three population centers, which also include Tokai (centered in Nagoya), thus constitute 58.2 percent of all respondents who identified where they lived (Figure 1-7). These shares roughly correspond to their shares in Japan's general population, where the three regions accounted for 56.9 percent (i.e., South Kanto 28.8 percent; Kinki 16.3 percent; and Tokai 11.8 percent) in 2021. Hokkaido (7 percent) and Okinawa (2.3 percent) appear overrepresented relative to the population shares of 4.2 and 1.4 percent, respectively, but these are two areas where Latter-day Saint missionary work has been

---

13. Unless otherwise noted, all Japanese data come from official government sources, available at www.e-stat.go.jp, designated as "e-stat" throughout this work.

**Figure 1-8. Frequency of Church Attendance
(Percent of respondents)**

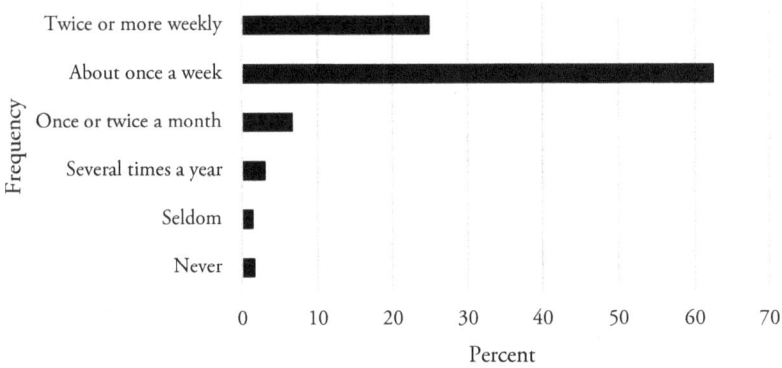

Notes: sample size (N)=498; respondents were asked to estimate their church attendance outside of pandemic restrictions present in 2021.
Source: Japan LDS Survey.

relatively more successful. Overall, the geographical distribution of the sample appears to be reasonably well balanced.

1-5. Religious and Socio-Economic Characteristics of Respondents

Religious Characteristics

Because survey respondents were requested to forward the link to their church friends and associates, it is to be expected that the survey predominantly reached those who attend church frequently enough to have developed friendships and relationships among the Latter-day Saint community. Indeed, out of the 498 individuals who reported the frequency of their church attendance, almost 25 percent stated that they attended church twice or more every week, while another 62.5 percent attended at least once a week; only about 3 percent of the respondents stated that they seldom or never attended church (Figure 1-8). While the sample is thus not representative of the overall Latter-day Saint population in Japan, as previously noted, they are precisely the kind of individuals who have found a way of successfully navigating the conflicting demands of church membership in the host society, whose religious beliefs and practices we are particularly interested in exploring. Our sample captures the kind of people one would expect to meet when he or she attends Latter-day Saint services in Japan.

Figure 1-9. Membership Status by Population Group
(Percent of respondents in each group)

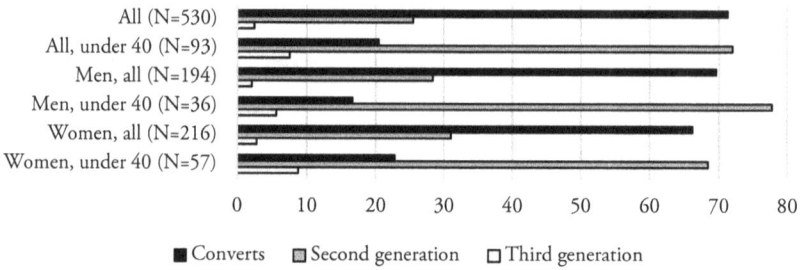

Note: the figure excludes four respondents who identified themselves as "other."
Source: Japan LDS Survey.

Figure 1-10. Membership Status: Japan–U.S. Comparison
(Percent of converts in each group)

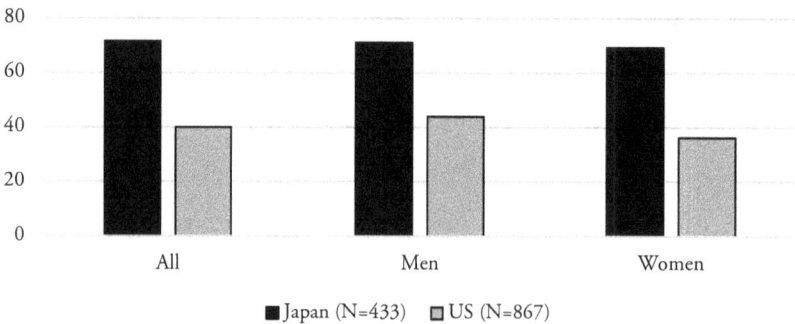

Note: for Japan, only 385 of the 433 respondents identified their gender; sample size is 173 for men and 212 for women.
Sources: Japan LDS Survey; Next Mormons Survey.

As to the respondents' church membership status, 71.3 percent were converts, 25.5 percent were second-generation members, and 2.5 percent were third-generation members (Figure 1-9). There was little gender difference (the share of converts was about 70 percent each for both men and women). This contrasts with the share of about 40 percent in a similar sample of American Latter-day Saints who attend church at least weekly (Figure 1-10). This reflects the fact that most of the membership growth in Japan has occurred since 1968, when the number of missions began to multiply. As expected, the share of converts declines as the sample becomes younger. For example, 72 percent of the respondents younger than the age

Table 1-1. Temple Endowment Status of Survey Respondents
(Percent of total)

	Yes	No	Total
All (N=511)	97.1	2.9	100

Source: Japan LDS Survey.

of 40 were second-generation members, and the share of third-generation members rises from 2.5 percent in the full sample to 7.5 percent in the subsample that includes only those under the age of 40.

Because the sample predominantly included actively practicing Latter-day Saints, over 97 percent reported that they had been endowed in the temple (Table 1-1),[14] and about 60 percent had served full-time proselytizing missions for the Church (Table 1-2). The share of those with full-time mission experience rises to about 66 percent among men; the share was as high as 89 percent among men under the age of 40, reflecting the fact that they were more likely to be second- or third-generation members. Not only was the share of respondents with full-time mission experience higher among those under the age of 40 (for both men and women), but the share of those who had served foreign missions was also higher. In fact, more than 11 percent of the male respondents under the age of 40 had served foreign missions. Interrupting work or school for an extended period of time to serve a mission is a uniquely Latter-day Saint institution, one that is highly unusual in Japanese society. The fact that so many of the practicing Japanese Latter-day Saints have done so, despite the potential social stigma or adverse educational or employment consequences, speaks volumes about the salience of their Latter-day Saint identity.

Socio-economic Characteristics

At the time of the survey, nearly 85 percent of both men and women reported that they were either married or widowed, and 3.5 percent of both men and women were divorced. About 12.5 percent had never been married, with a slightly higher percentage for men than for women (Figure 1-11). By focusing on those who attend church at least weekly in order to ensure comparability, we find that the share of married Latter-day Saints (around 80 percent) is nearly 10 percentage points higher than the com-

---

14. The temple endowment is a religious ordinance for members who have been in the Church at least for one year, in which sacred covenants are made; only those recommended by their ecclesiastical leaders as "worthy" are eligible.

Table 1-2. Full-time Mission Experience of Survey Respondents
(Percent of total)

	Yes	(Foreign mission)	No	Total
All (N=514)	60.3	(4.3)	39.7	100
All, under 40 (N=93)	72.0	(7.5)	28.0	100
Men, all (N=195)	65.6	(3.6)	34.4	100
Men, under 40 (N=36)	88.9	(11.1)	11.1	100
Women, all (N=246)	57.7	(4.1)	42.3	100
Women, under 40 (N=57)	61.4	(5.3)	38.6	100

Source: Japan LDS Survey.

parable U.S. figure (Table 1-3). Conversely, the share of active Latter-day Saints who have never been married is about 5 percentage points higher in the U.S. than in Japan. This should not be interpreted to mean that Japanese Latter-day Saints are necessarily more likely to be married than their American counterparts. It is widely observed that, for single women, opportunities for marriage within the church are extremely limited, given the higher share of women who join and then remain active in the church. In our view, the higher percentage of married members in our sample means that those who are married have a greater likelihood of remaining active in the church.

Finally, with respect to the respondents' employment status, only about 42 percent reported being employed full-time (Figure 1-12). This reflects the fact that a large proportion (about 37 percent) of women identify themselves as full-time homemakers.[15] The social participation of women outside the home remains limited in Japan, as they feel pressure to assume traditional gender roles.[16] The World Economic Forum's annual ranking of gender equality placed Japan 116th (out of 146 countries) in 2022 just behind Burkina Faso, though ahead of Turkey, Saudi Arabia, and India (WEF 2022).[17] The lack of adequate access to child care has meant that, when there is an economic need, women often obtain part-

---

15. The population average is about 21 percent, but the denominator includes a large student population. Thus, 37 percent may not be very different from the population average when the student population is excluded.

16. By "social participation," we mean assumptions of various roles in society other than that of wife or mother.

17. The United Kingdom was placed 22nd, Canada 25th, the United States 27th, and Australia 43rd, just to name a few countries.

**Figure 1-11. Marital Status of Survey Respondents
(Percent of total in each group)**

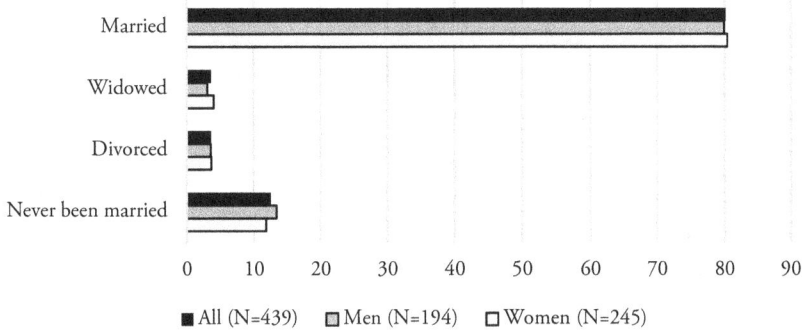

Source: Japan LDS Survey.

time or contractual work after they are married and have had children. About 30 percent (19 percent for those under 40) of the women reported being employed part-time.[18] When the sample is restricted to men, more than 62 percent reported being employed full-time.

Only 1.65 percent of the respondents stated that they were unemployed. This translates to about 2.7 percent, if those who were full-time homemakers, students, or retirees (and are therefore not in the labor force) are removed.[19] This is consistent with the national average of 2.7 percent in October 2021—when the survey was taken—suggesting that the Latter-day Saint population in Japan closely mirrors the general population when

---

18. Heaton (1998a), based on a survey of Japanese Latter-day Saints in five large cities during 1981–83, states that 63 percent of Latter-day Saint women were in the labor force and that the figure was notably higher than the rate for Latter-day Saint women in other countries (including the United States) as well as the Japanese population average. He does not distinguish between full-time and part-time work, but assuming that the 63 percent includes both, it compares with 54 percent in our sample. Presumably, the higher share reported by Heaton reflects the fact that the Latter-day Saint population in the early 1980s contained a significantly smaller elderly population. In our sample, the share rises to nearly 60 percent when it is restricted to those under 40. The labor force participation rate differs significantly by age. Thus, without knowing the age profile of the survey respondents, one must discount Heaton's comparison with the population average, which includes a large student population. We do not believe that the labor force participation of Latter-day Saint women in Japan was ever notably higher than the national average at any time.

19. Only 6 out of the 485 respondents identified themselves as students.

Table 1-3. Marital Status of Survey Respondents: Japan–U.S. Comparison
(Percent of total in each population group)

	Japan			U.S.		
	All (N=385)	Men (N=173)	Women (N=212)	All (N=867)	Male (N=423)	Female (N=444)
Married	80.0	80.4	79.7	71.1	71.1	71.0
Divorced	3.4	3.5	3.3	4.7	2.8	6.5
Widowed	3.9	3.5	4.3	2.6	2.1	3.0
Never been married	12.7	12.7	12.7	18.5	19.7	17.3
Other (U.S. only)	--	--	--	3.2	4.3	2.2
Total	100	100	100	100	100	100

Sources: Japan LDS Survey; Next Mormons Survey.

it comes to their participation in economic activities. Interestingly, a far smaller percentage of women than men reported being retired (7 vs. 26 percent). This may mean that women who identify as full-time homemakers do not identify as retirees even when their husbands retire.

An interesting observation from Figure 1-12 is that a higher percentage of women under the age of 40 reported that they were full-time homemakers (40.4 percent vs. 37 percent for all Latter-day Saint women), seemingly contradicting the generally held view that the social participation of women, however limited, has nonetheless been increasing in Japan. As a way to counter the demographic-driven decline in the labor force, the Japanese government has been actively promoting gender equality and the social participation of women over the past decade or so. As a result, the number of women in the labor force increased from 26.6 million in 2012 to 30 million in 2021; the share of women who hold executive positions in stock exchange-listed companies likewise rose from 1.6 percent to 7.5 percent over the same period, just to give an example (Cabinet Office 2023).

What we observe in our sample therefore appears to contradict our expectations that the share of younger women who are full-time homemakers should be smaller. However, this observation must be tempered by the higher percentage of women among the younger cohort who reported that they were employed full-time (40.4 percent vs. 24.8 percent for all Latter-day Saint women), which is consistent with the national trend pointing to greater social participation of women. Our speculative interpretation is that greater social participation of women in the larger society has meant greater opportunities for *full-time* (as opposed to *part-time* or *contractual*) positions for women who are pursuing employment,

Figure 1-12. Employment Status of Survey Respondents
(Percent of total in each group)

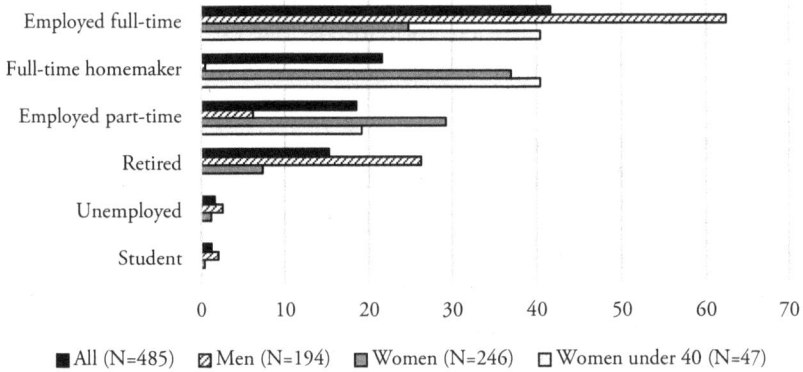

Source: Japan LDS Survey.

but this has not increased the number of women leaving the home to pursue work. This interpretation is consistent with the smaller share of the women under 40 who were employed part-time (19.2 percent vs. 29.3 percent for all Latter-day Saint women).

1-6. Conclusion

This introductory chapter has set the stage for the rest of the book. An important background to the study presented herein is the deceleration of membership growth experienced by The Church of Jesus Christ of Latter-day Saints in Japan in recent years. To be sure, the stagnation of membership growth, or religious activity more generally, is in part driven by an adverse demographic trend and is not unique to the Church. One can even claim that, thanks to the relative success of its missionary program, the Church has fared better than most other nontraditional religious groups in resisting an outright decline in membership for so many years. Even so, the stagnation of active membership presents challenges for the future prospects of the Church in Japan. This gives motivation for exploring the challenges and opportunities current and prospective members may face going forward, as Japan undergoes profound demographic, cultural, and other societal changes.

This is a data-driven study, set within the framework of identity theory and based on an anonymous survey of Latter-day Saints in Japan. Identity theory is a sociological framework that aims to understand how individuals align their behavior with the roles expected from membership in a particular group. As such, it is ideally suited to investigating the transplantation in a foreign cultural setting of The Church of Jesus Christ of Latter-day Saints. Identity theory, moreover, captures the reality of complex modern societies where individuals, having multiple identities, decide on the course of action when faced with competing expectations from the various social groups to which they belong. In this framework, individuals are seen as actively choosing their behavior within the bounds of norms dictated by the respective groups. Our focus is on how individual Latter-day Saints navigate the expectations of church membership against competing demands.

An anonymous survey ("the Japan LDS Survey") was administered in late 2021 to help understand the religious beliefs and practices, as well as the social identities, of Japanese Latter-day Saints, to which more than 500 individuals responded from all regions of Japan. They were, for the most part, religiously committed Latter-day Saints, with nearly 90 percent attending church at least weekly, nearly 97 percent having been endowed in the temple, and about 60 percent having served full-time proselytizing missions. The majority (about 56 percent) were women, which may reasonably mirror the gender composition of the active Latter-day Saint population today. The sample is somewhat overrepresented by those over the age of 60, but the share of the elderly for women (about 38 percent) was nearly identical to the general population share. Japan's aging population means that church membership is also aging. The sample represents a good cross-section of those Latter-day Saints who have fully embraced the Latter-day Saint identity and have learned to successfully manage the conflicting demands of membership in the larger society.

Chapter 2

Profiles of Japanese Latter-day Saints

2-1. Introduction

Having established the demographic, religious, and socioeconomic characteristics of the survey respondents in the previous chapter, our task now is to describe the personal and social profiles of religiously active members of The Church of Jesus Christ of Latter-day Saints in Japan, including their political and social views. The purpose of this chapter is to understand how they live and think as members of Japanese society. An important perspective we maintain throughout this chapter is how they compare to the larger Japanese population whenever comparable data are available. When we consider their political and social views, we obtain those of the general public from the widely reported surveys conducted from time to time by the *Asahi Shinbun*, a major national daily, and the Nihon Hōsō Kyōkai (NHK), Japan's public broadcasting station. These two outlets are deliberately chosen, first, to ensure that comparable data exists close to the time the Japan LDS Survey was taken and, second, to ensure that we have reasonably unbiased benchmarks for comparison. It is generally believed that the *Asahi* leans progressive on most political and social issues, while the NHK leans somewhat more conservative. In a few instances where comparable data are available, we also compare the profiles of Japanese and American Latter-day Saints to provide an additional perspective.

The rest of the chapter is organized as follows. Section 2-2 provides a glimpse of Latter-day Saint family life in Japan, including the relative shares of intra- and inter-faith marriages and the number of children a man or a woman typically has. Section 2-3 discusses the cultural background of Latter-day Saints, including their educational attainment and foreign experience. Section 2-4 is about what we call "sociability"; that is, the respondents' personal disposition that determines how they build friendships and relate to others. Section 2-5 discusses the respondents' own perception of their ideological inclination; that is, how they place themselves on the conservative/progressive spectrum. Section 2-6 turns to their political views, including political party support and the nationally contentious and divisive issue of national defense, while section 2-7 reports their social views related to such contemporary issues as same-sex

Figure 2-1. Member Status of Current or Former Spouses
(Percent of respondents in each group)

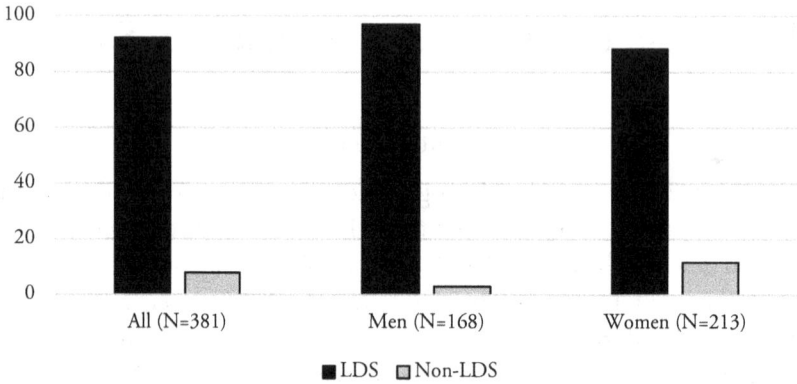

Source: Japan LDS Survey.

marriage, separate surnames for husband and wife, a female monarch, and government policy on immigration and refugees. Finally, section 2-8 presents a conclusion.

2-2. Family Life

Intra- vs. Inter-faith Marriage

We learned in the previous chapter that nearly 85 percent of men and women who reported their marital status were either married or widowed. Along with those who reported that they were divorced (about 4 percent of the respondents), this means that nearly 90 percent of the respondents had current or former spouses. The survey asked respondents if their current or former spouses were also Latter-day Saints, to which 381 individuals responded (Figure 2-1). Of these, 97 percent of men and 88 percent of women stated that their current or former spouses were also Latter-day Saints. The higher percentage for men probably means that women outnumber men both in convert baptisms and in active church membership, so women are more likely than men to be married or to have been married to nonmember spouses. It can also mean that, in Japan, as elsewhere in the world, men tend to have greater control over the selection of their marriage partners. Regardless, the overwhelming majority of religiously active Latter-day Saints in Japan appear to live in a Latter-day Saint household where both husband and wife are members.

Figure 2-2. Number of Children
(Percent of respondents in each group)

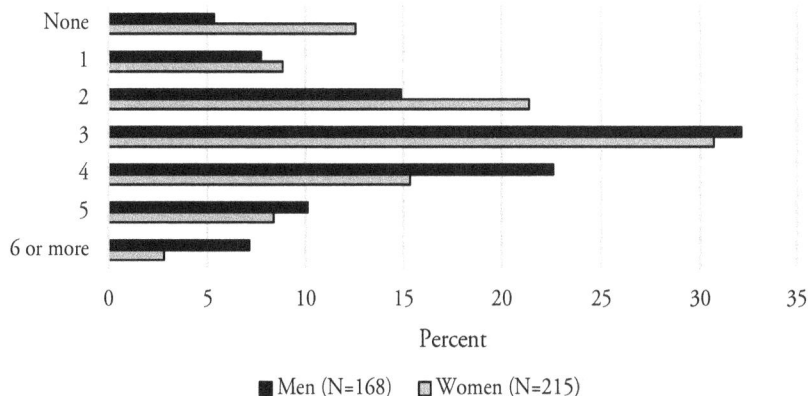

Source: Japan LDS Survey.

Number of Children

There were 383 currently or previously married individuals who reported the number of children they had (Figure 2-2). Here, we report the numbers separately for men and women in order to minimize possible double-counting (of husband and wife). We observe that, for men and women, the largest number of them (32.1 percent for men and 30.7 percent for women) had three children; 22.6 percent of men and 15.4 percent of women had four children. Comparing these percentages to a 2016 survey of American Latter-day Saints, as reported by Riess (2019), Japanese family sizes most closely resemble the size of American families that belong to the "Boomer/ Silent" generation, but they are greater than American "Generation X" families. Among Japanese survey respondents, the average number of children was 3.2 for men and 2.6 for women (the corresponding figures when those without children are excluded were 3.6 and 3.0, respectively). Latter-day Saint women in Japan on average appear to bear about one more child than their non–Latter-day Saint counterparts, whose total fertility rate (the average number of children born to a woman over her lifetime) was 1.3 in 2021 and has never exceeded 2 since 1961 (MHLW 2021a).

These findings can be compared to those reported by Heaton (1998b) based on a survey of Latter-day Saints in fifty-nine congregations in five cities between the summer of 1981 and the end of 1984 (Table 2-1).[1]

---

1. The sample consisted of all adults who attended church on a particular Sunday, with a follow-up random sampling of non-attenders.

Table 2-1. Comparing the Number of Children Born to a Latter-day Saint Woman in Japan between the Early 1980s and 2021
(Percent of total, unless otherwise noted)

Number of children	General population (1981–84)	LDS population (1981–84)	Japan LDS Survey (2021)
0	20.6	10.4	12.6
1	26.1	27.8	8.8
2	40.0	33.6	21.4
3 or more	13.3	28.1	57.2
Memorandum			
Average number of children	n.a.	1.9	2.6 (2.8 for those over 40; 1.9 for those under 40)

Notes: for 1981–84, the number of children born to a married woman over the age of 16 in a married-couple household; for the Japan LDS Survey, the number of children born to a woman.
Sources: Heaton (1998b), Table 14.1; Japan LDS Survey.

Heaton found that, while Latter-day Saints had above-average fertility, the differences from the national average were not as large as those observed in the United States. Moreover, he found no conclusive or consistent pattern between religiosity and the number of children (e.g., a more religiously active Latter-day Saint woman did not necessarily have more children than a less active one). He thus concluded that Japanese Latter-day Saints were "only weakly" influenced by their religious faith in making their reproductive decisions, ascribing this behavior to the failure of the "pronatalist tradition and cultural orientation" to take root against the background of more culturally acceptable fertility patterns.

The findings from the Japan LDS Survey seem to contradict such an interpretation based on the 1980s data. That Japanese culture affects reproductive decisions is indisputable, clearly evident from the fact that the average number of children has declined over time among religiously active Latter-day Saint women (2.8 for women over the age of 40 vs. 1.9 for those under 40)—even allowing for the possibility that some of those under 40 are yet to have more children. At the same time, the number of children a Latter-day Saint woman in Japan typically bears in our sample was significantly larger than the population average (NB: 57 percent of Latter-day Saint women had three or more children in 2021). It is therefore equally indisputable that pronatalist ideology—centered in Latter-day Saint theology that defines the purpose of procreation as providing homes for God's spirit children—has taken root among religiously active Latter-day Saints in Japan. Heaton's divergent findings may be explained by the nature of the Latter-day Saint population in Japan in the early 1980s, which predominantly consisted of relatively new converts who were just beginning to raise families, and also possibly by the sizable presence in his sample of religiously non-active Latter-day Saints.[2]

2-3. Cultural Background

Education

Sociologists have long observed a positive influence of education on religious participation, based almost exclusively on Christian samples in the United States (Iannaccone 1990; Stolzenberg, Blair-Loy, and Waite 1995). The most straightforward interpretation may be to consider education as contributing to the stock of religious human and social capital. Christianity is a rather sophisticated religion in the sense that it requires its devotees to read scripture and to conceptualize a system of abstract ideas. Religious participation also increases social capital (for example, connections to work and volunteer opportunities; mentors who can write letters of recommendation; social activities to practice soft skills), which may in turn increase educational attainment.

The impact of education on religiosity, however, seems to differ depending on how religiosity is defined. For example, highly educated Christians are more likely to report weekly church attendance than less educated Christians; but if religiosity is defined as belief in supernatural phenomena (such as belief in God) or daily prayer, the impact of education becomes negative (Schwadel 2011). This is complicated by variations across denominations; for example, education has a strong, positive effect on most religiosity measures for Latter-Day Saints, but a neutral effect for mainline Protestants in the United States (Pew Research Center 2017). In the non-Christian context of Japan, Miller (1995) found that education had a negative effect on the likelihood of membership in a new religious movement. Takagi (2016), observing that converts to The Church of Jesus

---

2. According to Heaton (1998b), the weight of non-attenders randomly sampled was adjusted to align with the population size. Given that some 80 percent of Latter-day Saints in Japan do not regularly attend church, it is uncertain how the weight was adjusted. If 80 percent of the adjusted sample indeed included those religiously non-active (many, if not most, of whom likely no longer identified themselves as Latter-day Saints), it is not clear what effect such a large proportion of these individuals would have on findings from the sample.

Figure 2-3. Educational Background
(Percent of respondents with postsecondary and graduate education)

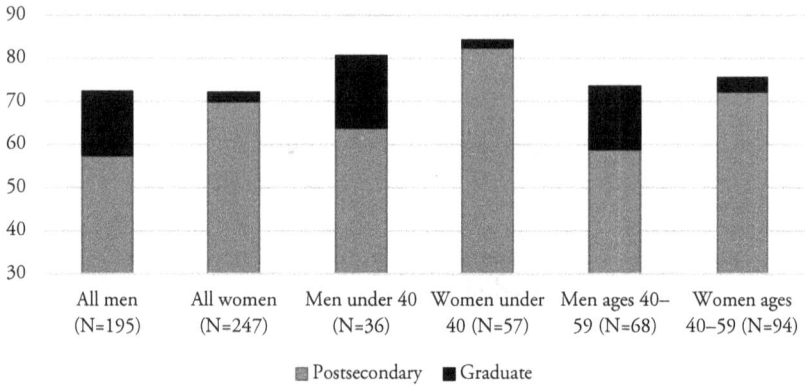

Source: Japan LDS Survey.

Christ of Latter-day Saints during the pre–World War II period predominantly came from those who were receiving (or had received) education at
the country's most prestigious institutions of secondary and higher education, argued that education allowed the individualization of religion and
thus made religion a matter of the choice for the individual. The positive
influence of education is broadly supported by the Japan LDS Survey,
which shows that the Latter-day Saint population is, on average, more
educated than the general population.

There were 442 individuals who identified their educational attainment in terms of the number of years of formal schooling, counting from
first grade in elementary school (Figure 2-3). Japan's educational system
changed drastically during the early post–World War II years, so we felt
that the best way to gauge educational attainment was to ask the number of years of schooling, as opposed to the identification of educational
institutions they had attended (such as high school, college, and university). In Japan, the first nine years are compulsory, so those who did not
complete nine years of schooling (six respondents) were either born before
the postwar educational reforms or had a special circumstance (such as ill-
ness). Though not compulsory, virtually everyone in recent years (though
not in the earlier years) receives an additional three years of education
through twelfth grade, so the focus here is on postsecondary and graduate
education. Clearly the share of Latter-day Saints with postsecondary education was higher among those under the age of 40 than among those ages
40–59: the share rises from 73.5 to 80.6 percent for men and from 75.5 to
84.2 percent for women. A slightly higher percentage of women received

postsecondary education, but far fewer of them went on to receive graduate education than men.

We are not in possession of comparable data for the Japanese population as a whole, though we have the time-series of the percentage of high school graduates each year who move on to receive postsecondary education, which increased from about 60 percent in the 1990s to about 80 percent currently (MEXT 2022). It appears safe to speculate that the general Latter-day Saint population (about 72 percent of whom had some postsecondary education in 2021) is more educated than the general Japanese population. This is consistent, at least qualitatively, with the findings reported by Heaton (1998a), who showed, based on the 1981–83 data, that Latter-day Saints in Japan were more than twice as likely as the general population to have some postsecondary education.[3] It is important to note, however, that any educational advantage Latter-day Saints may have had in the past over the general population is diminishing as more and more Japanese young adults attend postsecondary schools.

The findings from the Japan LDS Survey may be compared to those from the Next Mormons Survey (NMS) of American Latter-day Saints (Figure 2-4). Comparing men to men and women to women—and using the subsample that only includes those who attend church at least weekly to ensure comparability—the share of those with postsecondary education was 74.1 percent for Japanese men and 80.2 percent for American men, and 72.4 percent for Japanese women and 81.5 percent for American women. This suggests that, among active Latter-day Saints, American members are marginally better educated than their Japanese counterparts, although the gap may diminish over time as younger Japanese attain more years of formal education, in line with the national trend.

The share of American Latter-day Saints with some college education in the NMS was considerably higher than the findings reported by Heaton (1998a) based on the 1981–83 data, which gave a share of slightly less than 50 percent for men and women combined. Moreover, the share of those with some college education (80.2 percent for men and 81.5 percent for women) was considerably greater than the general population average (60.3

---

3. Heaton (1998a, Figure 4-17) does not say where he obtained the national average data, but the population average of about 20 percent (and the Latter-day Saint population share of about 40 percent) appears unreasonably low, given that, in 1985, 60 percent of high school graduates were receiving postsecondary education. It is possible that the survey specifically asked whether the respondent had attended university/college (*daigaku*), excluding other postsecondary educational institutions.

Figure 2-4. Educational Background, Japan–U.S. Comparison
(Percent of respondents with postsecondary education
who attend church at least weekly)

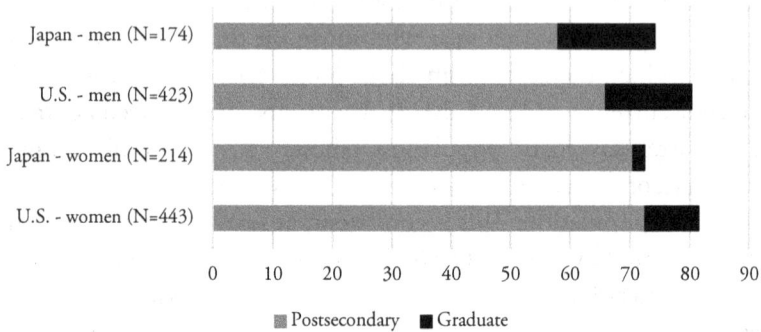

Source: Japan LDS Survey ; Next Mormons Survey.

percent for men and 63.5 percent for women in 2019), clearly establishing the positive influence of religiosity on educational attainment (U.S. Census Bureau 2020). In Japan, in contrast, The Church of Jesus Christ of Latter-day Saints may have attracted relatively more educated individuals in the past, but the educational profiles of Latter-day Saints appear to be converging to those of the general population as second- or third-generation members constitute a larger share of the population and as more young adults nationally are obtaining postsecondary education, as previously noted.

Foreign Experience

Foreign experience is another metric of cultural disposition, which may be particularly helpful in the Japanese context as it is expected to help individuals think or behave beyond the confines of societal norms. In the survey, respondents were asked if they had ever lived in a foreign country for school or work (including a spouse's or parent's work) for more than a year, to which 439 individuals responded (Figure 2-5). Missionary experience was excluded. The average share for the whole sample was 21.9 percent (of which, 15.3 percent was accounted for by those who had lived in the U.S.), which increases to 30.0 (22.2) percent for those respondents under the age of 40. Women tended to have more foreign experience than men, with 35.1 percent of those under 40 reporting to have lived in a foreign country, with the U.S. accounting for 24.6 percent.

Comparative data for the general population are not available, at least in the same form, but an educated guess may be attempted. Japan's ministry

Figure 2-5. Foreign Experience
(Percent of respondents in each group who have
lived in a foreign country for more than a year)

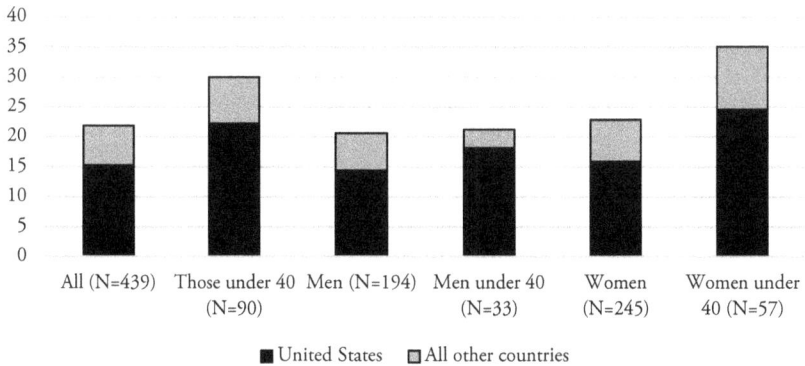

■ United States   □ All other countries

Source: Japan LDS Survey.

of foreign affairs reports every year the year-end number of Japanese citizens who are registered with its consular services abroad (MOFA 2022). We estimate from this that, over the years 1989–2021, at most seven to eleven million Japanese lived abroad as long-term residents in their host countries (excluding as permanent residents), depending on the assumptions we make for the average length of stay (our estimates assume between two and three years). This translates to between 6 and 9 percent of the general population, compared to nearly 22 percent for the Latter-day Saint population. The share of Japanese Latter-day Saints with firsthand exposure to foreign culture appears considerably greater than the general population average.

2-4. Sociability

What we call sociability is an important metric of the personal disposition of individuals, especially in gauging the type of people the Church attracts or the type of people who remain religiously active. To the extent that the Church in Japan still consists mainly of converts, this is a relevant question to ask. Insofar as second- and third-generation Latter-day Saints are concerned, we are interested in knowing how well they felt they were integrated into Japanese society as they were growing up. To pursue this line of inquiry, we posed the following question: "Reflecting back on your time in secondary school, on a scale of 1 through 4, how well did you feel you 'fit in' with your peers, with 1=poorly, 2=somewhat, 3= considerably, and 4=well?" There were 438 individuals who responded to this question (Table 2-2).

Table 2-2. Sociability of Survey Respondents:
"How well did you feel you 'fit in' with your secondary school peers?"
(Percent of respondents in each group)

	1	2	3	4	Total	Average score
	Poorly	Somewhat	Considerably	Well		
All (N=438)	11.9	27.2	40.0	21.0	100	2.7
Men (N=194)	11.3	30.9	39.2	18.6	100	2.6
Women (N=244)	12.3	24.2	40.6	23.0	100	2.7
Converts (N=167)	13.8	21.0	44.3	21.0	100	2.7
Non-converts (N=75)	9.3	29.3	33.3	28.0	100	2.8

Source: Japan LDS Survey.

No clear pattern emerges from this analysis, with the average score of 2.6–2.8 (on a scale of 1 through 4) for all groups (that is, on average, Latter-day Saints in Japan felt they fit in nearly "considerably" with their peers during their adolescence). Those who felt they fit in "poorly" with their peers were in the small minority, dispelling any notion that the Church predominantly attracts social misfits. On the contrary, 65 percent of those who joined the Church as converts had felt they fit in either "considerably" or "well" with their secondary school peers. Remarkably, 28 percent of second- and third-generation members felt they fit in "well" with their peers, despite various expectations their church places on their behavior and activities (a topic to be explored further in a subsequent chapter). Part of this result may have reflected the nature of the survey—the sample included many who were approached through social media networks.

Another aspect of sociability is the number of friendships that individuals develop. Respondents were asked to select one out of five statements that best describes the friendships they enjoy inside and outside of church (Figure 2-6). It is immediately clear that religiously active Latter-day Saints create their own community by forming friendships within the Church, with 37.9 percent of men and 33.7 percent of women reporting that they had more friends in the Church than outside of it (there was little difference between the full sample and the subsample that included only those who attended church at least weekly). In addition, 25.1 percent of men and 29.7 percent of women stated that they had many close friends in the Church. Only 2.6 percent of men (2.3 percent for "active" men only) and 1.2 percent of women (1.4 percent for "active" women only) stated that they did

Figure 2-6. Church Friendship
(Percent of respondents in each group)

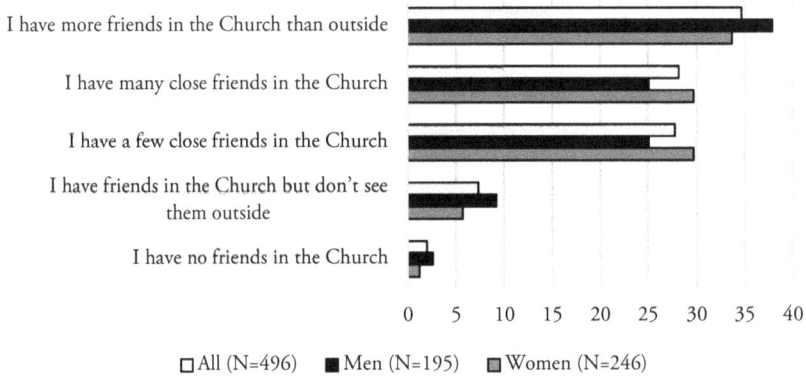

Source: Japan LDS Survey.

not have any close friends in the Church. Again, this result may also have reflected the sample bias inherent in this type of survey towards those with more active social networks within the Latter-day Saint community.

2-5. Ideological Inclination

In Japan, the common polarity to express the spectrum of political views is *hoshu* (lit. "to maintain or preserve") vs. *kakushin* (lit. "to innovate"). For convenience, we will use the term "conservative" for the former and the term "progressive" for the latter. In Japanese politics, to be conservative means to support maintaining the political system that largely emerged in the postwar period, after the country had regained sovereignty in 1952 under the San Francisco Peace Treaty that ended seven years of American occupation. The pillar of the system is the Japan–United States security alliance, renewed and formalized to its current form in 1960. Hence, those who are politically conservative tend to be pro-America. In terms of social values, the conservatives tend to uphold the Japanese family (*ie*) system of primogeniture and traditional gender roles, while the progressives (for which the term *shinpo* [lit. "to progress"] is more common) not only challenge traditional norms but favor adapting the system to meet changing societal needs. These elements of political and social views are explored in subsequent sections.

For the moment, we are interested in the respondents' own assessment of where they stand on the ideological spectrum. We asked them to characterize themselves as either conservative or progressive, without specifying what the terms mean. Given the definitions of these terms, it

Figure 2-7. Political and Social Views
(Percent of respondents in each group)

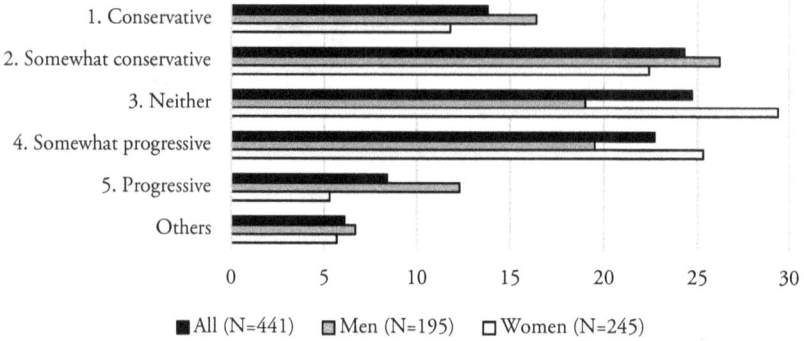

Source: Japan LDS Survey.

is possible to be politically conservative and socially progressive, and vice versa. At this stage, we are only exploring their own ideological perceptions of themselves. It turns out that, on a scale of 1 through 5 (with 1 being conservative and 5 being progressive), the average score was 2.8 for men and 2.9 for women. In other words, Japanese Latter-day Saints on average considered themselves to be about right in the middle of the ideological spectrum or, if anything, somewhat on the conservative side (Figure 2-7). Even so, the distribution included a significant number of respondents at the other end of the spectrum, with 12.3 percent of men and 5.3 percent of women considering themselves to be progressive. Japanese Latter-day Saints appear to represent a good cross-section of Japanese society.

2-6. Political Views

Moving on to explore the specific elements of the ideological makeup, the survey asked the respondents a few questions regarding their political views, including ones that would allow us to compare them with those of the general population. Their responses are organized in terms of (1) political party support, (2) the need for or desirability of political engagement, and (3) the nationally contentious and divisive issue of national defense, which involves a potential revision of the "peace" clause of the Japanese constitution and the Japan–U.S. security alliance, which will be explained below.

Party Support

The first question concerned their political party affiliation or support. A unique feature of the Japanese political landscape is that a large seg-

Figure 2-8. Political Party Support, Latter-day Saints vs. the General Population (Percent of respondents expressing particular party support)

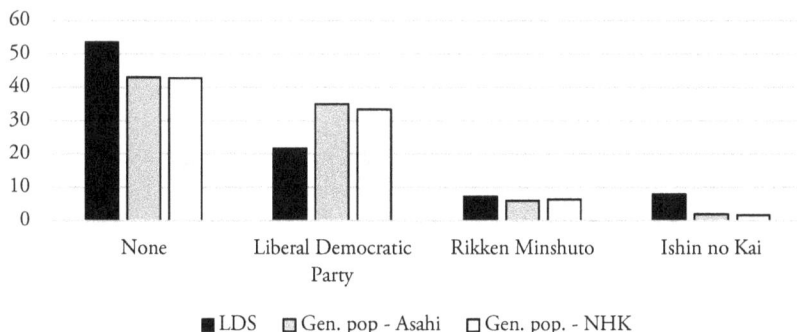

Notes: LDS sample size (N)=439; the Asahi survey was conducted in April 2021 and the NHK survey in August 2021.
Sources: Japan LDS Survey; the Asahi Shinbun; and NHK.

ment (sometimes constituting a majority) of the public does not claim to support a particular political party.[4] For example, in 2021, as much as 43 percent stated that they supported no particular political party (Asahi Shinbun 2021c; NHK 2021c).[5] At 53.5 percent, the share of Latter-day Saints who identified themselves with no party was significantly larger (at the 1 percent level) than the national average (Figure 2-8),[6] though the broad pattern was the same.[7] This translates into less support for the ruling conservative Liberal Democratic Party (21.6 percent) than the national average (33–35 percent). Fifteen Japanese Latter-day Saints supported the

---

4. The Japanese electoral system, in which the voter casts separate ballots for a candidate (in the district) and for a party (for proportional representation), allows multiple parties to survive as long as they can muster enough nationwide votes. Most conservatives tend to vote for the Liberal Democratic Party (LDP), which has been almost continuously in power since 1955 (except for August 1993–June 1994 and September 2009–December 2012).

5. The Asahi survey, conducted in early April 2021, had 1,551 respondents. The NHK survey, conducted in early August 2021, had 1,214 respondents.

6. Roughly, statistical significance at 1 percent means that the probability of obtaining the stated result by chance is only one percent. In this particular instance, we can state, with a 99-percent confidence, that the Latter-day Saint population differs from the national population.

7. In terms of political views, we can reject the hypothesis that the Latter-day Saint share does not differ from the general population share at the 1 percent level, except in one case to be noted below.

Japan Communist Party (not reported in the figure). Historically, Japanese Christians have often aligned themselves with socialism, if not outright communism, which in Japan has stood for the poor and the disadvantaged. A small trace of that tradition can be seen among the Latter-day Saints.

Political Engagement

Respondents assessed their agreement with three statements on personal political engagement and national defense (Table 2-3). On the first question, 55.1 percent of the 428 respondents (62.3 percent for men and 49.6 percent for women) either "somewhat" or "strongly" agreed with the statement "Latter-day Saints should be actively involved in politics to promote values consistent with the gospel." The average score (on a scale from 1 [strongly disagree] to 5 [strongly agree]) was 3.7 for men and 3.5 for women, suggesting that on average, Latter-day Saints in Japan have a moderate inclination to be involved politically. At the same time, 16.7 percent of men and 13.1 percent of women either "somewhat" or "strongly" disagreed with the idea that they should be involved in the political process. The same sense of patriotic duty many American Latter-day Saints express toward political engagement is not found among Japanese Latter-day Saints, possibly because of the widely held mistrust of politicians and the political process in Japan.[8]

National Defense

The next two questions were about national defense. The issues that divide conservatives and progressives in Japan concern the status of Article 9 of the Japanese constitution and the role of the 1960 Japan–U.S. security alliance. Japan's so-called pacifist constitution, a draft of which was presented to Japan by the United States during the early phase of the occupation, renounces war as a means of settling international disputes

---

8. In September 2019, a Japanese think tank conducted a survey of 1,000 people concerning their views of the state of democracy in Japan. Only 7.6 percent of the respondents considered, and another 33.9 percent somewhat considered, politicians to be their representatives. Being asked to rate their degree of trust in various democratic institutions, only 0.9 percent of the respondents answered that they "strongly" trusted politicians (another 19.2 percent "somewhat" trusted politicians). The combined total of 20.1 percent compares to 61.1 percent for the judiciary, 55.7 percent for universities, 53.9 percent for the mass media, 44.1 percent for the government bureaucracy, and 37.4 percent for the electoral system. See Genron NPO (2019).

Table 2-3. Political Views of Survey Respondents
(Percent of total in each group)

		1 Strongly disagree	2 Somewhat disagree	3 Neither agree nor disagree	4 Somewhat agree	5 Strongly agree	Total	Av.
Latter-day Saints should be actively involved in politics to promote values consistent with the gospel	All (N=428)	8.9	6.1	29.9	26.6	28.5	100	3.6
	Men (N=191)	9.9	6.8	20.9	26.7	35.6	100	3.7
	Women (N=236)	7.6	5.5	37.3	26.7	22.9	100	3.5
I am in favor of amending Article 9 of the Japanese constitution to allow legitimate self-defense capability	All (N=402)	26.6	12.4	24.9	13.2	22.9	100	2.9
	Men (N=188)	20.2	8.0	19.7	17.6	34.6	100	3.4
	Women (N=214)	32.2	16.4	29.4	9.3	12.6	100	2.5
I am in favor of a strong Japan–U.S. alliance as a means of securing peace in East Asia	All (N=399)	3.5	5.8	26.1	25.3	39.3	100	3.9
	Men (N=189)	4.2	4.2	14.3	21.7	55.6	100	4.2
	Women (N=210)	2.9	7.1	36.7	28.6	24.8	100	3.7

Source: Japan LDS Survey.

and abrogates the right to maintain armed forces.[9] The initial aim of the United States following the end of World War II was to disarm Japan, but it soon reversed its course when the Cold War with the Soviet Union escalated. During the Korean War, the United States instructed Japan to establish a paramilitary unit within the police force, which then developed into a major military organization that exists today known euphemisti-

---

9. Article 9 reads in part: "the Japanese people forever renounce war as a sovereign right of the nation and the threat or use of force as means of settling international disputes. In order to accomplish the aim of the preceding paragraph, land, sea, and air forces, as well as other war potential, will never be maintained." Official translation from the Prime Minister's office.

cally as the Self-Defense Forces, whose budget is comparable in size to the defense budget of France or the United Kingdom.[10]

The successive LDP governments have justified escalating defense spending solely for self-defense purposes and hence not as a violation of Article 9, but public debate has been raging for a few decades on whether or not the constitution should be amended to legitimize the Self-Defense Forces explicitly. The conservatives favor revising the constitution as a way to allow Japan to play a more assertive role in the world, while the progressives are opposed, fearing that a revision of the constitution may lead to a resurgence of militarism.

In our survey, 34.6 percent of men and 12.6 percent of women "strongly" supported amending Article 9, while 17.6 and 9.3 percent, respectively, "somewhat" supported. On the opposite end, 20.2 percent of men and 32.2 percent of women "strongly" opposed amending the article. Men were more hawkish than women. Likewise, a similar gender difference could be observed for the Japan–U.S. alliance. With the escalating geopolitical tension in the East China Sea, support for the Japan–U.S. security alliance has generally been rising among the Japanese public in recent years. In the Japan LDS Survey, 55.6 percent of men and 24.8 percent of women either "somewhat" or "strongly" agreed with the statement "I am in favor of a strong Japan–U.S. alliance as a means of securing peace in East Asia." Support was stronger for the Japan–U.S. alliance among both men and women than for the constitutional amendment. Only 4.2 percent of men and 2.9 percent of women expressed "strong" opposition to the Japan–U.S. alliance.

Comparison with the National Population

Where are Latter-day Saints situated on the national opinion spectrum? The Japan LDS Survey can be compared to the *Asahi* and NHK surveys to answer this question (Figure 2-9). A 2021 Asahi survey reported support for the constitutional amendment at 30 percent (Asahi Shinbun 2021b),[11]

---

10. In 2021, Japan budgeted ¥5.34 trillion (approximately $49.4 billion at the prevailing exchange rate) for military expenditure, including ¥619.9 billion for expenses associated with the stationing of United States forces in Japan (MOD 2021). In 2021, Global Firepower ranked Japan's military strength fifth out of 140 countries (Global Firepower 2021).

11. Conducted from March and April 2021, with 2,175 respondents. We cannot reject the hypothesis that the LDS share of 32.9 percent does not differ from the Asahi share of 30 percent at the 5 percent level of significance.

Figure 2-9. Views on National Defense,
Latter-day Saints vs. the General Population
(Percent of respondents who express support)

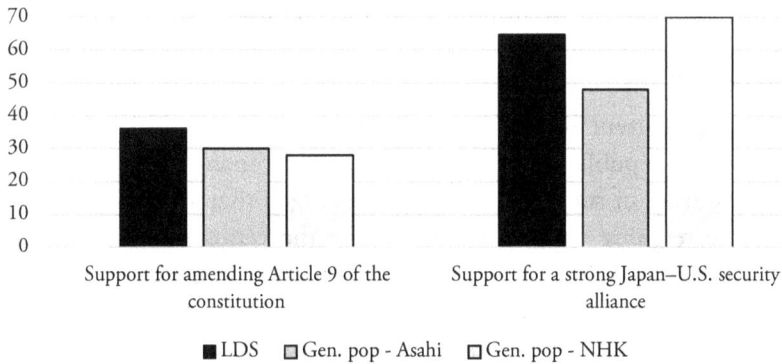

Notes: the figures for Latter-day Saints combine those who "support strongly"
and those who "support somewhat"; Asahi surveys were conducted in March/
April 2021 for the first item and February 2017 for the second item, while
NHK surveys were conducted in April 2021 for both.
Sources: Japan LDS Survey; the Asahi Shinbun; and NHK.

while a 2021 NHK survey reported at 28 percent (NHK 2021b),[12] compared to the support of 36.1 percent in the Japan LDS Survey (where we
have combined those who responded "somewhat agree" and "strongly
agree" as a measure of support). As to the Japan–U.S. alliance, the support of 64.6 percent among the Latter-day Saints was comparable to the
70 percent in another 2021 NHK survey who thought that Japan should
strengthen its alliance with the United States (NHK 2021a),[13] and the 48
percent in a 2017 Asahi survey who thought that strengthening the Japan–
U.S. alliance would contribute to peace and stability in East Asia (Asahi
Shinbun 2017).[14] On both of these issues, the views of Japanese Latter-day
Saints appear to differ little from those of the general public.

2-7. Social Views

The last main section of this chapter explores the views of Japanese
Latter-day Saints on several contemporary social issues. Once again,
where feasible, we compare our survey results with those conducted by
the progressive-leaning *Asahi* and the somewhat more conservative-lean-

12. Conducted in late April 2021, with 1,533 respondents.
13. Conducted in April 2021, with 1,222 respondents.
14. Conducted in February 2017, with 953 respondents.

ing NHK news organizations. The responses are organized in terms of (1) contemporary issues, including approval of a female monarch, gender equality, same-sex marriage, separate surnames for husband and wife; and (2) government policy on immigration and refugees.

Contemporary Issues

First, the current emperor does not have a male heir, which has given rise to an active public debate as to whether a woman should be allowed to become head of state. The conservatives argue that allowing a woman to become reigning empress would violate the centuries-long tradition. Second, gender equality has belatedly become a pressing social issue, especially in the light of a declining population that has highlighted the need for greater social participation of women. Third, there is broad support for legalizing same-sex marriage, but little progress has been made because of opposition from the ultra-conservative wing of the LDP. Fourth, with their greater social participation, an increasing number of women are finding it inconvenient to change their legal surnames when they become married.[15] Several attempts by opposition parties to introduce legislations to legalize separate surnames for husband and wife since the 1990s have been blocked by ultra-conservative members of the LDP, despite broad public support.

In our sample of largely active Latter-day Saints, the overwhelming majority (85.9 percent of men and a surprisingly smaller 77.7 percent of women) "strongly"—and another 9.4 and 14.1 percent, respectively, "somewhat"—supported gender equality as a citizenship right (Table 2-4), but the support for specific aspects of gender equality was much weaker. For example, only 35.9 percent of men and 28.2 percent of women "strongly"—and another 18.2 and 22.5 percent, respectively, "somewhat"—supported a female monarch, while only 31.2 percent of men and 39.7 percent of women either "somewhat" or "strongly" supported separate surnames for husband and wife. As to same-sex marriage, Japanese Latter-day Saints expressed a strong aversion (even though the question was explicitly posed in such a way as to allow a religious reservation), with

---

15. Japan's Civil Code, consistent with the traditional family system, requires that husband and wife adopt the same surname. Except when the husband is received into the wife's family when there is no male heir, the general practice is for the wife to adopt the husband's name. Universities allow women to use their maiden names (so that they can claim all due credit for their academic work), and the government has since 2019 allowed maiden names to be parenthesized along with the legal names on official documents, including passports and driver's licenses.

Table 2-4. Views of Survey Respondents on Contemporary Social Issues
(Percent of total in each group)

		1 Strongly disagree	2 Somewhat disagree	3 Neither agree nor disagree	4 Somewhat agree	5 Strongly agree	Total	Av.
I support legally allowing a woman to become reigning monarch	All (N=408)	11.3	4.7	31.9	20.6	31.6	100	3.6
	Men (N=181)	18.2	7.2	20.4	18.2	35.9	100	3.5
	Women (N=227)	5.7	2.6	41.0	22.5	28.2	100	3.7
I support gender equality as a citizenship right	All (N=433)	1.6	0.7	4.4	12.0	81.3	100	4.7
	Men (N=191)	1.1	0.5	3.1	9.4	85.9	100	4.8
	Women (N=242)	2.1	0.8	5.4	14.1	77.7	100	4.6
I support same-sex marriage as the right of a citizen, even though I have doctrinal reservation	All (N=422)	42.9	15.9	17.8	10.9	12.6	100	2.3
	Men (N=192)	49.0	14.1	13.0	9.9	14.1	100	2.3
	Women (N=230)	37.8	17.4	21.7	11.7	11.3	100	2.4
I am in favor of granting separate surnames for husband and wife	All (N=413)	24.2	12.8	27.1	18.9	17.0	100	2.9
	Men (N=186)	27.4	12.9	28.5	14.5	16.7	100	2.8
	Women (N=227)	21.6	12.8	26.0	22.5	17.2	100	3.0

Source: Japan LDS Survey.

49 percent of men and 37.8 percent of women expressing objection to it even as a citizenship right.

Immigrants and Refugees

We next asked the respondents what they thought of government policy on immigration and refugees. With a declining and rapidly aging population, Japan has been suffering an acute labor shortage in occupations that are typically filled by younger workers, leading to a heated public debate

Table 2-5. Views of Survey Respondents on Immigration and Refugee Policy
(Percent of total in each group)

		1 Strongly disagree	2 Somewhat disagree	3 Neither agree nor disagree	4 Somewhat agree	5 Strongly agree	Total	Av.
I am in favor of allowing more immigrants to come to Japan	All (N=413)	13.3	15.5	30.0	25.4	15.7	100	3.2
	Men (N=190)	16.9	16.3	23.2	23.7	20.0	100	3.1
	Women (N=233)	10.3	14.8	35.9	26.9	12.1	100	3.2
Japan should grant refugee status more liberally to displaced individuals	All (N=417)	12.0	12.7	30.9	26.6	17.8	100	3.3
	Men (N=192)	17.2	13.5	23.4	25.5	20.3	100	3.2
	Women (N=225)	7.6	12.0	37.3	27.6	15.6	100	3.3

Source: Japan LDS Survey.

on whether Japan should ease its restrictive immigration policy. As to its refugee policy, some feel that Japan has not lived up to its responsibility as an industrial nation to accept a more meaningful number of displaced persons as refugees. Japan does accept them temporarily but recognizes very few of them as refugees eligible to settle in the country. According to the nonprofit Japan Association for Refugees (JAR), in 2020, Japan recognized as refugees only 47 of the 3,936 displaced persons it had temporarily received, compared to 63,456 in Germany, 19,596 in Canada, and 18,177 in the United States (JAR 2020). There has been a strong resistance to changing the historical homogeneity of the Japanese population, but there are individuals and organizations in Japan calling on the government to accept refugees more liberally. The views of Latter-day Saints were divided on both immigration and refugee policy (Table 2-5), with the average score of around 3 ("neither agree nor disagree") for men and women.

Comparison with the National Population

We can compare the social views of Latter-day Saints with those of the general Japanese population in four of these areas where comparable data are available (Figure 2-10). We note that, except for immigration, Latter-day Saints are more socially conservative than the general population,[16] no doubt influenced by their religious beliefs. Their support, in particular, for legalizing same sex-marriage (at 23.5 percent) was significantly lower than the general population share of 65 percent (Asahi Shinbun 2021a),[17] even generously allowing for a potential margin of error (in fact, the proportion of Japanese Latter-day Saints who approved legalizing same-sex marriage was similar to that of their American counterparts).[18] The proportion of Latter-day Saints who expressed support for a female monarch was 52.2 percent, compared to 76 percent in an *Asahi* survey (Asahi Shinbun 2019),[19] and 74 percent in a NHK survey (NHK 2019),[20] while only 35.9 percent of Latter-day Saints, as opposed to 67 percent in the general population (Asahi Shinbun 2021c),[21] supported legalizing separate surnames.

Support for more immigration among Latter-day Saints (at 41.2 percent) was the only metric that was comparable to the general population average: 40 percent (Asahi Shinbun 2018) and 32.7 percent (NHK 2020).[22] Responses to survey questions on immigration can vary widely, depending on the sample and how the questions are phrased. This accounts for the considerable discrepancy between the 2020 NHK survey and the 2018 Asahi survey. Responses tend to become more favorable to "immigration" when a question is posed in terms of a need for foreign workers,

---

16. In terms of social views, we can reject the hypothesis that the Latter-day Saint share does not differ from the general population share at the 1 percent level of significance, except in one case to be noted below.

17. Conducted in late March 2021, with 1,564 respondents.

18. Comparing Japanese and American Latter-day Saints who attended church at least weekly, we find that 20.7 percent of men and 18.8 percent of women supported legalizing same-sex marriage in Japan while 19.8 percent of men and 21.2 percent of women did so in the United States (where the NMS phrased the question in terms of legalizing it in all fifty states).

19. Conducted in March and April 2019, with 2,093 respondents.

20. Conducted in September 2019, with 1,539 respondents.

21. Conducted in early April 2021, with 1,551 respondents.

22. The Asahi survey was conducted in November and December 2018, with 2,038 respondents. The NHK survey was conducted in March 2020, with 1,572 respondents. We cannot reject the hypothesis that the Latter-day Saint share of 38.5 percent does not differ from the Asahi share of 40 percent at the 5 percent level of significance. Roughly, this means that we accept the equality of the two populations with a 95-percent confidence.

Figure 2-10. Social Views on Controversial Contemporary Issues,
Latter-day Saints vs. the General Population
(Percent of respondents who express support)

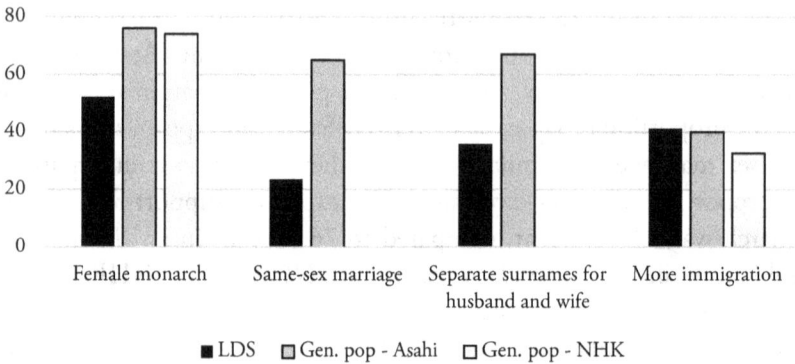

Notes: the figures for Latter-day Saints combine those who "support strongly"
and "support somewhat." Asahi surveys were conducted in March/April 2019
for the first item, March 2021 for the second, November/December for the
third, and April 2021 for the fourth, while NHK surveys were conducted in
September 2019 for the first item and March 2020 for the third. No comparable
NHK surveys exist for the second and the fourth.
Sources: Japan LDS Survey; the Asahi Shinbun; and NHK.

as opposed to "foreigners living in the neighborhood." Our survey simply
asked whether the respondent supported more immigration, and, for comparison, we selected the figures from the Asahi and NHK surveys that we
thought were the most comparable. The proportion of Latter-day Saints
who supported greater immigration was only slightly larger than the *Asahi*
survey, and about 9 percentage points larger than the NHK survey. This
may indicate that, despite their generally more socially conservative lean-
ing, the views of Latter-day Saints on immigration are either on par with or
somewhat more progressive than those of the general public.

2-8. Conclusion

This chapter has discussed the personal and social profiles of religiously
active Latter-day Saints in Japan, with the objective of understanding how
they live and think as members of Japanese society. A clear picture that
emerges from this analysis is that, far from forming a distinct subculture,
these Latter-day Saints represent a cross-section of Japanese society, from
the most conservative to the most progressive on contemporary political
and social issues. If anything, they are somewhat more conservative on
social issues, especially on same-sex marriage but not on immigration, un-

doubtedly informed by their religious convictions. The range of views on political issues, however, differs little from the general population. Even so, they form their own community by developing extensive friendships and predominantly marrying within the faith. While Japanese cultural influence on reproductive decisions cannot be denied (the average number of children in Latter-day Saint families has been declining along with the national trend), the pronatalist ideology of Latter-day Saint theology has taken root among religiously active Latter-day Saints. The average fertility rate among Latter-day Saints has consistently exceeded the national average by about one child per woman.

Compared to the population average, members of The Church of Jesus Christ of Latter-day Saints tend to be more educated (in terms of years of formal schooling), though the gap may be diminishing as more young adults obtain postsecondary education in Japan. Japanese Latter-day Saints are marginally less educated than their American counterparts, and the positive influence of religiosity on education (not vice versa) observed in the United States does not seem as strong in Japan. The overwhelming majority considered themselves to be sociable (only about 10 percent felt they had fit in "poorly" with secondary school peers), dispelling the notion that the Church attracts social misfits. The share of Latter-day Saints with firsthand exposure to foreign culture (through living abroad for more than a year) is two or three times the national average, possibly reflecting their membership in a worldwide church. Interestingly, the self-assessment of their ideological inclination is distributed almost evenly on the conservative/progressive spectrum, indicating that, despite their commitment to the same religious beliefs and practices, Japanese Latter-day Saints are indeed a diverse group of individuals.

CHAPTER 3

RELIGIOUS CONVERSION

3-1. Introduction

This chapter, focusing on a subset of the survey respondents who identified themselves as converts to The Church of Jesus Christ of Latter-day Saints, discusses how they came to acquire a new religious identity. Our purpose is to understand what facilitates and what impedes the process of new identity formation—that is, religious conversion. Converts constitute the overwhelming majority of church membership in Japan. The sample of Latter-day Saints collected from the Japan LDS Survey reflects this reality. Of the 530 respondents who identified their membership status, 71.3 percent (numbering 378) were converts (see Figure 1-9 in chapter 1). There was little gender difference. Of the 410 respondents who identified both their membership status and their gender, 69.6 percent of men (numbering 135) and 66.2 percent of women (numbering 143) were converts. Thus, these 378 individuals (when gender is not specified) and 278 individuals (when gender is specified) are the subject of this chapter. About 82 percent of them reported attending church at least once a week.

The rest of this chapter is organized as follows. Section 3-2 discusses identity-theoretic perspectives on religious conversion, explaining how the survey responses can be interpreted as a way of describing the process of new identity formation. Section 3-3 reports the demographic profiles of Latter-day Saint converts in Japan in terms of the (calendar) year and the (biological) age of their conversion. Section 3-4 identifies various influences on conversion, such as prior knowledge of the Church, prior exposure to Christianity, consequential Latter-day Saint doctrines and teachings, and social relationships, especially the significant role missionaries play. Section 3-5, in turn, discusses influences that work against conversion, with a focus on family opposition that many reported having experienced. Section 3-6 attempts to ascertain if there has been a discernible change among converts in terms of their demographics or prior background over time, as Japanese society has clearly been changing. Finally, section 3-7 presents a conclusion.

3-2. Identity-theoretic Perspectives on Conversion

Within the framework of identity theory, conversion to a new religion can be thought of as the acquisition of a new identity. To a person who has previously professed no religion, this is an additional identity, whereas a person who has previously professed a religion must abandon it, at least in part, before the new identity can be acquired. In either case, the new religious identity must coexist with multiple other identities he or she maintains as members of various social groups. Then, by invoking Stryker's theory of salience (Stryker and Burke 2000), we may surmise that conversion to a new religion is generally only possible when the new identity does not heavily conflict with existing identities. The very fact that few in Japan have embraced Christianity, let alone The Church of Jesus Christ of Latter-day Saints, suggests that for many Japanese there is a fundamental conflict, among other things, between the Christian worldview and the worldview rooted in Japanese culture. On the metaphysical (spiritual or intellectual) level, the very act of conversion means that the person has reconciled the conflicting worldviews by fusing a new one. On the practical level, one must translate the metaphysical conversion into *social* conversion by committing oneself to the norms of behavior expected from being a Latter-day Saint.

The concept of cultural or religious capital, as proposed by Bourdieu (1986), may be useful in this context. Cultural capital is comprised of the intangible assets possessed by those who have absorbed the dominant culture in terms of knowledge, ways of speaking, manners, and the like. Religious capital, a subset of cultural capital, may include knowledge of scripture, familiarity with religious rituals and obligations, and even a network of people one develops in a particular faith community. The process of participating in a religion transforms time and effort into knowledge and worldviews that constitute religious capital (Iannaccone 1990). Framed in this way, adopting a new religious identity means favoring new capital over old capital. Cultural capital forms the basis for social structure and one's position within this structure. Displaying this capital through symbolism embedded in such intangible assets as behaviors, customs, possessions, and credentials enables individuals to improve or secure their status within the social hierarchy. By understanding religious conversion through this lens, we understand why it is difficult for individuals to abandon their accumulated capital entirely. Participation in a religion that conflicts with the widely accepted values and norms of the individual's community means abandoning the accumulation of valuable capital, thereby threatening his or her status within that community.

Even though the claims of The Church of Jesus Christ of Latter-day Saints to Christianity are sometimes contested by other Christian denominations, many of its doctrines and practices are clearly aligned with Western Christian perspectives, perspectives alien and even hostile to much of Japanese society. Transition to a Western religion in general, and the Latter-day Saint faith in particular, is difficult within this social context for two reasons. First, the adoption of this religion requires acquiring a vast amount of new religious capital, including: belief in a Judeo-Christian deity; belief in the Christian concepts of sin, atonement, and mortality; and belief in the Latter-day Saint–specific perspective of mortality, salvation, and deity as well as an understanding of the social and structural organization of the Church. On top of this, adopting the new faith further requires abandoning some prior knowledge and worldviews that have been accumulated over years of participating in Japanese society, the most prominent among which may be polytheism and moral relativism (i.e., the idea that there is no absolute good or evil). Second, as another kind of difficulty, abandonment of cultural capital can take a heavy toll on social status as it means abandoning some of the resources necessary for maintaining and negotiating status in the community. In the case of the Latter-day Saint faith, declining jobs that would require working on Sundays, constantly refusing an offer of green tea, and navigating the expectations of social drinking in the workplace are just a few such examples in Japan.

While this understanding of cultural capital explains why only a tiny proportion of the Japanese population has embraced any Christian denomination, we must not become too dismissive of the potential for The Church of Jesus Christ of Latter-day Saints to enjoy wider acceptance in Japan than it does today. For one thing, a Japanese person who acquires Latter-day Saint identity does not have to give up all of his or her cultural capital. That is to say, there is some cultural continuity between being Japanese and being a Latter-day Saint. In fact, some of the Latter-day Saint teachings resonate well with what is considered important in Japanese culture, such as humility, honesty, filial and familial duties, and reverence for one's ancestors. Another reason for the potential for wider acceptability is that culture does not prescribe a single choice but allows a range of possible actions in a given situation, as we earlier observed in our discussion of cultural sociology (Swidler 1986). This is true of Japanese culture. Individuals, while subject to cultural constraints, are able to prac-

Figure 3-1. Year of Conversion
(Percent of respondents in each group)

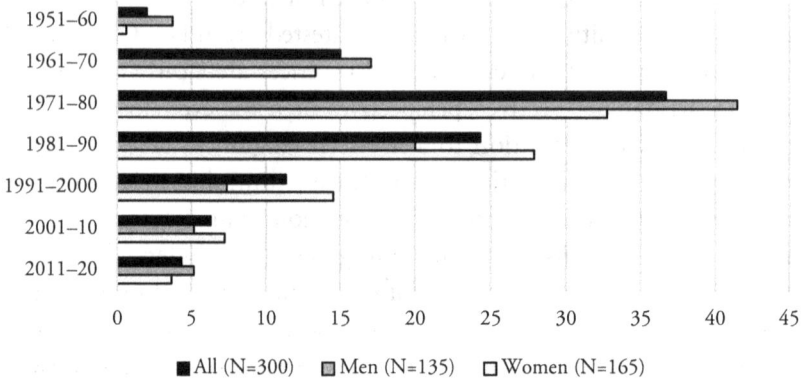

Source: Japan LDS Survey.

tice a religion of their choice, as dictated by their own conscience, personal disposition, prior experience, family background, and the like. The fact that the Church in Japan boasts a membership of more than 130,000 today (though admittedly not all of them are religiously active) is prima facie evidence that it is possible to be both Japanese and a Latter-day Saint. The survey questions were designed to explore this very issue, namely, how one comes to the decision to become a Latter-day Saint.

3-3. Demographic Profiles of Latter-day Saint Converts

Year of Conversion

Exactly 300 individuals identified both their age of conversion and their birth year, allowing us to know when (in terms of calendar year) they had joined the Church (Figure 3-1). More than half (56.7 percent) of them joined the Church in the decades between 1971 and 1990, the period that saw the largest number of converts during any period in the history of the Church in Japan, when the membership increased by more than five times (see Figure 1-2 in chapter 1). Having been baptized more than thirty years ago, many of these converts have become seasoned members, likely middle-aged or older. In contrast, more of the younger respondents in the study tended to be second- or third-generation members (who are not being represented in this chapter). Only about 20 percent of those under the age of 40 were converts (see Figure 1-9 in chapter 1). The survey did not ask the respondents where they had joined the Church.

Figure 3-2. Age of Conversion
(Percent of respondents in each group)

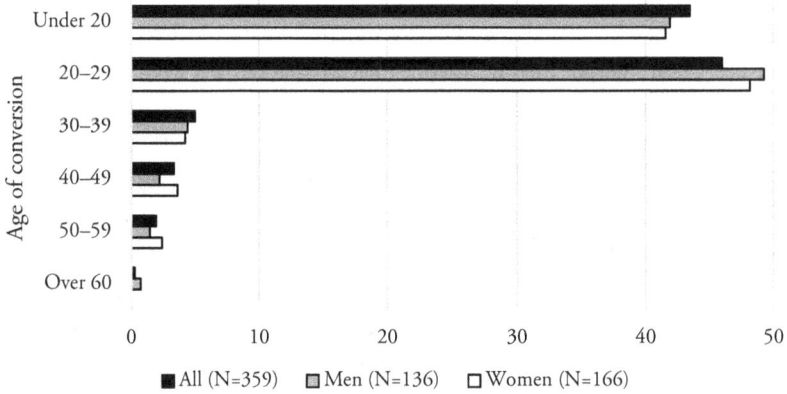

Source: Japan LDS Survey.

We presume that many of these converts came from the larger urban areas where the Church was more established in earlier years.[1]

Age of Conversion

The overwhelming majority of converts in the survey joined the Church at a relatively young age (Figure 3-2). This should not be surprising to anyone familiar with the missionary work of the Church in Japan, or perhaps anywhere for that matter, but the size of this majority may be somewhat of a surprise. In fact, almost 90 percent of all converts in our sample joined the Church under the age of 30, with little gender difference. The average age of conversion was 22.1 for all; and, for those who identified their gender, 21.9 for men and 22.0 for women.[2] Very few joined the Church after the age of 50, and even a smaller number joined

---

1. Takagi (2016) observes that, before the split of the Northern Far East Mission in 1968, more than 50 percent of converts in the mid-1960s came from the two population centers of Tokyo and Osaka. A survey of 104 converts between 1955 and 1975 reported by Numano (2000) shows that 60 percent of them came from the three population centers around Tokyo, Osaka, and Nagoya (the number rises to 77 percent if those who were converted in the principal regional cities of Sapporo, Sendai, Hiroshima, and Fukuoka are included).

2. Sugiyama (1997) conducted a survey of 140 Latter-day Saints in Sendai, Morioka, and Fukushima between 1994 and 1996 to find that the average age of conversion was 22. Coming from a different sample, the number is remarkably similar to ours.

after the age of 60 (in fact, no identified woman in our sample did). These findings—that religious conversions tend to take place at a young age—are consistent with the large empirical literature on the sociology and economics of religion: those who switch religions tend to do so early in their life cycle (Verter 2003; Stark 1998; Iannaccone 1990). A remarkably similar phenomenon was observed in the Japan Mission of The Church of Jesus Christ of Latter-day Saints before World War II (Takagi 2016). From 1901 to 1924, about 70 percent of the Latter-day Saint converts in Japan were between 16 and 25 years of age at the time of baptism, with the average age of 22.9.

The reasons are quite intuitive. Young people are open to new ideas, they do not have the family or work commitments of older people, and they do not feel the pressure of society that comes with age. More formally, these tendencies may be explained in terms of religious human capital in the following way (Iannaccone 1998; Stark and Finke 2000).[3] To enjoy the benefits of a particular religion requires human capital specific to that religion. Thus, the cost of conversion to the Church is expected to be lower for a younger person who is likely to possess a smaller stock of capital (which is acquired through "on-the-job training") because the return from the existing stock of capital, or the cost of giving up the current religion, is smaller. In the case of a younger person, moreover, the benefit of switching to a new religion will be enjoyed over a longer period, making its expected net present value greater.

3-4. Influences that Contribute to Conversion

Prior Knowledge and Background

The Japan LDS Survey asked the respondents about their knowledge and background prior to their conversion, requesting them to select all that applied from a list of five possible forms of religious knowledge rel-

---

3. The basic framework used in the economics of religion is to assume that, in making a religious decision (whether to join a new religion, attend church more frequently, or donate more money), the individual maximizes their intertemporal utility (or, in simpler terms, makes decisions with their resources and time to seek out the highest level of satisfaction) defined over this life and the next. Individuals who increase their religious activity will spend more resources in this life (such as time, purchased goods, and effort building up religious human capital), but do so believing that their investment increases their utility in the afterlife. Those who do not believe in an afterlife, or do not believe that such religious investment will affect their afterlife's utility, will focus on maximizing utility for this lifetime only.

Figure 3-3. Prior Knowledge and Background
(Percent of respondents in each group)

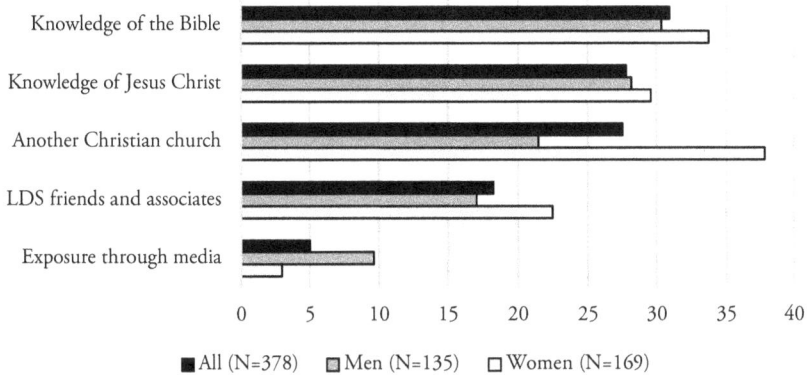

Notes: respondents were requested to select all that apply; "others" are excluded
from the figure.
Source: Japan LDS Survey.

evant to the Church (Figure 3-3). It is clear from their responses that
some previous knowledge of or familiarity with Christianity was more
common than any other factor, including having Latter-day Saint friends
and associates (which about 18 percent identified as having prior to their
conversion). Indeed, as much as 31 percent of all respondents identified
knowledge of the Bible prior to conversion, followed by 27.8 percent who
identified knowledge of Jesus Christ and 27.5 percent (37.9 percent for
women alone) who identified having attended another Christian denomination. Exposure to the Church through the media was not as common
among converts, selected only by 5 percent of the respondents. We will
investigate later in the chapter how the more recent role of the media has
impacted missionary work.

The finding of the importance of prior Christian experience in the
process of religious conversion is also consistent with the large empirical
literature on the sociology and economics of religion: those who switch
religions tend to choose religions similar to theirs (Iannaccone 1998; Stark
and Finke 2000). This, too, can be explained in terms of religious capital. To enjoy the benefits of a particular religion requires human capital
specific to that religion, making the expected cost of conversion to The
Church of Jesus Christ of Latter-day Saints lower for someone who is
already familiar with Christianity and can therefore continue to use part
of the same religious human capital. There is thus an element of truth in

**Figure 3-4. The Most Helpful Latter-day Saint
Doctrines and Teachings in Conversion
(Percent of respondents in each group)**

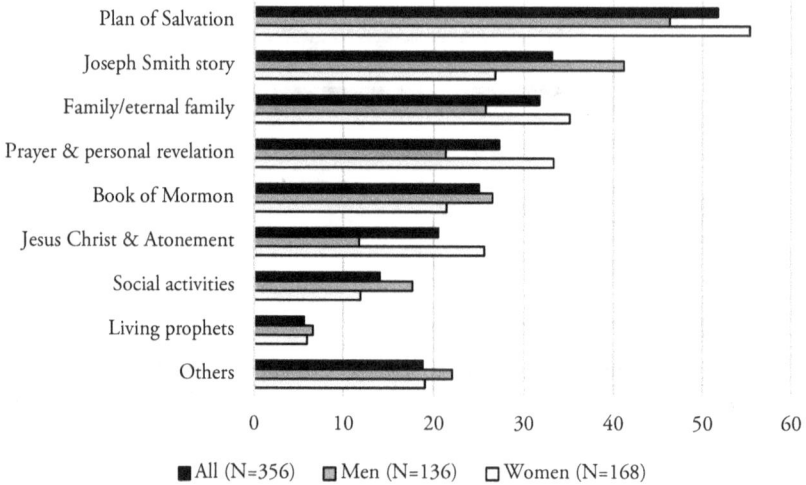

Note: respondents were asked to select up to three.
Source: Japan LDS Survey.

what Figuerres (1999, p. 26) stated as a former mission president in Japan: "The Japanese people . . . must often be converted to Christianity first, then to the restored gospel."

Consequential Doctrines and Teachings

The survey then inquired about the doctrines or teachings of The Church of Jesus Christ of Latter-day Saints that had resonated with them or helped them form their commitment to the Church, asking them to select up to three from a list of nine (Figure 3-4). The most consequential doctrine or teaching was the plan of salvation, which 51.7 percent of the respondents (46.3 percent for men and 55.4 percent for women) identified. We did not define "plan of salvation" but left it to the individual's understanding of the Church's teaching. In responding to an open-ended invitation, many respondents stated that knowing where they came from, why they are here, and where they are going after this life resonated strongly with them. It is possible that, in this, they saw a strong contrast with the Buddhist doctrine of reincarnation or the absence in the Shinto doctrine of life after death.

In second place was the Joseph Smith story, which 33.1 percent of all respondents (46.3 percent for men and 51.7 percent for women) identified as having been consequential. This was more important than the Book of Mormon, which 25.0 percent of all respondents (26.5 percent for men and 21.4 percent for women) identified as having been consequential to their conversion. The reason may be that the Joseph Smith story is simple and easy to understand even for those unfamiliar with a foreign religion, whereas many, including members but especially those investigating the Church, often find the Book of Mormon to be difficult to understand. Clearly, the Joseph Smith story highlights the unique position of The Church of Jesus Christ of Latter-day Saints, setting it apart from all other Christian denominations while affirming its belief in Jesus Christ.

In third place was the doctrine on the family and the eternal family, a teaching closely related to the plan of salvation. As stated earlier, this may be one area where there is some cultural continuity between the Church and Japanese society, where one's ancestors are revered. The survey question did not specifically address family history or temple work, considering that this concept was subsumed in the doctrine of eternal family. Some, but not many, commented on family history work or the temple in their responses to our open-ended invitation. In contrast, few identified the doctrine of continuous revelation ("living prophets") or social activities as having played a significant role in their conversion.

The Role of Human Relations

The survey inquired about individuals who had played a significant role in the respondents' conversion, asking them to select all that applied from a list of six (Figure 3-5). Perhaps it is not surprising that the largest share (87.1 percent) of the respondents identified missionaries as having played a significant role. Missionaries are central to the Church's proselytizing work because all converts are in principle required to take missionary discussions before their baptisms. Only 1.4 percent and 3.4 percent of the respondents identified neighbors and coworkers, respectively, as having played significant roles. Admittedly, Latter-day Saint neighbors and coworkers are very rare in Japan, making them an unlikely source of information about the Church. Even so, this may also suggest the difficulty in Japanese society of talking about one's religious faith openly, when the relationship is not close and there is concern about how they may be viewed. In contrast, there may not be so much hesitancy about discussing one's religion more openly with a close school friend. The relatively small share

Figure 3-5. The Person Who Played a Significant Role in Conversion
(Percent of respondents in each group)

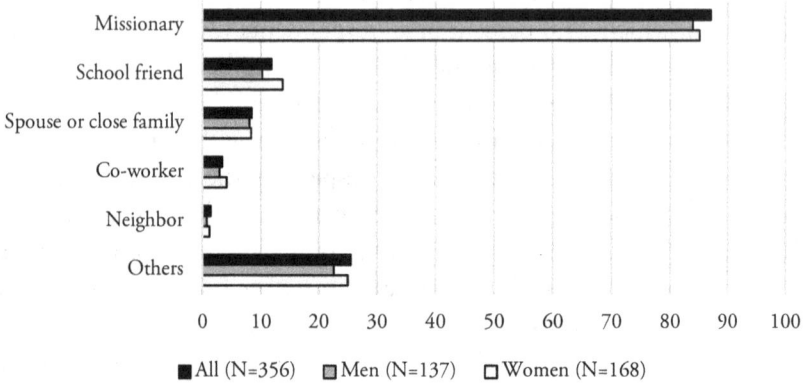

Note: respondents were requested to select all that apply.
Source: Japan LDS Survey.

(11.8 percent) of the respondents who identified school friends as having
played a significant role in their conversion probably reflects the small absolute number of friends who are Latter-day Saints, which in turn reflects
the small absolute number of Latter-day Saints in Japan more generally.

A large number (172) of survey respondents accepted the open-ended
invitation to comment on the influence of others in their conversion.
Some comments were about members who had helped them in their conversion process. "Every member a missionary" has been preached from
the pulpit in Latter-day Saint meetings for many years, and members are
encouraged to assist in missionary work. These comments, often referring
to simple words or acts of kindness, included: "The members were kind";
"[It was] the good relationships in the families of the church members";
and "It was the gentleness, kindness, and purity of the . . . members." In a
culture of reticence, the uncharacteristic expressiveness of Japanese Latter-
day Saints, instead of coming across as abrasively foreign, may appear re-
freshing and indeed welcoming in some cases. One respondent remarked:
"One member said to me, 'Please come again,' and I felt this is the place
where I belong." Few would object to being told they are welcome, irrespective of what their culture says about the proper norm of behavior.

Yet, many more of the comments were about the missionaries, not so
much about what they had said or taught, but more about their display
of love and friendship. One respondent said, "They became friends, and
I wanted to become a church member because of my admiration and

Figure 3-6. Latter-day Saint Missionaries in Japan, 1974–2021
(Year-end number; percent share of native missionaries)

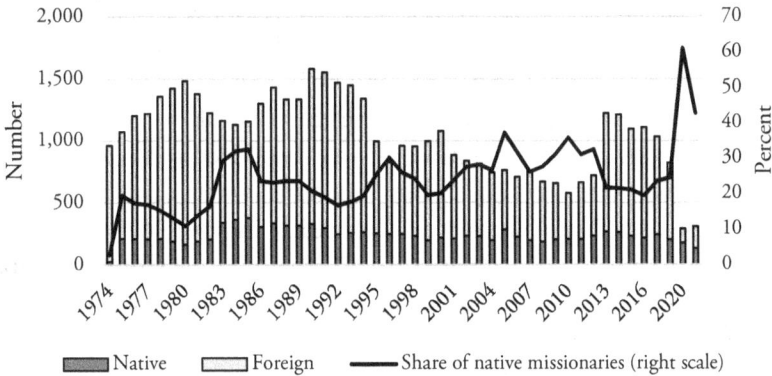

Native Foreign ——Share of native missionaries (right scale)

Note: the numbers for 2019 are missing.
Source: Bunkachō, *Shūkyō Nenkan*, annual issues.

respect for them," while another reported, "I felt the spirituality of the missionaries, and they brought the Spirit." Yet another said, "My final decision was the love I felt from the missionaries." Other characteristics mentioned about the missionaries were their brightness, energy, smiles, character, lifestyle, and seriousness. One mentioned their handshake, suggesting the strong and lasting impression this uncustomary practice of greeting leaves upon the minds of first-time investigators in Japan. Serving as a missionary is more than learning the language and reciting the lessons. This must be true almost anywhere, but especially so in Japan, where the missionaries must cross a cultural boundary.

Religious conversion—understood as the replacement, partial or whole, of existing cultural capital—suggests the possible advantage of native Japanese over foreign missionaries. Unfortunately, the Japan LDS Survey did not address this issue directly but, given the finding of the central role missionaries play in the conversion process, some preliminary thoughts may be offered. Japanese Latter-day Saints have provided a relatively steady supply of missionaries every year, generally ranging between two and three hundred men and women, though their share in the total number of missionaries has fluctuated from year to year, depending on the number of foreign missionaries allocated to Japan in each year (Figure 3-6). For example, the share, which typically ranged between 25 and 35 percent from the latter part of the 2000s into the early 2010s, drastically declined to about 20 percent after 2013, when the decision of the Church to lower the eligible ages for full-time missionary service (to 18 for men and 19 for women) in the previous year nearly doubled the number of missionaries allocated to Japan. A reversal occurred in 2020 when the global COVID-19 pandemic halted the arrival of new foreign missionaries serving in Japan. The share of local missionaries at the end of 2020 was as high as 61 percent (the share declined to 42.9 percent at the end of 2021).

This pattern begs the question of what happened to the effectiveness of proselytizing work in Japan when it became largely carried out by native missionaries. Normally, it would be nearly impossible to identify the contribution of native missionaries to the growth of the Church in Japan, separate from the influences of many other factors that are at play (such as member involvement and local leadership). However, the pandemic of 2020–21 may be used proximately as a natural experiment to isolate the unique contribution of native missionaries. Even though the pandemic itself was likely a negative factor impacting missionary work, the number of baptisms per missionary during this period actually increased. Of course, this may be just a simple reflection of the fact that fewer missionaries were assigned to each unit (a branch or ward), but one mission president serving in Japan during this time commented that many of his colleagues and local members interpreted this as a welcome sign of the unique effectiveness of local missionaries. If so, this may be a result, not of the native missionaries' language proficiency per se, but of their ability to translate the culture of the religion for their compatriots, their ability to bridge the gap between the culture of Japan and the culture of the Church, and even the mere ability to assure that it is possible to be both Japanese and a Latter-day Saint. One mission president remarked to us that foreign missionaries were better able to stop people and talk to them or open doors in homes, but that the Japanese missionaries were more effective in teaching the gospel.

3-5. Opposition to Conversion

The survey asked the respondents, "What was the biggest hurdle to overcome in your decision to join the Church?" One might have expected the answer to be the Word of Wisdom, Sabbath observance, or paying tithing—namely, Latter-day Saint practices that are not part of Japanese culture.[4] It turns out, however, that by far the most serious opposition

---

4. According to a recent mission president in Japan, tithing appears to be a serious obstacle to conversion among married couples. This may well be the case, but tithing was identified as the biggest obstacle only by 3.3 percent of the respondents to this survey. This may be due to the bias inherent in the sample.

Figure 3-7. The Biggest Hurdle to Conversion
(Percent of respondents in each group)

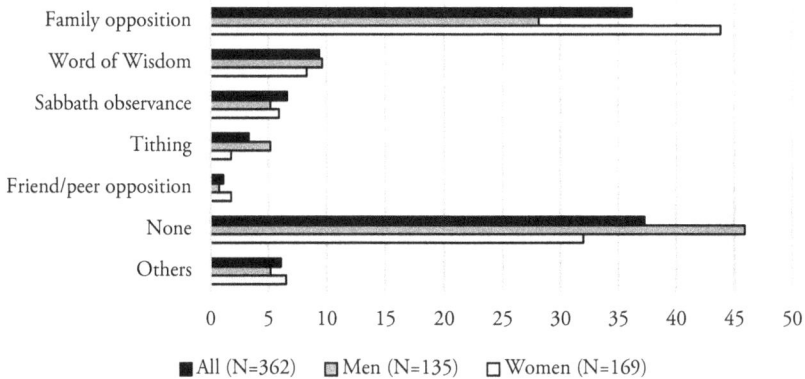

Source: Japan LDS Survey.

came from family members, with 36.2 percent of all respondents (43.8 percent of those who identified as women) reporting having experienced family opposition (Figure 3-7). Opposition from friends or peers, at 1.1 percent, was almost negligible. Remarkably, 37.3 percent reported having experienced no opposition of any kind. Only a few respondents (numbering twenty-two) chose to state other hurdles to their conversion, which included the law of chastity, social prejudice against the Church, repentance, and difficulty obtaining testimony of certain doctrines (such as Jesus Christ as the only god). The large share of respondents who experienced no opposition may have reflected a selection bias—the sample included only those who had actually joined the Church and largely remained active. It should not be taken as suggesting the average experience of all Japanese who investigated the Church.

The significant incidence of family opposition in the conversion process may well be a reflection of Japan's collective (as opposed to individualistic) culture, where harmony is respected and religious choice is not considered entirely personal. In families, the father or the husband may exercise oversight in maintaining harmony. We are familiar with the interesting, if not amusing, experience of a young woman whose mother opposed her baptism because, after she had started taking missionary discussions, she began doing the dishes at home ("something is wrong

_____

Our sample consists of respondents who had actually converted to the Church (and mostly while they were young) and does not include those who had faced tithing as a serious obstacle and decided not to convert.

Figure 3-8. Family Opposition as a Hurdle to Conversion, by Gender and Age
(Percent of respondents in each group)

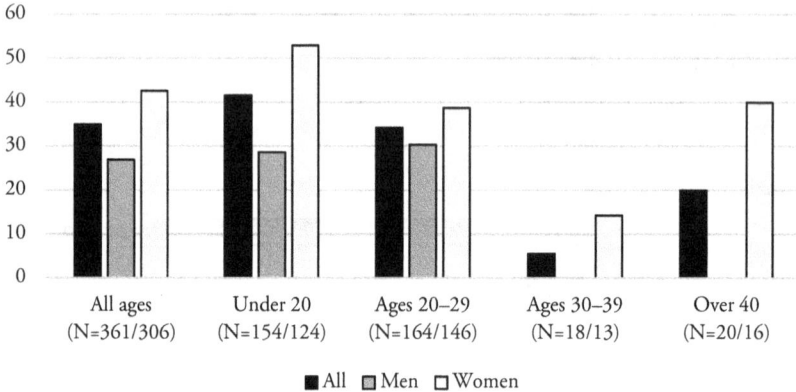

| | All ages (N=361/306) | Under 20 (N=154/124) | Ages 20–29 (N=164/146) | Ages 30–39 (N=18/13) | Over 40 (N=20/16) |

■ All   ▨ Men   ☐ Women

Note: the second number in parentheses refers to the number of respondents in each group who identified their gender.
Source: Japan LDS Survey.

with her!"). We believe that this mother was trying to find any excuse she could find to oppose her daughter joining the Church. Hoffmann (2007) observed, based on selected interviews in a small branch in Hokkaido, that women appeared to face more family opposition than men while speculating that those investigating the Church, both men and women, likely faced less opposition as they grew older. The Japan LDS Survey broadly confirms Hoffmann's conjecture (Figure 3-8). When all converts are considered, 42.6 percent of women, as opposed to 26.9 percent of men, stated family opposition as the biggest hurdle to their conversion.

Gender differences persist when the sample is divided into four age groups. None of the male respondents reported experiencing family opposition when they had converted after their thirtieth birthday. In contrast, women reported having experienced family opposition even in their forties and fifties. In fact, the share of such women (40.0 percent) was about the same as the share of those having experienced opposition in their twenties (38.8 percent). We believe that women are more likely than men to face family opposition because when they are young, their parents are concerned about their marriage prospects, and when they are married, they have (at least historically) been subject to greater spousal authority (unlike their male counterparts). To be sure, the absolute number of those who converted after their thirtieth birthday in our sample is so small that we cannot place full confidence in these percentage numbers. Even so, our personal observation suggests that some older women do face opposition from their husbands when they express a desire to join the Church.

For those under the age of 30, a good share (about 30 percent) of not just women but also men faced family opposition. This fact must be assessed against the earlier finding that about 91 percent of them had joined the Church before their thirtieth birthday (see Figure 3-2). This suggests that the relatively high incidence of family opposition converts experienced in our sample is a reflection of the relatively young ages at which many of the survey respondents joined the Church. The fact that they joined the Church despite family opposition means that the opposition was not insurmountable. At the same time, there certainly must have been others who were prevented from joining the Church by family opposition. As our sample consists only of active membership, those who were unable to overcome such challenges are missing from the survey. One might think that parental opposition is stronger today than in earlier years as skepticism about religion and concerns about privacy have grown. It may also be true that parents are more protective of children today than in the past as concerns about safety in society have likewise grown. This is the conundrum the Church's missionary work faces going forward: whereas individuals are more receptive when they are young, they are also more likely to face family opposition.

3-6. Changing Patterns of Conversion

Missionary work can never be expected to be static in a dynamic society such as Japan. What was once accepted as a norm may no longer be widely observed today. This penultimate section of the chapter addresses the question of whether—and if so, how—the patterns of conversion may be changing over time, focusing on the composition of converts and their prior knowledge and background.

Composition of Converts

In order to ascertain whether the composition of converts in terms of their demographic and other characteristics has changed over time, we compared five metrics across two cohorts of converts (with the second further subdivided into two), namely those baptized during 1951–80 and those baptized during 1981–2020 (Table 3-1). Two significant differences between the two cohorts of converts are clearly visible. First, the average age of conversion rose from 19.8 to 24.5. This aging of converts is even more striking when the second cohort is divided into two: the average age

Table 3-1. Changing Composition of Converts

	Those baptized during 1951–80 (N=153–61)	Those baptized during 1981–2020 (N=131–39)	Of which: 1981–2000 (N=101–07)	Of which: 2001–2020 (N=30–32)
Gender composition (% men)	52.2	36.7	34.6	43.8
Average age at conversion	19.8	24.5	22.4	31.5
Postsecondary education (% respondents)	67.1	67.6	65.4	75.0
Ideological inclination, average score (1=conservative; 5=progressive)	2.9	3.0	3.0	3.1
How fit with school peers, average score (1=poorly; 4=well)	2.8	2.6	2.6	2.4

Source: Japan LDS Survey.

rises to 31.5 for those baptized during 2001–20. Second, the share of men among converts declined from 52.2 percent to 36.7 percent (this trend was partially reversed during 2001–20 where the share went back to 43.8 percent). There was little difference in the other metrics, except that the share of converts with some postsecondary education spiked to 75 percent during 2001–20. The sociability of converts (how well they felt they had "fit in" with secondary school peers) marginally declined (from 2.8 to 2.4, where 1 represents poorly and 4 represents well), but the difference is not statistically significant at the 5 percent level.

Prior Knowledge and Background

To ascertain further how the patterns of conversion may have changed over time, we compared the prior knowledge and other background of converts across three cohorts: those baptized during 1951–80, those baptized during 1981–2000, and those baptized during 2001–20 (Figure 3-9). Three significant differences emerge immediately from this exercise. First, the prevalence of prior exposure to Christianity in the conversion process declined consistently, for example, from 61.1 to 38.5 percent for knowledge of the Bible and from 52.6 to 38.5 percent for having attended another Christian denomination. Second, the prevalence of having Latter-day Saint friends and associates rose from 27.4 to 38.5 percent. Third, likewise, the prevalence of social and mass media as a source of informa-

Figure 3-9. Changing Prior Knowledge and Background
(Percent of respondents in each group)

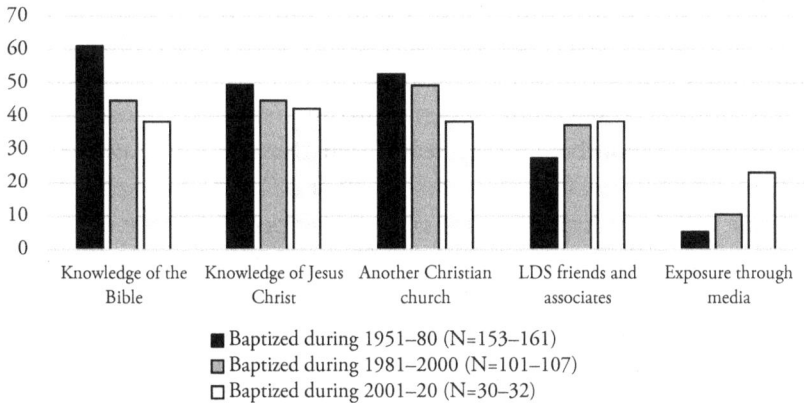

■ Baptized during 1951–80 (N=153–161)
▨ Baptized during 1981–2000 (N=101–107)
□ Baptized during 2001–20 (N=30–32)

Source: Japan LDS Survey.

tion about the Church increased from a mere 5.3 percent for those baptized during 1951–80 to 23.1 percent for those baptized during 2001–20. It is possible that, as the Church has grown in membership, human connections and the media have increasingly become the first point of contact with the Church for the Japanese public.

3-7. Conclusion

This chapter has discussed the findings from the Japan LDS Survey that relate to religious conversion. The large majority (more than 70 percent) of the respondents who identified their membership status in the survey were converts to The Church of Jesus Christ of Latter-day Saints, nearly 60 percent of whom joined the Church during the decades of 1971–90 when the Church saw more than a five-fold growth in its membership. Remarkably, close to 90 percent joined the Church before the age of 30 (about half of them before the age of 20), with the average age of around 22. Among the factors contributing to their conversion were prior familiarity with Christianity, with around 30 percent each identifying knowledge of the Bible, knowledge of Jesus Christ, and attending another Christian denomination as having been consequential. Nearly 90 percent of the respondents stated that the missionaries had played the largest role in their conversion, while 52 percent of them identified the plan of salvation as a Latter-day Saint teaching or doctrine most consequential to their conversion, followed by the Joseph Smith story (33 percent) and doctrines about the eternal family (32 percent). In terms of obstacles to joining the Church, family opposition was identified by 36 percent of respondents as the largest hurdle. Rather surprisingly, however, a larger share (37 percent) of the respondents reported having experienced no opposition to their joining the Church.

Given the overwhelming evidence that individuals are most receptive to a foreign religion before they reach their thirtieth birthday, the proselytizing work of The Church of Jesus Christ of Latter-day Saints should continue to benefit from focusing on younger people. At the same time, the survey found that the incidence of family opposition tended to be greater when conversion took place before the thirtieth birthday (no male respondent reported having experienced family opposition after his thirtieth birthday). The mitigating fact, we believe, is that family opposition in Japan (where only a few profess an organized religion) is rarely religiously motivated but comes from parental concern over the minor child, including the child's ability to make a mature, informed decision about what may affect his or her future. This means that family opposition can be overcome by helping the parents dispel any anxiety about the Church and by helping them better understand the positive aspects of church membership. We are familiar with an initiative in one of the missions in Japan, where something of an informal "contract" between a minor and his or her parents was used for this purpose, replacing a legalistic parental consent form designed to protect the Church or its officers from any legal liability or blame that could arise from baptizing a minor child.[5] We are told by local leaders that the contractual approach to obtaining parental consent significantly improved the consent rate by the parents and led to an increase in baptisms, possibly by allowing parents to see the positive aspects of church membership for their children.

---

5. Before the Japan Sendai Mission was reorganized in 2019, the mission used a form that focused on the improved behavior the Church expects from the minor, to be signed by both the minor and their parents. In this form, the minor promises that, "By learning the teachings of Jesus Christ, I will strive to respect my parents and family, cherish our home, encourage education, work diligently, keep my heart and body clean, honor the law, strive for health and a healthy lifestyle, be grateful to my ancestors, be a good student and citizen in the community," among other character traits that are appealing to parents within the context of Japanese culture. The parents, on their part, sign the form stating their hope that their minor will observe those things he or she has just promised "by learning the teachings of Jesus Christ." A copy of the form is in the possession of the authors.

The survey found a significant rise in the average age of converts, from about 20 years old for those baptized during 1951–80 to 24.5 years old for those baptized during 1981–2020 (31.5 years old for those baptized during 2001–20 only), and an equally significant decline in the share of men among the converts, from 52.2 percent to 36.7 percent over the same period (though it recovered to 43.8 percent for those baptized during 2001–20 only). We are not sure if the rise in the average age and the fall in the share of men are permanent, nor do we know what caused these changes. The recent rise in the average age of converts may mean that family opposition (which primarily affects those under the age of 30) is taking a toll on membership growth, possibly reflecting Japanese society's increasing hostility to nontraditional religions, a topic to be addressed in the penultimate chapter. If the fall in the share of men is permanent or does not recover, it may further exacerbate the gender balance in Japan, where active women already outnumber active men (thus further diminishing the prospect for marrying in the faith).

Finally, the survey found that, as the Church experienced growth in membership, social connections and the media increasingly became the first points of contact with the Church for the Japanese public, even as the relative importance of familiarity with Christianity declined in the conversion process (for example, the share of the respondents who identified knowledge of the Bible prior to their conversion declined from 61.1 percent for those baptized during 1951–80 to 38.5 percent for those baptized during 2001–20). In particular, among the latest cohort of converts, 23.1 percent (compared to a mere 5.3 percent among the earliest cohort) identified exposure to the Church through social and mass media prior to their conversion. Given the way our world has been changing in recent years, we believe that this trend will continue, providing the Church with opportunities to further benefit from increased use of social and mass media, including greater use of new technology.

CHAPTER 4

RELIGIOUS BELIEFS AND PRACTICES

4-1. Introduction

Having reviewed the profiles, backgrounds, and experiences of religiously active Latter-day Saints in Japan, including as converts to The Church of Jesus Christ of Latter-day Saints, this chapter turns to the central questions of what they believe and how they practice their religion. The purpose of this chapter is to understand how and how thoroughly they have adopted or developed their identity as Latter-day Saints. Where comparable data are available from the Next Mormons Survey (NMS), we compare the religious beliefs and practices of Japanese Latter-day Saints with those of American Latter-day Saints, after adjusting for church activity status (we only compare those who attend church at least weekly). This helps eliminate any bias attributable to differences in level of devotion. To eliminate any possible gender bias, we also compare men to men and women to women since our sample is skewed to women while the NMS survey is corrected for gender imbalance.

The rest of the chapter is organized as follows. Section 4-2 discusses how Japanese Latter-day Saints worship on Sundays, including how they travel to their meetinghouses. Section 4-3 explores religious beliefs and convictions, including their belief about God and their acceptance of Latter-day Saint teachings. Section 4-4 considers their devotion to such religious practices as prayer, scripture reading, temple worship, and tithing (voluntary donation of a tenth of their income); it also addresses their adherence to the Word of Wisdom (that is, abstention from tea, coffee, tobacco, alcoholic drinks, and illicit drugs) and the law of chastity (that is, abstention from sex outside marriage). Section 4-5 discusses respondents' views on gender issues within the Church, including whether they think women have enough voice in the Church as well as what they think of abortion and the Latter-day Saint practice of ordaining only men to the priesthood. Finally, section 4-6 presents a conclusion.

4-2. Aspects of Religious Life

We first address the manner in which Japanese Latter-day Saints worship on Sundays. In describing the size of their congregations (in terms

Figure 4-1. Congregation Size in Terms of Active Membership
(Percent of respondents attending)

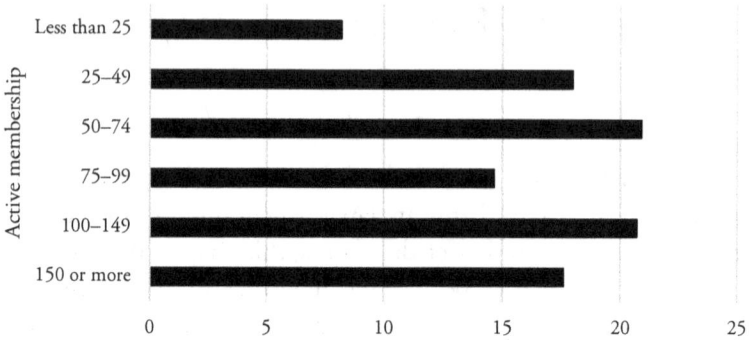

Note: sample size (N)=512.
Source: Japan LDS Survey.

of active membership) we asked the respondents to base their answers on what it was like before the COVID-19 pandemic or what it was expected to be once all pandemic-related restrictions were lifted (Figure 4-1). As larger units have a larger number of members, the percentage distribution is inevitably skewed towards larger units. Thus, the fact that more than 15 percent of the respondents attend congregations of more than 150 active members does not mean that more than 15 percent of the congregations in Japan have more than 150 active members. What is important here is the perspective and personal experience of individual Latter-day Saints.

From the perspective of individuals who worship in their local congregations, more than a quarter (26.2 percent) reported attending congregations of less than 50 active members; of this, 8.2 percent reported attending congregations of less than 25 active members. These individuals did not necessarily live in less populated areas. In fact, a few respondents in large metropolitan areas stated that they attended congregations smaller than 25 active members. What this means is that, as multiple congregations exist in these areas, even internal migration (e.g., out to the suburbs) can create membership imbalances. For example, a city ward and a suburban ward may meet in the same building, with some members of the city ward who live in high-rise apartments purchasing affordable suburban homes located in the boundary of the other ward. On the other hand, those who reported attending congregations larger than 150 active members were concentrated in population centers (especially in South Kanto, Tokyo's suburbs). None reported attending such units who lived

Figure 4-2. Mode of Transportation to Church
(Percent of respondents)

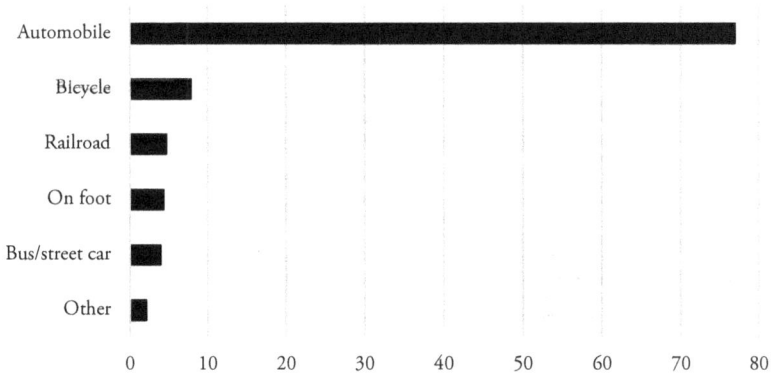

Note: sample size (N)=531.
Source: Japan LDS Survey.

in Tohoku, Hokuriku, or Shikoku. Active membership in these units is largely affected by external migration of members from rural areas to population centers, especially to the region around Tokyo.

Second, we asked the respondents how they typically traveled to their meetinghouses (Figure 4-2). The overwhelming majority (77.0 percent) reported that they traveled by automobile, followed by 7.9 percent who traveled by bicycle. Although public transportation is well developed in most populated areas of Japan and many use it to commute to work or school, it tends to become expensive when multiple family members need to travel together. A typical bus or subway ride may cost the Japanese yen equivalent of $1.50 to $2.00, which means that a family of five would need to pay upwards of $15 just to go to church and back. Expenses can add up if one needs to go to the meetinghouse multiple times, for example, in the case of someone who holds a major responsibility in the organization. Driving may well be a more economical means of transportation in such instances.[1] In less populated areas, frequency of public

_____

1. Of course, we are only considering the marginal cost of attending church, which assumes that those who drive already own automobiles. The cost of owning an automobile in Japan can be more expensive than in other countries, as it involves the cost of the automobile itself but also the expenses associated with high property tax, periodic comprehensive vehicle inspection, insurance, and often even securing a parking space.

Figure 4-3. Latter-day Saints Who Travel to Church by Automobile,
by Gender, Region, and Age Group
(Percent of total in each group)

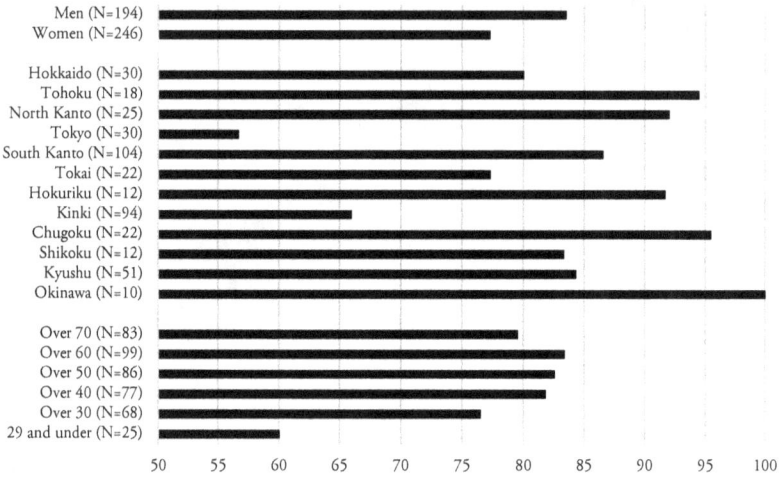

Source: Japan LDS Survey.

transit service may dictate that driving is the only reasonable option even if public transportation is available.

These suppositions are corroborated by comparing the percentage share of Latter-day Saints who traveled to church via automobile according to gender, region, and age group (Figure 4-3). Men tended to drive to church more than women (83.5 vs. 77.2 percent), likely reflecting the fact that fewer women—at least from an older generation—have driver's licenses. In terms of regional variation, the smallest share of those who drove to church was 56.7 percent for Tokyo, followed by 66.0 percent for Kinki (where Osaka, Kyoko, Kobe are located), suggesting that those who live in large population centers are more likely to travel by public transportation.[2] In contrast, 100 percent in Okinawa, and 95.5 percent in Shikoku, drove to church. In terms of variation by age, the youngest (those under 30) and the oldest (those over 70) were less likely to drive, possibly suggesting that

2. According to the Japan Automobile Inspection and Registration Information Association (JAIRIA) (2021), at the end of March 2021, the number of passenger vehicles per capita (per household) was 0.487 (1.037) for all of Japan. The number falls to 0.224 (0.422) for Tokyo and 0.314 (0.633) for Osaka, two of the most urbanized prefectures where extensive public transportation networks are established. In contrast, the comparable numbers for Fukui and Toyama (both in the Hokuriku region) were 0.663 (1.715) and 0.678 (1.660).

Figure 4-4. Distance to Church
(Percent of respondents)

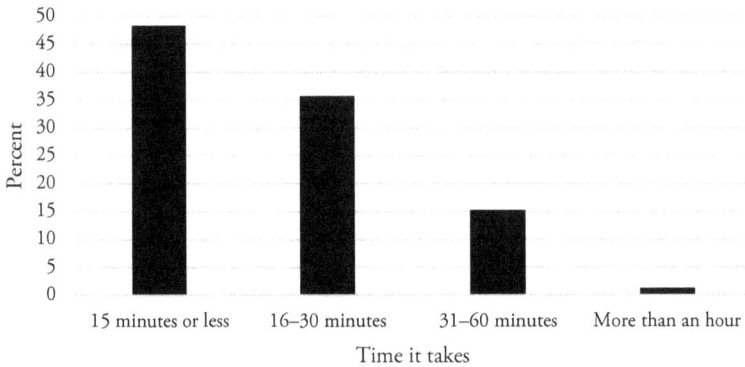

Note: sample size (N)=529.
Source: Japan LDS Survey.

those without children find public transportation a less expensive or less stressful means of transportation when it is convenient and available.

Finally, we asked the respondents about the distance to their meeting-houses in terms of the time it typically took to travel there (Figure 4-4). Nearly half the respondents (48.2 percent) stated that it took them less than 15 minutes, while another 35.5 percent said it took between 16 and 30 minutes. Only six respondents (1.1 percent) reported more than an hour. Comparing average distance across regions (Figure 4-5), moreover, we find that it exceeded 30 minutes (designated by the number 2 or above on the horizontal axis) only in two regions:[3] Hokuriku (2.4) and North Kanto (2.2). Even so, the average distance in these regions only slightly exceeds 30 minutes. Remarkably, the overwhelming majority of religiously active Latter-day Saints in Japan seem to live within 30 minutes of their meetinghouses.

The relative ease the respondents reported of attending church probably means that (1) The Church of Jesus Christ of Latter-day Saints has historically followed the strategy of locating meetinghouses in central and convenient locations (typically, in the case of large cities, within a few minutes' walk from a major train station), (2) Japanese cities are relatively compact, making it easy to travel (especially on Sunday mornings when traffic is light), and (3) when active members relocate themselves for various reasons, they select areas convenient to attending church. However, this

---

3. 1=1–15 minutes; 2=16–30 minutes; 3=31–45 minutes; 4=46–60 minutes; and 5=61 minutes or more.

Figure 4-5. Average Distance to Church by Region

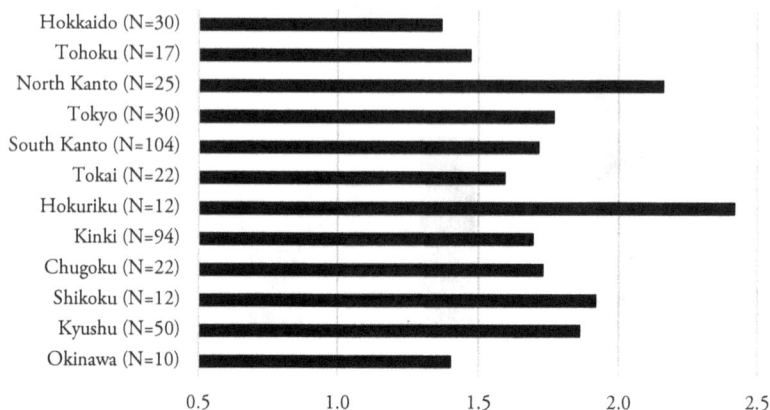

Note: 1=1–15 minutes; 2=16–30 minutes; 3=31–45 minutes; 4=46–60 minutes; and 5=61 minutes or more.
Source: Japan LDS Survey.

should not minimize the hardships a few members experience attending church. Given that most respondents in our survey are religiously active, and that distance likely makes church attendance harder, it is possible that many more Latter-day Saints actually live quite far from their meeting-houses but have ceased to remain active (i.e., there is a selection bias in the sample). As the Church is not increasing the number of congregations at the moment, distances can increase, for example, when an active member who is attending church in a large city is transferred by his or her employer to a place where no congregation is located nearby. One respondent voluntarily commented how hard it was to attend church, living so far away.

4-3. Religious Beliefs and Convictions

To evaluate the religious beliefs and convictions of Japanese Latter-day Saints, we asked the respondents the same four questions Jana Riess and Benjamin Knoll asked American Latter-day Saints in the Next Mormons Survey (NMS). This permits a comparison of Japanese and American Latter-day Saints after making appropriate adjustments to ensure comparability.

The Favorite Part of Being a Latter-day Saint

The first question asked what their favorite part of being a Latter-day Saint was, requesting them to select up to three options from a list of nine (Table 4-1). The three most widely selected "favorite parts," irrespective of

Table 4-1. The Favorite Parts of Being a Latter-day Saint
(Percent of respondents in each group; up to three selected)

	All members (N=497)	Of which, under 40 (N=93)	Men (N=194)	Of which, under 40 (N=36)	Women (N=246)	Of which, under 40 (N=57)
A. Its emphasis on the Savior, Jesus Christ	60.4	52.7	59.8	52.8	61.0	52.6
B. The knowledge that families can be together forever	65.4	62.4	59.3	44.4	68.3	73.7
C. The comfort of having a prophet on the earth today	31.4	19.4	26.8	19.4	35.0	19.3
D. The opportunities the church provides me to serve other people	13.9	16.1	17.0	19.4	10.6	14.0
E. The freedom from addiction that comes with keeping the Word of Wisdom	3.6	7.5	5.7	11.1	2.0	5.3
F. The strong community I enjoy at church	16.9	25.8	21.6	25.0	14.2	26.3
G. The peace my faith provides in hard times	47.9	53.8	41.8	52.8	54.1	54.4
H. The focus on children and youth	5.4	2.2	7.7	5.6	3.7	0.0
I. Temple worship	25.8	21.5	26.3	22.2	25.2	21.1
Total	270.6	261.3	266.0	252.8	274.0	266.7

Source: Japan LDS Survey.

their gender or age, were (1) the Church's emphasis on Jesus Christ, (2) the knowledge of eternal family togetherness, and (3) the peace the faith brings in hard times. Younger Latter-day Saints on average gave less importance to the unique Latter-day Saint belief of having a prophet on the earth today (31.4 percent for all members vs. 19.4 percent for those under the age of 40). Men were more likely than women to appreciate somewhat the opportunities the Church provides to serve others (17.0 vs. 10.6 percent).

The NMS allows us to compare Japanese and American Latter-day Saints who attended church at least weekly, focusing on the five most important aspects selected (Figure 4-6). A striking observation is that U.S. responses were somewhat more evenly distributed, so that smaller percentages of American men and women selected "eternal families" and "emphasis on Jesus Christ" as their favorite parts of being a Latter-day Saint compared

Figure 4-6. The Favorite Part of Being a Latter-day Saint: Japan–U.S. Comparison
(Percent of respondents)

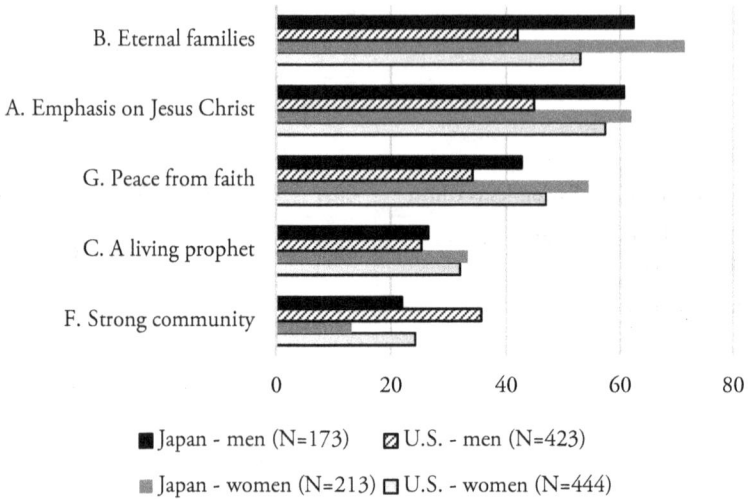

Note: based on a subsample that includes only those who attend church at least weekly.
Sources: Japan LDS Survey; Next Mormons Survey.

Table 4-2. Belief about God
(Percent of respondents in each group)

	All (N=498)	Men (N=195)	Women (N=246)
A. I know God really exists and I have no doubts about it.	84.5	80.5	87.4
B. While I have doubts, I feel that I do believe in God.	12.7	14.9	11.4
C. I find myself believing in God sometimes, but not at other times.	1.8	2.6	1.2
D. I don't believe in a personal God, but I do believe in a Higher Power of some kind.	0.6	1.0	0.0
E. I don't know whether there is a God, and I don't believe there is any way to find out.	0.2	0.5	0.0
F. I don't believe in God.	0.2	0.5	0.0
Total	100	100	100

Source: Japan LDS Survey.

Figure 4-7. Belief about God: Japan–U.S. Comparison
(Percent of respondents in each group)

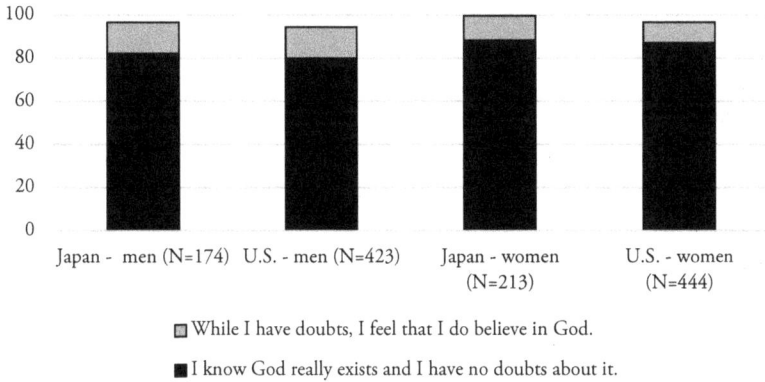

☐ While I have doubts, I feel that I do believe in God.

■ I know God really exists and I have no doubts about it.

Note: based on a subsample that includes only those who attend church at least weekly.
Sources: Japan LDS Survey; Next Mormons Survey.

to their Japanese counterparts. Moreover, considerably larger percentages of American men and women (35.7 and 24.3 percent vs. 22.0 and 13.2 percent for Japan) valued the community-belonging aspect of being a Latter-day Saint. Our own speculative interpretation is that Japanese Latter-day Saints, for the most part, have not overcome the seniority- and gender-based relational barriers their culture imposes, finding it difficult to develop genuine friendships across generations and gender boundaries within their congregations. Also contributing to this may be a particular lifestyle of Japanese Latter-day Saints that tends to limit their personal interactions to Sundays.

Belief about God and Acceptance of Latter-day Saint Teachings

The next two questions concerned Japanese Latter-day Saints' belief about God and their acceptance of Latter-day Saint teachings. In the first question, respondents were provided with six statements expressing a range of levels of belief in God (from "I know God really exists and I have no doubts about it" to "I don't believe in God"). Respondents were asked to select the statement that came the closest to describing their own belief. Results show that 84.5 percent said they knew God really exists and they had no doubts about it; a greater share of women (87.4 percent) than men (80.5 percent) stated such a belief (Table 4-2). Another 12.7 percent stated that they had doubts, but they felt that they believed in God. Less than 3 percent of the respondents expressed a weaker belief about God. Comparing Japanese and American Latter-day Saints who attended church

Table 4-3. Acceptance of Latter-day Saint Teachings
(Percent of respondents in each group)

	All (N=493)	Men (N=194)	Women (N=244)
A. I believe wholeheartedly in all of the teachings of the LDS Church.	76.9	74.7	81.1
B. I believe many or most of the teachings of the LDS Church.	19.5	19.6	17.6
C. Some of the teachings of the LDS Church are hard for me to believe.	2.8	5.2	0.8
D. Many or most of the teachings of the LDS Church are hard for me to believe.	0.6	0.0	0.4
E. I do not believe in the teachings of the LDS Church.	0.2	0.5	0.0
Total	100	100	100

Source: Japan LDS Survey.

at least weekly, the share of those who expressed such strong beliefs were a few percentage points higher among the Japanese respondents (Figure 4-7).

In the second question, respondents were similarly given five statements representing differing levels of belief in Latter-day Saint teachings and were asked to identify the statement that most closely resembled their own views. Results show that 76.9 percent of respondents reported that they believed wholeheartedly in all of the teachings of the Church, while another 19.5 percent believed in many or most of its teachings (Table 4-3). Very few (3.6 percent) expressed a weaker acceptance of Latter-day Saint teachings. As was the case with belief about God, a greater share of women (81 percent) than men (74.7 percent) expressed a stronger acceptance, with 5.2 percent of men finding it difficult to believe some or most of the teachings and only 1.2 percent of women feeling the same. Comparing Japanese and American Latter-day Saints who attended church at least weekly, a striking pattern emerges (Figure 4-8): a far larger share of Japanese men and women (74.7 and 81.2 percent, respectively) believed wholeheartedly in all of the teachings of their church than American men and women (57.9 and 65.8 percent, respectively).

The Source of Spiritual Authority

One of the unique teachings of The Church of Jesus Christ of Latter-day Saints is that members are entitled to receive personal revelation to guide their lives. At the same time, another important teaching of the Church is that there is a prophet on the earth today who speaks for God,

Figure 4-8. Acceptance of Latter-day Saint Teachings: Japan–U.S. Comparison
(Percent of respondents in each group)

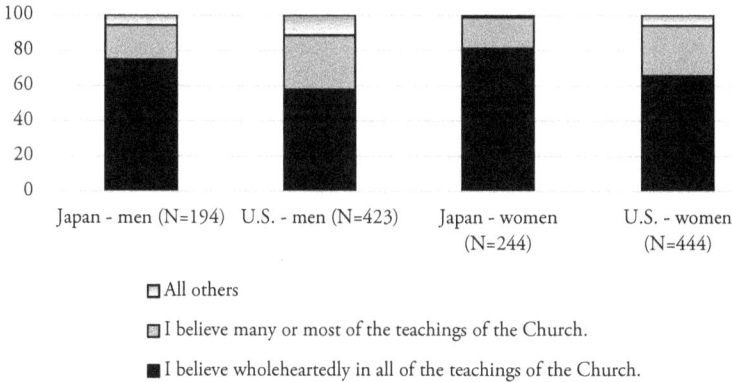

☐ All others

▨ I believe many or most of the teachings of the Church.

■ I believe wholeheartedly in all of the teachings of the Church.

Note: based on a subsample that includes only those who attend church at least weekly.

Sources: Japan LDS Survey; Next Mormons Survey.

and that local priesthood (ecclesiastical) leaders are divinely called to preside over their respective congregations under the direction of the prophet. Heeding the counsel of the prophet (and local priesthood leaders) and seeking one's own personal revelation can potentially conflict, and how one weighs these conflicting demands can be an important gauge of the nature of his or her practical faith. We followed the NMS in asking the respondents to select one of two statements that comes closer to their view even if neither is 100 percent accurate: (A) Good Latter-day Saints should obey the counsel of priesthood leaders even if they don't necessarily know or understand why; and (B) Good Latter-day Saints should first seek their own personal revelation on a matter and act accordingly, even if it is in conflict with the counsel of priesthood leaders. There were 493 respondents who answered this question (Table 4-4).

The overwhelming majority of respondents stated that they would give precedence to priesthood leaders over personal revelation (73.0 percent for the full sample). A greater share of women (79.2 percent) than men (68.0 percent) did so.[4] The popular caricature of stereotypical Japanese is that, given the centuries-old Confucian upbringing, they respect authority and seldom assert themselves (at least openly) when they disagree with an

---

4. The difference is statistically significant at the 1 percent level. Roughly, this means that, with a 99-percent confidence, we can state that the average is greater for women than for men.

Table 4-4. Belief about the Source of Spiritual Authority
(Percent of respondents in each group)

	All (N=493)	Of which, under 40 (N=93)	Men (N=194)	Of which, under 40 (N=36)	Women (N=245)	Of which, under 40 (N=57)
A. Good Latter-day Saints should obey the counsel of priesthood leaders even if they don't necessarily know or understand why.	73.0	76.3	68.0	69.4	79.2	80.7
B. Good Latter-day Saints should first seek their own personal revelation on a matter and act accordingly, even if it is in conflict with the counsel of priesthood leaders.	27.0	23.7	32.0	30.6	20.8	19.3
Total	100	100	100	100	100	100

Source: Japan LDS Survey.

authoritative figure. The fact that such an overwhelming majority (and more women than men) would heed outside authority more than their own conscience seems consistent with such a cultural trait. The slightly larger share of those under 40 who gave priority to priesthood leaders is puzzling, but the difference is not statistically significant for all samples.

The larger share of those who gave precedence to priesthood leaders among the younger generation may be in part due to the larger share of non-converts. When the share was compared between converts and non-converts (second- and third-generation members), a slightly smaller share of converts gave precedence to priesthood leaders (Figure 4-9), though the difference is not statistically significant. For whatever it's worth, it is possible that second- and third-generation members are more likely to show greater deference to authority as they have been taught from a young age to do so. Little difference was found in the extent to which the respondents gave precedence to priesthood leaders between active and less active members or between those who served full-time missions and those who did not. If there was any correlation, it was with the strength of their belief in God (the correlation coefficient of 0.2) and their acceptance of Latter-day Saint teachings (the correlation coefficient of 0.26). In other words, those who express no doubt about their belief in God and believe wholeheartedly in Latter-day

**Figure 4-9. Those Who Give Precedence to Priesthood
Leaders over Personal Revelation, by Population Group
(Percent of total in each)**

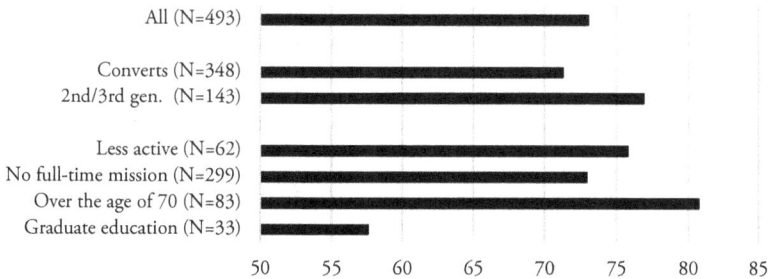

Note: "less active" means attending church less frequently than once a week.
Source: Japan LDS Survey.

Saint teachings are also more likely to give precedence to priesthood leaders over personal revelation, when pressed by the survey question.[5]

The exceptions were those over the age of 70 and those with some graduate education. A slightly larger share (80.7 percent) of older respondents,[6] and a considerably smaller share (57.6 percent) of the more educated respondents,[7] gave precedence to priesthood leaders (compared to 73.0 percent of the overall survey sample).[8] The larger share for the older members is consistent with the possibility that they were more exposed to the influences of Confucian philosophy in their formative years. The relationship between education and religion, however, is more complex (Mitchell 2017). Sociologists of religion have identified two competing patterns. First, education has been seen to be positively associated with religion, perhaps because religious practice requires religious capital (see

---

5. To calculate the correlation coefficient, the number 1 was assigned to precedence of priesthood leaders (0 otherwise), to the strongest expression of belief about God (0 otherwise), and to the strongest expression of acceptance of Latter-day Saint teachings (0 otherwise). Both correlations are relatively small but statistically significant at the 1 percent level.

6. At 78.8 percent, those over the age of 60 also had a higher share, but the difference was not statistically significant.

7. There was no noticeable difference between those with some postsecondary education and those without any postsecondary education. Only graduate education had any noticeable impact.

8. With the z-statistics of 1.49 and 1.91, respectively, the hypothesis that the percentage share comes from the same population is rejected at the 10 percent level for those over the age of 70, and at the 5 percent level for those with graduate education.

chapter 1), which increases with the level of education. Second, at the same time, many have observed a decline in religiosity within the general population, accompanied by an increase in the level of education (an observation consistent with the so-called secularization thesis).[9]

It is important, in the particular context of interpreting our result, that there are marked differences across countries and religions (or denominations within Christianity) in the way religion and education interact with each other. In the United States, for example, religiosity and education are tied more closely together because religion is a major source of cultural capital. This is not the case in such countries as China, where religion is viewed less favorably (Glaeser and Sacerdote 2008). How these inter-societal differences manifest themselves is also influenced by how religiosity is defined (e.g., belief in God and church attendance). One cannot establish the relationship between education and religion without first making judgements about which metric represents "true" devotion. In the case of Japanese Latter-day Saints, educational differences in giving precedence to personal revelation over priesthood authority underscores that religiosity looks different across demographic groups, with different levels of education shaping their views on which aspects of their religion are personally more meaningful.

The impact of cultural factors on the nature of practical faith seems evident when we compare Japanese and American Latter-day Saints who attended church at least weekly (Figure 4-10). In the Japanese sample, it was earlier observed that those under 40 were more likely to give precedence to priesthood leaders over personal revelation (though the difference was not statistically significant), and we ascribed this to the larger presence of second- or third-generation members who have been taught

---

9. To reconcile the consistent empirical findings pointing to a positive impact of education on religiosity with the broader historical observation requires isolating the effect of education on religiosity from the influences of all other variables that are correlated with education. Hungerman (2014) used changes in compulsory education laws in Canada as a controlled experiment. Tracing a cohort of individuals by use of census data and identifying educational attainment by the timing of the laws, the author found that individuals who faced higher school-leaving ages had higher rates of religious nonaffiliated status as adults. Further, Becker and Woessmann (2013) used the natural experiment provided by a panel data of income and church attendance during 1886–1911 for 175 Prussian counties. The authors found that, once the county and time effects are controlled for, the observed negative association between income and church attendance disappears and education has no independent effect on church attendance.

Figure 4-10. Belief on the Source of Spiritual Authority: Japan–U.S. Comparison (Percent of respondents in each group)

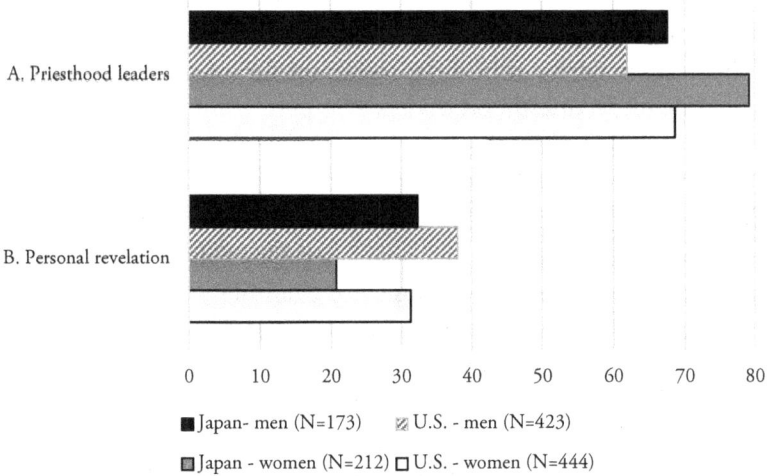

A. Priesthood leaders

B. Personal revelation

0   10   20   30   40   50   60   70   80

■ Japan- men (N=173)   ▨ U.S. - men (N=423)
▦ Japan - women (N=212)   ☐ U.S. - women (N=444)

Note: based on a subsample that includes only those who attend church at least weekly.
Sources: Japan LDS Survey; Next Mormons Survey.

to respect church leaders from a young age. If this interpretation is correct, we would expect to find a larger share of American Latter-day Saints (more of whom are non-converts) who give precedence to priesthood leaders. This is not the case. On the contrary, a smaller share of American men and women (62.0 and 68.7 percent, respectively) gave precedence to priesthood leaders than did Japanese men and women (67.6 and 79.3 percent, respectively).[10]

Once again, we are not implying that those who give precedence to personal revelation are any more or less religious than those who give precedence to priesthood leaders. Heeding the counsel of one's spiritual leaders and listening to one's own conscience are both important aspects of being a Latter-day Saint. The relative importance of each can legitimately vary across individuals who are equally committed religiously, and we must not read too much into a forced either/or choice that the survey respondents were asked to make. Even so, the higher share of Japanese Latter-day Saints, especially women, who gave precedence to priesthood

10. Even though the difference is not statistically significant for men, the difference for women, at more than 10 percentage points, is significant at the 1 percent level. That is, roughly speaking, we can state, with a 99-percent confidence, that we did not obtain the larger average for Japanese women by chance.

leaders aligns with the popular characterization of stereotypical Japanese traits. It is also consistent with our earlier finding that a greater share of American Latter-day Saints hold doubt about some of the Latter-day Saint teachings. Yet, despite these differences, it is remarkable that the overwhelming majority of both Japanese and American Latter-day Saints gave precedence to priesthood leaders over personal revelation.

4-4. Religious Practices

Moving from beliefs to practices, we are interested in knowing exactly how and how faithfully Japanese Latter-day Saints observe outward religious practices. For this purpose, we examine a series of questions concerning the respondents' compliance with or observance of important religious practices widely expected of practicing Latter-day Saints. This includes different aspects of what we may call personal devotion (daily prayer, scripture reading, temple attendance, member missionary work, and voluntary service in the church), the Word of Wisdom (abstention from the consumption of tea, coffee, tobacco, alcoholic drinks, and illicit drugs), the law of chastity (abstention from sex outside marriage), and the voluntary payment of tithes (that is, one tenth of annual income) and offerings. Cultural adaptation dictated that we alter the wording or format of the questions from the NMS. Even so, proximate comparisons with American Latter-day Saints are possible in most cases.

Personal Devotion

First, with respect to what we call personal devotion, the respondents were asked to assess their compliance or observance in five areas, as noted above, on a scale of 1 through 4, where 1 means no or little compliance and 4 means full compliance (Table 4-5). An interesting pattern that emerges across the five areas is that the share of those who reported "full" compliance was higher for men than for women. How to interpret this is not clear. It can mean that, as women are more involved in taking care of their children and household affairs, they have less time for personal devotion. It could alternatively be that women are more critical of themselves than men, so that few of them are satisfied with their religious practice. We are inclined toward the second interpretation. Another pattern we observe is that, except for member missionary work, the average score was around 3 on a scale of 1 (meaning little or no compliance) to 4 (meaning full compliance), that is, "good" compliance. The average for temple attendance was somewhat lower (around 2.5), but one must remember that,

Table 4-5. Devotion to Latter-day Saint Teachings
(Percent of respondents in each group)

		1 Little or no compliance	2 Some compliance	3 Good compliance	4 Full compliance	Total	Average score
Daily prayer	All (N=491)	6.9	9.2	23.8	60.1	100	3.4
	Men (N=192)	7.8	12.0	17.7	62.5	100	3.3
	Women (N=266)	6.4	6.4	28.9	58.3	100	3.4
Scripture reading	All (N=493)	9.7	22.7	29.6	37.9	100	3.0
	Men (N=195)	11.8	20.5	24.6	43.1	100	3.0
	Women (N=265)	8.3	23.8	33.2	34.7	100	2.9
Temple attendance	All (N=481)	17.5	31.2	31.4	20.0	100	2.5
	Men (N=188)	18.1	30.3	29.3	22.3	100	2.6
	Women (N=262)	15.6	33.2	32.1	19.1	100	2.5
Member missionary work	All (N=484)	25.0	54.8	16.1	4.1	100	2.0
	Men (N=189)	22.8	56.1	15.3	5.8	100	2.0
	Women (N=264)	25.8	53.8	17.4	3.0	100	2.0
Church service	All (N=493)	5.9	25.4	43.6	25.2	100	2.9
	Men (N=194)	4.6	20.6	44.3	30.4	100	3.0
	Women (N=267)	5.6	28.8	43.8	21.7	100	2.8

Source: Japan LDS Survey.

in Japan, it was an expensive and time-consuming activity for those who lived far from Tokyo, Fukuoka, or Sapporo, where the country's only three temples were located at the time of the survey in late 2021.

In four of these areas, proximate data can be obtained from the NMS for comparison purposes, if we interpret "full" and "good" compliance in Japan as equivalent to practicing "weekly" and "at least once a week" (except for daily prayer, for which "full" and "good" compliance is taken to mean practicing "daily"). Adjusted for church activity status, we find that Japanese men and women gave more devotion to daily prayer (82.7 and 88.7 percent vs. 73.1 and 77.7 percent for American men and women, respectively), but they gave less devotion to scripture reading (72.0 and 68.4 percent vs. 80.1 and 82.8 percent for American men and women, respectively) (Figure 4-11). Japanese Latter-day Saints' perception of their devotion to member missionary work was far lower than their American counterparts (22.2 and 21.0 percent vs. 70.3 and 59.2 percent for American men and women,

Figure 4-11. Devotion: Japan–U.S. Comparison
(Percent of respondents who reported high devotion)

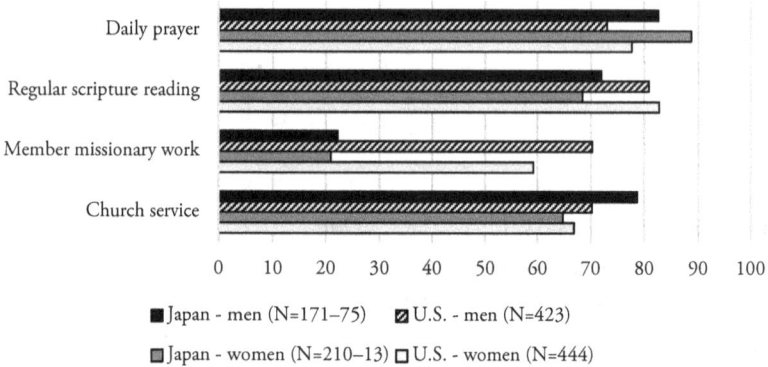

Notes: based on a subsample that includes only those who attend church at least weekly; high devotion means "full" and "good" compliance for Japan, "daily and at least once a week" ("daily" for daily prayer only) for the U.S.
Sources: Japan LDS Survey; Next Mormons Survey.

respectively). Part of the reason may have something to do with the way the question was phrased: we asked the respondents about their compliance with "member missionary work," whereas the NMS asked them about "sharing [their] views on God or religion with others." It is thus possible that Japanese Latter-day Saints' view of missionary work was more formal, though it is also possible that their lower devotion to missionary work reflects cultural reticence about expressing one's religious belief openly.

Word of Wisdom

Second, concerning their adherence to the Word of Wisdom, respondents assessed their compliance in four areas (abstaining from green tea, black tea/coffee, tobacco, and alcoholic drinks) (Table 4-6). Compliance was extremely high, with an average score of 3.9 or 4 (on a scale of 1 through 4). Very few in our sample reported that their compliance was less than "full" (although not reported in the table, there was little difference between the full sample and the subsample that included only those who attended church at least weekly). The high compliance of Japanese Latter-day Saints can be contrasted with the compliance of American Latter-day Saints (Figure 4-12), where we interpreted "not having consumed the substance in question for the last six months" to be equivalent to "full" and "good" compliance in the Japan survey (admittedly, the threshold of compliance is much higher for Japan than for the United States). In the NMS,

Table 4-6. Adherence to the Word of Wisdom
(Percent of respondents in each group)

		1 Little or no compliance	2 Some compliance	3 Good compliance	4 Full compliance	Total	Average score
Green tea	All (N=495)	2.6	0.6	3.2	93.5	100	3.9
	Men (N=195)	2.1	1.5	3.6	92.8	100	3.9
	Women (N=269)	1.9	0.4	2.6	95.2	100	3.9
Black tea/ coffee	All (N=496)	2.2	0.2	4.2	93.3	100	3.9
	Men (N=195)	2.1	0.0	4.1	93.8	100	3.9
	Women (N=268)	1.1	0.4	4.5	94.0	100	3.9
Tobacco	All (N=491)	1.2	0.2	1.8	96.7	100	3.9
	Men (N=193)	1.0	0.0	2.1	96.9	100	3.9
	Women (N=265)	0.8	0.4	1.5	97.4	100	4.0
Alcoholic drinks	All (N=493)	1.4	0.2	2.8	95.5	100	3.9
	Men (N=195)	1.0	0.5	3.6	94.9	100	3.9
	Women (N=265)	0.8	0.0	1.5	97.7	100	4.0

Source: Japan LDS Survey.

as much as 22.6 percent of American men and 12.6 percent of American women who attended church at least weekly admitted that they had consumed alcoholic drinks during the last six months; the comparable figure for black tea/coffee was 32.1 percent for men and 22.9 percent for women.

These findings should not be taken to mean that American Latter-day Saints on average are less faithful than their Japanese counterparts. A much smaller share of Latter-day Saints in Japan attend church regularly (our estimate suggests at most 20 percent). This means that those who are not compliant with the Word of Wisdom are less likely to be attending church (and did not participate in the survey). On the other hand, church-attending American Latter-day Saints, constituting a larger share of the overall Latter-day Saint population (perhaps 40–60 percent), include a much more diverse group of people with varying degrees of religious commitment. The higher level of Word of Wisdom compliance in Japan may also suggest a stronger peer pressure for conformity, as we discuss further in the penultimate chapter. A respondent voluntarily commented that those who did not keep the Word of Wisdom in Japan would almost always drop out of activity. The high compliance of those who are

Figure 4-12. Word of Wisdom: Japan–U.S. Comparison
(Percent of respondents who reported high compliance)

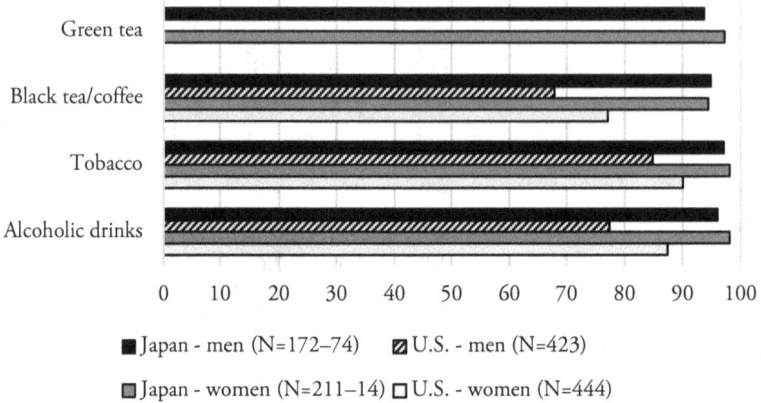

Japan - men (N=172–74) U.S. - men (N=423)

Japan - women (N=211–14) U.S. - women (N=444)

Notes: based on a subsample that includes only those who attend church at least weekly; high compliance means "full" and "good" compliance for Japan, "not having consumed the substance in the last six months" for the U.S.; no comparable U.S. figures are reported for green tea; for black tea/coffee, the figures for the U.S. are the higher of the respective figures for black tea and for coffee. Sources: Japan LDS Survey; Next Mormons Survey.

attending church can even be considered as an indictment of the church in Japan as an inhospitable place for those who are trying to keep the Word of Wisdom but for various reasons find it difficult.

Chastity and Tithing

Finally, the last set of questions on religious practices concerned the respondents' compliance with the law of chastity and the voluntary payment of tithes and offerings (Table 4-7). Similar to their adherence to the Word of Wisdom, compliance in both areas was extremely high with an average score of 3.9 for chastity and 3.8 for tithes and offerings (on a scale of 1 through 4), irrespective of gender. Yet, the percentage share of those who reported full compliance, in the high 80s, was considerably smaller for tithes and offerings than for any other area of religious practice. This possibly reflects, among other things, the reality that economic circumstances are sometimes beyond the control of individuals.

Roughly comparable data are available for the payment of tithes and offerings from the NMS, where we interpret regular payment of tithes "before" and "after" tax as equivalent to "good" and "full" compliance in our survey (Figure 4-13). Here again, the compliance of Japanese Latter-day Saints was 12–14 percentage points higher than that of American

Table 4-7. Chastity and the Payment of Tithes and Offerings
(Percent of respondents in each group)

		1 Little or no compliance	2 Some compliance	3 Good compliance	4 Full compliance	Total	Average score
Chastity	All (N=487)	1.6	0.6	3.9	93.8	100	3.9
	Men (N=192)	1.6	1.0	4.2	93.2	100	3.9
	Women (N=263)	1.1	0.4	3.8	94.7	100	3.9
Tithes and offerings	All (N=492)	3.5	1.8	7.5	87.2	100	3.8
	Men (N=193)	4.1	1.6	6.2	88.1	100	3.8
	Women (N=266)	1.9	1.9	9.0	87.2	100	3.8

Source: Japan LDS Survey.

Latter-day Saints. Even allowing for definitional differences, it is probably safe to conclude that Japanese Latter-day Saints who attended church at least weekly were on average more compliant in the payment of tithes than their American counterparts. The same argument we made about adherence to the Word of Wisdom (that is, the U.S. sample included a broader spectrum of members) can be made against concluding from this evidence that American Latter-day Saints were on average less faithful.

4-5. Views on Women and Priesthood

The issues of abortion, women's voice in the church, and women and priesthood are dealt with here, separate from other religious beliefs, given their multidimensional nature and their broader nonreligious implications. Respondents were asked to assess their agreement with three statements designed to gauge their beliefs (two of which were taken from the NMS). The first question asked the respondents if they thought that abortion was against the teachings of God. In Japan, abortion is neither a political nor a social issue, and societal tolerance for the practice is high. It is for this reason that we phrased the statement strictly as a moral issue. There were 436 individuals who responded to the question (of this number 195 men and 240 women identified their gender). More than 76 percent (across three groupings) "strongly" agreed that abortion was against the teachings of God, while another 11 to 12 percent agreed "somewhat" (Table 4-8). Around 4 percent "strongly" disagreed.

Figure 4-13. Tithes and Offerings: Japan–U.S. Comparison
(Percent of respondents who reported high compliance)

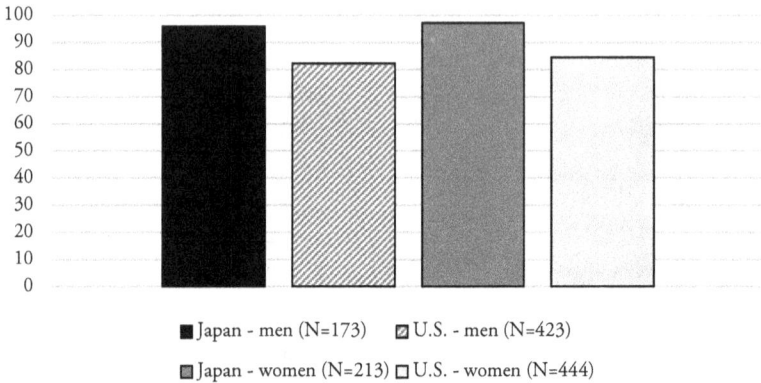

■ Japan - men (N=173)   ▨ U.S. - men (N=423)

▨ Japan - women (N=213) ☐ U.S. - women (N=444)

Notes: based on a subsample that includes only those who attend church at least weekly; high compliance means "full" and "good" compliance for Japan and regular payment of tithes "before" and "after" tax for the U.S.
Sources: Japan LDS Survey; Next Mormons Survey.

The Next Mormons Survey did not ask this question in the same way, but an attempt can still be made to compare Japanese and American Latter-day Saints who attended church at least weekly. Here, we interpret "strongly agree" as equivalent to "morally wrong" in the NMS, as we do not expect anyone who considers abortion as morally wrong to only "somewhat" agree with the statement that it is against the teachings of God. Assuming that this equivalency is valid, we find an interesting pattern (Figure 4-14). A higher share of Japanese men (76.4 percent) than American men (72.9 percent) morally opposed abortion, but a higher share of American women (83.7 percent) than Japanese women (76.3 percent) opposed the practice.[11] Another interesting pattern is that, in Japan, more men than women opposed abortion, while the opposite was true in the United States. If we include those who "somewhat" agreed with the statement (see Table 4-7), the share of Japanese Latter-day Saints, male or female, who opposed abortion becomes unambiguously larger. The same argument we made about the Word of Wisdom (that is, the U.S. sample included a broader spectrum of members) can be invoked here against concluding that American Latter-day Saints are on average more tolerant of a divisive moral issue.

The next two statements about the status of women in the Church come straight from the NMS. The first of these asked the respondents to assess

---

11. The difference is not statistically significant for men, but it is significantly different for women at the 1 percent level.

Table 4-8. Views on Women and Priesthood
(Percent of respondents in each group)

		1 Strongly disagree	2 Somewhat disagree	3 Neither agree nor disagree	4 Somewhat agree	5 Strongly agree	Total	Av.
A. Although abortion is legal and acceptable in Japan, I feel it is against the teachings of God except in certain cases allowed by the church	All (N=436)	3.7	1.8	6.7	11.5	76.4	100	4.6
	Men (N=195)	3.1	1.0	8.2	11.3	76.4	100	4.6
	Women (N=240)	4.2	2.5	5.4	11.7	76.3	100	4.5
B. Women do not have enough say in the church	All (N=425)	37.2	17.6	23.8	13.6	7.8	100	2.4
	Men (N=190)	28.4	18.4	26.3	18.4	8.4	100	2.6
	Women (N=235)	44.3	17.0	21.7	9.8	7.2	100	2.2
C. The fact that women do not hold the priesthood sometimes bothers me	All (N=438)	76.9	9.4	8.7	2.1	3.0	100	1.4
	Men (N=194)	71.1	9.8	9.8	3.6	5.7	100	1.6
	Women (N=244)	81.6	9.0	7.8	0.8	0.8	100	1.3

Source: Japan LDS Survey.

their agreement with the statement "Women do not have enough say in the Church," while the second asked about their agreement with the statement "The fact that women do not hold the priesthood sometimes bothers me." There were 425 respondents (190 men and 235 women among those who identified their gender) who responded to the first question ("voice"), and 438 (194 men and 244 women) responded to the second ("priesthood"). The overwhelming majority disagreed with these statements, with the average scores (on a scale of 1 through 5, with 1 for "strong" disagreement) of 2.6 and 1.4, respectively (see the bottom two-thirds of Table 4-7). In both areas, women expressed stronger disagreement than men; for the statement on voice, the responses were clustered around the middle ("neither agree nor disagree"), whereas the responses were clustered in the bottom for the statement on priesthood ("strongly disagree"). As much as 81.6 percent of

Figure 4-14. Opposition to Abortion: Japan–U.S. comparison
(Percent of respondents who attend church at least weekly)

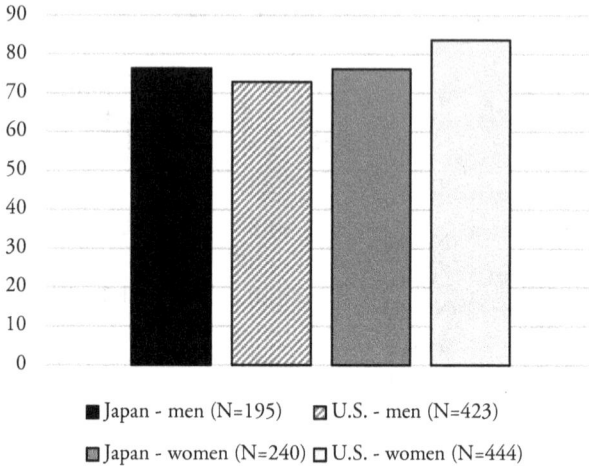

■ Japan - men (N=195)   ▨ U.S. - men (N=423)

▨ Japan - women (N=240) □ U.S. - women (N=444)

Notes: based on a subsample that includes only those who attend church at least weekly; opposition means "strongly agree" for Japan and "morally wrong" for the U.S.

Sources: Japan LDS Survey; Next Mormons Survey.

women and 71.1 percent of men stated that they were never bothered by the fact that women do not hold the priesthood.

A remarkable result emerges when we compare the responses of Japanese and American Latter-day Saints who attended church at least weekly, even though the basic pattern of overall disagreement, with a higher share for women, remains the same in each country (Figure 4-15). For both statements, a much higher share of American Latter-day Saints, male or female, expressed agreement. That is, American Latter-day Saints were more likely to think that women do not have enough voice and more likely to be bothered by women not being given the priesthood. For the first statement, the difference was statistically significant only for agreement (at the 1 percent level), while the difference for the second statement was statistically significant for both agreement and disagreement (at the 1 percent level).

The small share of Japanese women (less than 1 percent; two out of 211 individuals) bothered by women not holding the priesthood is striking, compared to 18 percent of American women (see panel B). The result was less striking for women's voice, but the basic pattern was the same. Whereas 18 percent of religiously active American women strongly felt the lack of their voice in the Church, the corresponding share of religiously active Japanese women was only 6.4 percent (see panel A). The broad takeaway

Figure 4-15. Views on Women in the Church: Japan–U.S. Comparison (Percent of respondents who strongly agree or disagree with respective statements)

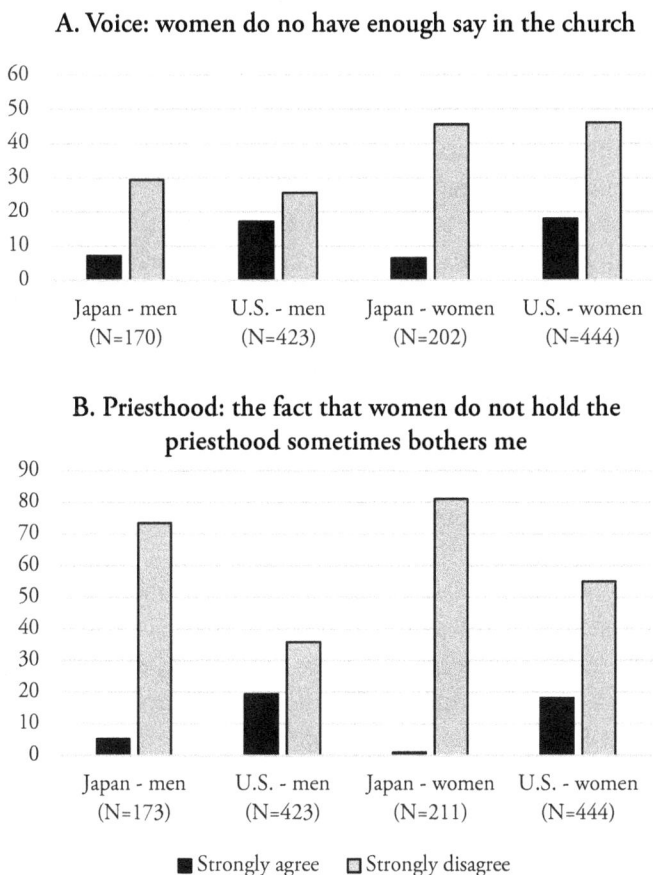

A. Voice: women do no have enough say in the church

| | Japan - men (N=170) | U.S. - men (N=423) | Japan - women (N=202) | U.S. - women (N=444) |

B. Priesthood: the fact that women do not hold the priesthood sometimes bothers me

| | Japan - men (N=173) | U.S. - men (N=423) | Japan - women (N=211) | U.S. - women (N=444) |

■ Strongly agree   □ Strongly disagree

Notes: based on a subsample that includes only those who attend church at least weekly.
Sources: Japan LDS Survey; Next Mormons Survey.

from this comparison is that, while both Japanese and Americans broadly endorsed the status quo for women, Japanese Latter-day Saints, and especially the women, were more supportive than their American counterparts of the current status of women in the Church. One possible explanation is the cross-cultural differences in expectation of gender parity in organizational leadership. Another possible explanation may be that, given the greater obstacles to remaining active in the Church in Japan and the fact that women are more likely than men to be in inter-faith marriages (see chapter 2), Latter-day Saint women who struggle with gender parity in church leadership are more likely to drop out of activity in Japan.

4-6. Conclusion

This chapter has reviewed the religious beliefs and practices of religiously active Latter-day Saints in Japan, with a view to understanding how and how thoroughly they have adopted or developed their identity as Latter-day Saints. In our survey, the overwhelming majority of them stated that they attended congregations with an active membership of more than seventy-five members (75 percent) and traveled to their meetinghouses by automobile (77 percent; 56–66 percent for densely populated urban areas). Nearly 50 percent of them lived within fifteen minutes' distance from their meetinghouses (by using their preferred means of transportation) and another 36 percent lived within thirty minutes' distance. We have argued that the relative ease with which Japanese Latter-day Saints seem to attend church reflects (1) their deliberate locational choices; (2) the strategic decision by The Church of Jesus Christ of Latter-day Saints to locate their meetinghouses in central and convenient locations; and (3) the relative compactness of Japanese cities.

About 85 percent stated that they had no doubt about the existence of God, with more women (88 percent) expressing such a conviction than men (81 percent). About 77 percent stated that they wholeheartedly accepted all of the Latter-day Saint teachings, with another 20 percent accepting many or most of the teachings. Again, more women (81 percent) than men (75 percent) stated the strongest expression of acceptance. These percentages were higher than those of American Latter-day Saints, adjusted for church activity status. The difference was not statistically significant for the strength of belief about God, but for the strength of acceptance of Latter-day Saint teachings, the difference (17 and 15 percentage points for men and women, respectively) was statistically significant. The most appealing teaching of The Church of Jesus Christ of Latter-day Saints was the idea that families can be together forever, with more than 65 percent stating that having this knowledge was their most favorite part of being a Latter-day Saint. This was closely followed by the Church's emphasis on Jesus Christ (60 percent).

In the observance of personal devotion (such as daily prayer, scripture reading, and temple attendance) and other unique religious practices (such as the Word of Wisdom, chastity, and tithing), the compliance of Japanese Latter-day Saints was high. Except for member missionary work and tithing, the self-assessed compliance averaged somewhere between "good" and "full" (more than 93 percent reported full compliance in the observance of the Word of Wisdom and the law of chastity). Exact comparison with American Latter-day Saints was not possible because the questions were worded differently. Proximate comparison suggests, however, that when adjusted for church activity status, Japanese Latter-day Saints on average scored higher on daily prayer but lower on scripture reading and member missionary work. In addition, their compliance of different aspects of the Word of Wisdom was greater than that of American Latter-day Saints, in some cases by as much as 10 percentage points.

An interesting picture that emerges from the survey is that of stereotypical Japanese men and especially women who give deference to authority and rarely express their opinion when they disagree with those in authority. Adjusted for church activity status, 68 percent of men (cf. 62 percent in the U.S.) and 79 percent of women (cf. 69 percent in the U.S.) gave precedence to their priesthood (ecclesiastical) leaders over personal revelation in guiding their personal affairs. A greater share of Japanese Latter-day Saints seem to approve the current status of women in the Church. In our survey, only 7 percent of men (cf. 17 percent in the U.S.) and 6 percent of Japanese women (cf. 18 percent in the U.S.) did not think women had "enough say in the Church," while only 5 percent of men (cf. 19 percent in the U.S.) and less than 1 percent of women (cf. 18 percent in the U.S.) were bothered by women not having the priesthood. The difference between Japanese and American Latter-day Saints was striking, consistent, and statistically significant in all cases for women.

We conclude that the overwhelming majority have developed a strong identity as Latter-day Saints. On average, they seem more devoted to their faith than their American counterparts in terms of both beliefs and practices. The higher share of those fully committed in Japan likely reflects the smaller share of the total Latter-day Saint population who attend church regularly. An estimated less than 20 percent attend church regularly in Japan, but the share in the United States might be as high as 40–60 percent. In consequence, whereas active membership in Japan includes only those fully committed, a much more diverse group of people with varying degrees of commitment attends church in the United States. It may be that only those fully committed have managed to remain religiously active in Japan.

CHAPTER 5

IDENTITY CONFLICT

5-1. Introduction

Having thus far considered the religious identity of Japanese members of The Church of Jesus Christ of Latter-day Saints, in this chapter we explore any conflict they may experience between that identity and the multiple identities they maintain in the larger Japanese society. The purpose is not only to find evidence of identity conflict but also to investigate how this conflict is managed or mitigated. We first discuss how they perceive their social acceptance as practitioners of a minority religion, which defines the nature and intensity of any conflict they may face, before discussing specific life situations. We select three life situations in which they may face conflict, namely, family relationships, the workplace, and the larger society. In addressing identity conflict in the family, we focus on the cultural practices of institutional Buddhism. For identity conflict in the workplace, we focus on the challenges posed by endemic long working hours and social drinking. For identity conflict within the larger Japanese society, we focus on the custom of serving green tea and the challenges posed by Japan's education system.

The rest of this chapter is organized as follows. Section 5-2 discusses Japanese Latter-day Saints' perception of their social acceptance by asking, among other things, how their family and peers support their membership in The Church of Jesus Christ of Latter-day Saints, how comfortable they feel about practicing a minority religion, and if they ever feel embarrassed to admit their church membership. Section 5-3 explores identity conflict in the family, where the focus is on the socially mandated participation in institutional Buddhism, but we also discuss conflicts involving Sabbath observance, Shinto rituals, and the Word of Wisdom. Section 5-4 shifts attention to the workplace, where we focus on long working hours and social drinking as potential sources of conflict, while section 5-5 discusses how Latter-day Saints avoid conflict through career choices, especially in the context of Sabbath observance. Section 5-6 takes up identity conflict in the larger Japanese society, where our focus is on the Japanese custom of serving green tea as an act of hospitality and on Japan's education system, whose demands can become so encroaching as to keep students and their families from participating in church activities. Finally, section 5-7 presents a conclusion.

Table 5-1. Perception of Social Acceptance
(Percent of all respondents)

		1 Strongly disagree	2 Somewhat disagree	3 Neither agree nor disagree	4 Somewhat agree	5 Strongly agree	Total	Average score
A. Latter-day Saints are highly regarded as good neighbors and colleagues	N=472	1.5	5.1	32.0	38.3	23.1	100	3.8
B. Latter-day Saints are not very well known in Japan. People don't pay much attention.	N=481	1.7	6.4	25.2	36.8	29.9	100	3.9
C. My peers support my choices as a result of my church membership.	N=483	0.4	1.4	10.6	31.3	56.3	100	4.4
D. My nonmember family/relatives support my choices as a result of my church membership.	N=486	0.6	1.0	7.8	24.5	66.0	100	4.5
E. I feel comfortable in practicing my beliefs even if they are different.	N=487	0.8	2.3	5.5	30.2	61.2	100	4.5

Source: Japan LDS Survey.

5-2. Perception of Social Acceptance

To gauge the overall perception by Latter-day Saints of their social acceptance as practitioners of a minority religion, the survey requested respondents to assess their agreement with five separate statements describing how society, family, and peers view their church membership, on a scale of 1 (strongly disagree) to 5 (strongly agree) (Table 5-1). Except for the second statement (B), which asked how well Latter-day Saints are known in Japan, greater agreement means a higher perception of their social acceptance. For these four statements, the average score ranged between 3.8 and 4.5, suggesting a relatively high assessment of social acceptance.

While the average score of agreement is similar across the four statements, there is a clear difference between how individuals perceive their own acceptance (C–E), and how they perceive the collective acceptance of Latter-day Saints (A). For example, the share of those who "strongly" agreed with the statements about their personal acceptance or personal religious

Table 5-2. Response to the Question "Do you feel embarrassed to admit that you are a member of The Church of Jesus Christ of Latter-day Saints?" (Percent of respondents in each group)

	All (N=444)	All, active (N=390)	Men (N=195)	Men, active (N=174)	Women (N=246)	Women, active (N=213)
Never	68.9	70.0	73.3	73.6	65.5	67.1
Sometimes	28.8	28.2	24.1	24.1	32.5	31.5
Often	1.1	1.0	1.0	1.2	1.2	0.9
Always	1.1	0.8	1.5	1.2	0.8	0.5
Total	100	100	100	100	100	100

Note: "active" means "attending church at least weekly."
Source: Japan LDS Survey.

practice was 56–66 percent, compared with 23.1 percent for those who "strongly" agreed with the statements about the social acceptance of Latter-day Saints as a group. If we combine those who "strongly" agreed and those who "somewhat" agreed, 87.6 and 90.5 percent felt support from their peers and families, respectively, in the choices they make, and 91.4 percent felt comfortable practicing their beliefs even if they are different.

Such a positive view of the experience with practicing a minority religion in Japan is corroborated by asking them the question: "Do you feel embarrassed to admit that you are a member of The Church of Jesus Christ of Latter-day Saints?" There were 444 individuals who responded to the question (Table 5-2). About 70 percent, irrespective of their gender or activity status, stated "never"; the share was marginally higher among those who attended church at least weekly, and the share was somewhat smaller among women. Only the male-female difference for the total Latter-day Saint population is statistically significant (at the 5 percent level).[1] Conversely, around 30 percent felt embarrassed at least "sometimes."

The share of those who always felt embarrassed was extremely small at 0.8–1.5 percent. As small as these numbers may be, Latter-day Saints do appear to encounter socially awkward situations from time to time. In the previous survey question (see Table 5-1), about 67 percent either "somewhat" or "strongly" agreed with statement B: "Latter-day Saints are not very well known in Japan. People don't pay much attention." We believe that the evidence of occasional conflict experienced or perceived by some Latter-day Saints is not contradictory to the rest of the evidence showing a generally

---

1. That is, roughly speaking, we can state with a 95-percent confidence that we did not obtain the smaller share for women by chance.

positive experience of Japanese Latter-day Saints. Our interpretation is that many have found a niche by establishing friendships and long-term relationships in their spheres of daily life, and many feel comfortable among those who understand their religious practices, if not their religious beliefs. When they are outside the niche, conflict could emerge.

5-3. Conflict in the Family

Family, both nuclear and extended, is the first area of focus in our exploration of identity conflict. Here, we highlight the role of Buddhism, which may be considered as much a social institution as a religious one. The pervasive social influence of Buddhism may explain why, despite the constitutionally guaranteed freedom of religion since 1889, many continue to feel constrained by Buddhism in their free exercise of religious practice. The institutionalization of Buddhism is traced to the beginning of the Edo period (1603–1867) in the seventeenth century, when Buddhist temples assumed the official role of registering births and deaths (and, in the case of a male, as the likely site of his funeral and burial). This system was officially terminated at the beginning of the Meiji period (1868–1912), when the right to rule was abrogated by the Tokugawa family and returned to the imperial household, which instead attempted to elevate Shinto as the state religion (Takagi 2016).

The fortunes of institutional Buddhism recovered subsequently, and it has continued to keep a grip on the ritualistic part of Japanese life, in large part because family temples are where dead ancestors are memorialized and where many of them remain buried. Two aspects of institutional Buddhism could present Japanese Latter-day Saints with a potential conflict. One is a family altar (*butsudan*)—which the first-born son is typically expected to inherit from generation to generation—where a visual or physical representation of the Buddha and mortuary tablets (*ihai*, representing each deceased ancestor) are placed. The other is periodic memorial rituals (*hōji*), where extended family gathers for a service conducted by the family monk. Edo Buddhism added a number of such rituals as a way to acquire more resources from parishioners. At present, such rituals are held every seventh day from the date of death through the forty-ninth day as well as on the hundredth day.[2]

---

2. Thereafter, rituals are performed on the first, third, seventh, thirteenth, seventeenth, twenty-third, twenty-seventh, thirty-third, thirty-seventh, forty-third, forty-seventh, fiftieth, and one hundredth anniversaries of death. Some are more important than others, to which only the immediate family members are expected to attend.

Figure 5-1. Conflict in the Family
(Percent of respondents experiencing conflict)

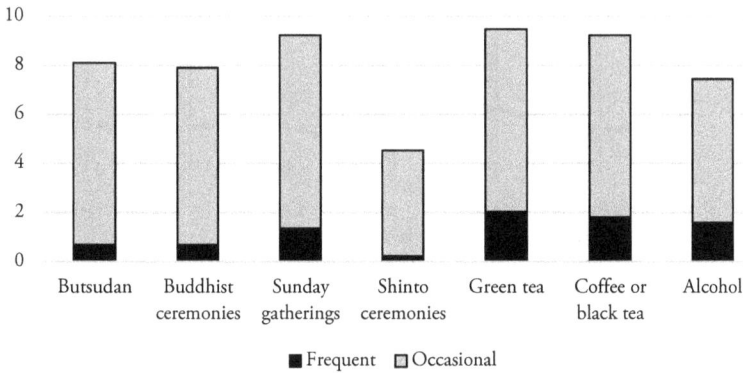

Notes: sample size (N)=442/443/444 (depending on the area of potential conflict); percent of the respondents who reported experiencing frequent or occasional conflict in a given area of family life.
Source: Japan LDS Survey.

Respondents were asked to indicate the frequency of the conflict they experienced regarding seven different family-related activities, including Buddhist and Shinto traditions, on a scale from 1 (never) to 4 (frequent). According to the survey, very few Latter-day Saints in Japan considered the *butsudan* and periodic memorial rituals as frequent or even occasional sources of conflict (Figure 5-1). This may be explained as follows. First, matters related to the *butsudan* and memorial rituals are not everyday occurrences. One is at most a one-time event involving only the eldest son of a family when he inherits the *butsudan*, and the other is occasional or at most periodic, as explained above. Second, most Japanese Latter-day Saints have assumed a practical approach to institutional Buddhism, not as a religious practice, but as a cultural or social obligation devoid of any religious content. This is similar to American Latter-day Saints attending a funeral or wedding officiated by a priest or minister of another Christian denomination. This also explains why so few (about 4.5 percent) reported any conflict with Shinto ceremonies, which may involve the blessing of an infant and annual festivals to celebrate the growth and health of children.

Somewhat more consequential was the impact of family obligations on the observance of the Sabbath and the Word of Wisdom. Weddings, for example, are often held on Sundays. Alcoholic drinks are served when relatives gather. Green tea can become a constant source of conflict when a member lives in a nonmember household (which is no different from a situation that

Figure 5-2. Acceptance and Conflict in the Family
(Average score in each group, on a scale of 1–4)

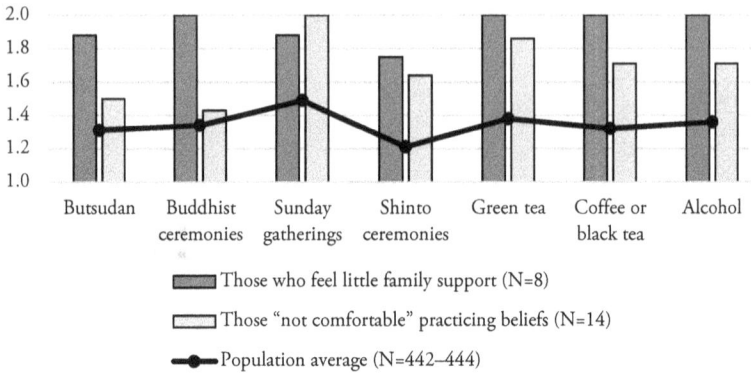

Notes: two subgroups are those who in Table 5-1 "strongly" or "somewhat" disagreed with the statements: "D. My nonmember family/relatives support my choices as a result of my church membership" and "E. I feel comfortable in practicing my beliefs even if they are different." The scale is: 1=never; 2=hardly/seldom; 3=occasionally; and 4=frequently.
Source: Japan LDS Survey.

may exist in the United States). The survey indicates that, while Latter-day Saints experienced conflict more often in these areas than with institutional religious ceremonies, the share of those who reported "frequent" conflict was small, ranging between 1.4 percent (Sabbath observance) and 2.0 percent (green tea); the share increases to between 7.5 percent (alcoholic drinks) and 9.5 percent (green tea) if those who reported "frequent" and "occasional" conflict are combined. The relatively small incidence of conflict suggests that Latter-day Saints in Japan have for the most part accommodated any sources of conflict with their nonmember families.

It may be recalled that 89.5 percent of the 490 respondents agreed ("strongly" or "somewhat") with the statement: "My nonmember family/relatives support my choices as a result of my church membership," and 91.4 percent likewise agreed with the statement: "I feel comfortable in practicing my beliefs even if they are different" (see Table 5-1). It is observed that those few who disagreed ("strongly" or "somewhat") had a higher-than-average number of conflicts in the family (Figure 5-2). For example, those who felt little family support had an average conflict score of 2.0 (on a scale of 1 through 4) with respect to Buddhism and Word of Wisdom observance (c.f. the Latter-day Saint population average of around 1.3). Those who did not feel comfortable practicing their beliefs had an average conflict score of 1.9–2.0 with respect to Sunday gatherings and green tea (c.f. the Latter-day Saint population average of 1.3–1.5). The lack of family support or acceptance typically translated to a greater incidence of conflict. Even so, the conflict score was at most 2.0; that is, hardly or seldom. Conflict even in these cases was never occasional, much less frequent.

5-4. Conflict in the Workplace

In our discussion of identity conflict in the workplace, we highlight (1) the long working hours of typical Japanese workers and (2) wide-spread social drinking. A fuller discussion of other aspects of Word of Wisdom observance in the workplace will be deferred to a later section where we discuss identity conflict in society. For many people, the workplace is an in-separable part of the larger society that shares the same societal customs and norms, and conflicts in society often take place in the context of making a living. There is thus only a fine line between what we call the workplace and what we call society. For the purposes of this book, we view "anonymity" as defining the dividing line. In the workplace, work associates typically know (and often respect) the religious practices of their Latter-day Saint colleagues. On the other hand, when a Latter-day Saint employee of a retail establishment sells a product to a customer, his or her religious practices are less likely to be known. We consider the former situation as a workplace situation, and the latter as a situation that occurs in the larger society.

Long Working Hours

First, as to long working hours, we have earlier noted their likely legal origins. Yet, Japan's Labor Standards Law, in principle, stipulates the legal maximum of eight hours a day and forty hours a week, and that anything beyond must be negotiated between the employer and the labor union. It is difficult to obtain the accurate reality of overtime work from official govern-ment statistics, but 93.8 percent of some 12,300 firms surveyed in 2017 responded that they had either occasional (36.4 percent) or perennial (57.4 percent) overtime work (TSR 2017). Excessive overtime work, for which employees are not always fully compensated, has become a major social issue, so much so that the government revised the Labor Standards Law to specify an annual maximum of 720 hours and a monthly maximum of 100 hours of overtime work, to become effective for larger firms from April 2019 and for small and medium-sized enterprises from April 2020 (MHLW 2019). What this means is that the government has legally sanctioned over-time work of three hours a day on average (assuming that this is enforce-able), a staggering official admission of endemic overtime work in Japan.

Figure 5-3. Overtime Hours in a Typical Week
(Number of respondents)

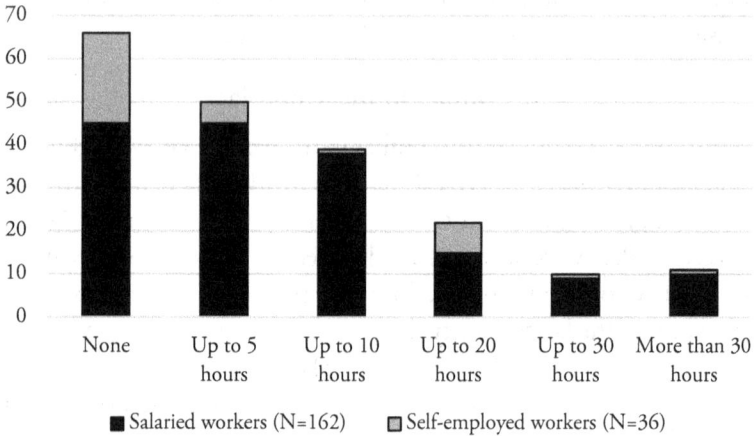

Notes: sample size (N)=198; the sample includes only those who reported that they worked full time.
Source: Japan LDS Survey.

Our survey of Japanese Latter-day Saints does not support the notion of endemic and pervasive overtime work (Figure 5-3). Based on a subsample of 198 Latter-day Saints who were employed full time, a third (66 individuals) reported no overtime work and 10 percent (21 individuals) stated that they had more than 20 hours of overtime work in a typical week. The mean response was 8.7 hours (9.2 hours if the self-employed were excluded), with the median being 3.8 hours (5 hours). What one thinks of these numbers is a matter of interpretation. On the one hand, endemic overtime work did not characterize the population of Latter-day Saints in Japan who worked full time. On the other hand, 10 percent still worked more than 20 hours overtime (and 20 percent worked more than 10 hours), which might pose some challenges in balancing family, church, and work obligations. In the full sample of 280 Latter-day Saints who responded to the question, only 7.1 percent reported that work "frequently" prevented them from attending weekday church activities, roughly corresponding to the 10 percent who reported endemic overtime work. The share of those whose work "occasionally" prevented them from attending weekday activities was 12.1 percent, which again roughly corresponded to those who reported overtime work of more than 10 but less than 20 hours (Figure 5-4). Among respondents in the survey, 6.8 percent reported "frequent" conflict in Sabbath observance because of work, while another 7.2 percent reported "occasional" conflict.

Figure 5-4. Conflict in Work and Society
(Percent of respondents)

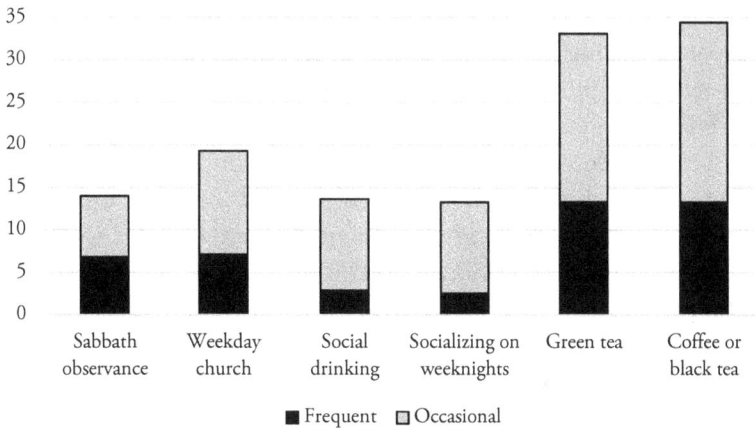

Notes: sample size (N)=279/280 (depending on the area of potential conflict); percent of the respondents who reported experiencing conflict in a given area of work or social life.
Source: Japan LDS Survey.

Social Drinking

Second, social drinking is a term that grossly downplays the ceremonial or ritualistic role drinking plays in Japanese society. Social drinking in Japan is a group-oriented, formalized part of a worker's life. It takes place in a highly permissive drinking culture that gives a positive social perception of drinking (especially by men), and liberally forgives drunkenness in public places. In fact, one is expected to drink to get drunk (Shimizu 1990). Partanen (2006, p. 194) quotes from D. E. Bayley, who observed how police officers in Japan displayed an "exaggerated solicitude for drunken people" by treating them "according to the general view that they are children and not responsible for what they do and say."[3] Few restrictions exist against the consumption of alcohol, except for a severe legal penalty for drunk driving, and social sanctions, including a dismissal from employment, for those who accidentally kill someone while driving under the influence of alcohol.

Partanen (2006, p. 191) describes the purpose of social drinking as "the attainment of uninhibited sociability," as drinking breaks down the barriers of hierarchy and creates "egalitarian relations." Drinking estab-

---

3. This author provides an excellent historical background of social drinking in Japan.

lishes new relationships, renews old relationships, restores broken relationships, and enhances group solidarity. Shimizu (1990) argues that these relational purposes of drinking explain why per capita alcohol consumption expanded along with economic growth and urbanization, which increased social mobility. A drinking session begins with a formal ceremony where social hierarchy is respected. Typically, the most senior participant gives a speech, followed by a toast, and as the session progresses, social barriers begin to break down, permitting direct and intimate conversations. Business deals can be made in such an atmosphere of trust, and workers try to establish personal relationships with their superiors. There is limited room for personal discretion. Participants do not choose a drink but drink a cup as it is filled by others. Refusing an offer of a drink requires, in the words of Partanen, "profuse apologies" (Partanen 2006, p. 192).

Of course, not all social drinking is this formal, but it is a routine occurrence for coworkers to go out drinking on the way home. Given that, at least historically, Japanese have tended to remain with the same firm for a long time, they find social drinking as a networking opportunity with their peers elsewhere in the firm. With close coworkers who understand their religious faith, Latter-day Saints may not feel as uncomfortable hanging out with them occasionally,[4] but going to drinking places is not something they would like to do frequently, especially when they know that conversations could turn vulgar and everyone else gets drunk. On less intimate occasions, they could experience awkwardness if not outright embarrassment.

The Japan LDS Survey suggests that instances of conflict involving alcoholic drinks do occur but do not seem very prevalent (see Figure 5-4). According to the survey of 279 respondents who were currently employed, unemployed, or retired,[5] only 2.9 percent of them reported that they "frequently" experienced (or had experienced) tension or difficulty with entertaining clients where alcohol is served (denoted as "social drinking"), with another 10.8 percent experiencing such conflict "occasionally."

---

4. Anonymity plays an important role in defining the type of conflict that may occur even in the workplace. We are acquainted with the experience of a Latter-day Saint who was put on public display in a relatively large drinking session at the workplace, where he was given a glass to drink up. All eyes were on what he was going to do. His close friends and associates, who knew his faith, became alarmed. Just then, a sympathetic boss stepped in to rescue him from the predicament by taking the glass from him and drinking it up.

5. For those unemployed or retired, we asked them to think of their experience with their previous or longest-held jobs.

Figure 5-5. Acceptance and Conflict in Work and Society
(Average score in each group, on a scale of 1–4)

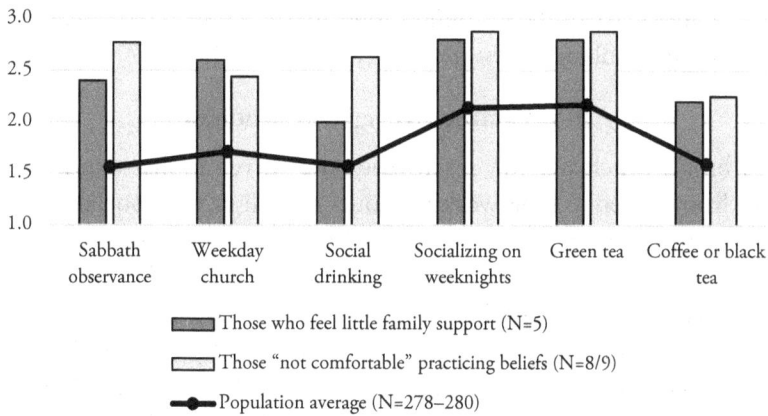

Those who feel little family support (N=5)

Those "not comfortable" practicing beliefs (N=8/9)

Population average (N=278–280)

Notes: two subgroups are those who in Table 5-1 "strongly" or "somewhat" disagreed with the statements: "C. My peers support my choices as a result of my church membership" and "E. I feel comfortable in practicing my beliefs even if they are different." The scale is: 1=never; 2=hardly/seldom; 3=occasionally; and 4=frequently.
Source: Japan LDS Survey.

Likewise, only 2.5 percent reported that they "frequently" experienced (or had experienced) such conflict with going for drinks with colleagues (denoted as "socializing on weeknights"), with another 10.8 percent reporting "occasional" conflict (Figure 5-4).

Acceptance and Conflict

Similar to the case of conflicts in the family, there is a strong correlation between the incidence of conflicts in the workplace and the lack of acceptance or support from work associates. It may be recalled that 87.5 percent of the 490 respondents agreed ("strongly" or "somewhat") with the statement: "My peers support my choices as a result of my church membership," and 91.4 percent likewise agreed with the statement: "I feel comfortable in practicing my beliefs even if they are different" (see Table 5-1). As was the case in the family, those few who disagreed with these two statements ("strongly" or "somewhat") had a higher-than-average number of conflicts in the workplace (Figure 5-5). For example, those who felt little peer support had an average conflict score of 2.6–2.8 (on a scale of 1 through 4) with respect to weekday church and socializing on weeknights (c.f. the Latter-day Saint population average of 1.7–2.1); those who felt less comfortable practicing their beliefs had an average conflict score of 2.6–2.8 with respect to social drinking and Sabbath observance (c.f. the Latter-day Saint population average of around 1.6). The incidence of these conflicts is greater in the workplace than in the family, but they still occur less frequently than "occasionally."

5-5. Conflict-Mitigating Choices

A broad conclusion we reach from the survey is that conflicts that derive from endemic long working hours as well as from social drinking do occur in the workplace, but the incidence is surprisingly infrequent. In fact, 55–60 percent of the respondents stated that they experienced no conflict at all, with another 25–27 percent experiencing conflict only rarely. In part, this suggests the tendency for workplace conflicts to be accommodated or resolved as long-term relationships are established. We have already observed that, of the 490 respondents, 86.3 percent agreed with the statement: "My peers support my choices as a result of my church membership" (see Table 5-1). Also contributing to the relatively low incidence of identity conflict in the workplace, we believe, is deliberate conflict-avoiding career choices, with respect to the place of employment (e.g., whether one is self-employed or works for the public sector) or the type of work (whether one is a professional or works in the retail business).

Evidence of such conflict avoidance is suggested by the respondents who were currently working, unemployed, or retired (in the case of unemployed or retired workers, we asked them to respond on the basis of the last or the longest-held jobs) (Figure 5-6). First, in terms of place of employment, only 45.5 percent ("none of the above," in panel A) stated that they were (or had been) employed in the private sector, presumably as salaried workers or wage earners. That is to say, the majority had selected places of employment that would pose less conflict with their Latter-day Saint identity, including public-sector jobs and self-employment. In fact, 11.8 percent were or had been self-employed, and another 6.8 percent were or had been business owners (that is, self-employment with one or more employees). The self-employment share of 18.6 percent far exceeded the share in the Japanese population, which was about 10 percent in 2020, including the family members.[6] Another striking feature, evident in the type of work, is that the share of Latter-day Saints in the retail business,

---

6. The lack of a universally agreed definition of self-employment makes it difficult to find a comparable figure from the general population, but we believe that 12 percent would be the upper bound (and the actual comparable figure might be close to 10 percent). Bureau of Statistics (2023a).

Figure 5-6. Types of Employment and Work
(Percent of all respondents currently working, unemployed, or retired)

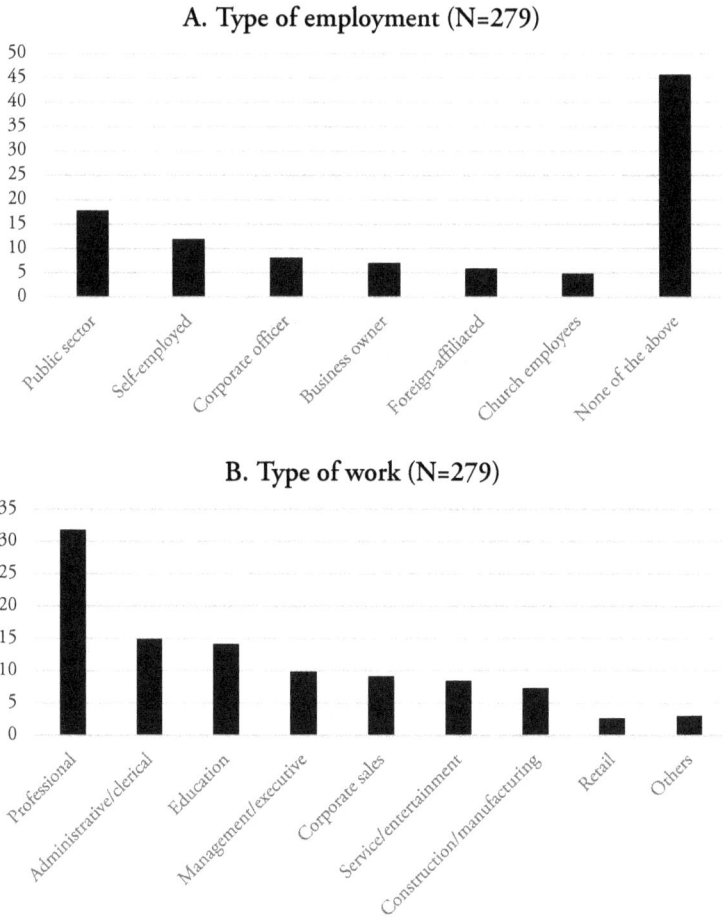

A. Type of employment (N=279)

B. Type of work (N=279)

Source: Japan LDS Survey.

at 2.5 percent, was far smaller than the estimated share in the Japanese population of 12.7–15.7 percent in 2019.[7]

On the other hand, the share of professionals in the Latter-day Saint population (28.4 percent) was far larger than the estimated general population share (17.5 percent in 2019). The definition of professional jobs may not be perfectly comparable across the two populations. As the govern-

---

7. The smaller number (12.7) represented the share of workers in sales, while the larger (15.7) was the share of workers in the retail and wholesale sectors. Bureau of Statistics (2023b).

ment data do not have "teachers" as a separate category, teachers (treated separately in the Japan LDS Survey) may be included among the professionals. If so, the more comparable Latter-day Saint share of professionals (28.4+13.3=41.7 percent) far exceeded any reasonable estimate of the general population share of professionals provided by government data (in sectoral employment data, education accounted for only 5 percent, making 22.5 percent the extreme upper bound).[8] A professional position allows the worker greater flexibility to live his or her religion more freely and strengthens the leverage vis-à-vis the employer on the terms of employment.

These patterns are the direct outcome of a deliberate decision to choose an occupation that would make it easier to practice their faith. The Japan LDS survey asked the respondents to select up to three options from a list of seven possible factors responsible for the current employment decision (or the last or the longest-held job in the case of unemployed or retired persons). We had 281 respondents answer this question (Figure 5-7). The most common factor was Sabbath observance, which about 62 percent of the respondents selected, followed by personal interest or aptitude (58.4 percent), salary (46.3 percent), and location (27.8 percent). Being able to attend weekday church activities (16.4 percent) or the ease of keeping the Word of Wisdom (3.2 percent) was not a very important consideration. Nearly 90 percent of respondents had been converted to The Church of Jesus Christ of Latter-day Saints in their teens or twenties. Converting at a relatively young age has allowed them to choose a path that would facilitate the continued practice of their minority religion.

5-6. Conflict in the Larger Japanese Society

For the discussion of potential tension between Latter-day Saint identity and identity as a member of Japanese society, we highlight (1) endemic tea drinking and (2) extracurricular school activities, including those on Sundays. Though our focus is on green tea, conflict regarding green tea is a special case of a broader conflict that can arise concerning Word of Wisdom observance more generally, which also includes absten-

---

8. Heaton (1998a), based on the 1981–83 data, estimated that about 20 percent of Japanese Latter-day Saints were employed as professionals, which he said was about double the national average. Without knowing how he obtained the estimate, we cannot be certain whether the larger share in our sample reflects only the definitional difference or the maturing of church membership over the past forty years.

**Figure 5-7. Factors that Influenced the Employment Decision
(Percent of respondents; up to three selected)**

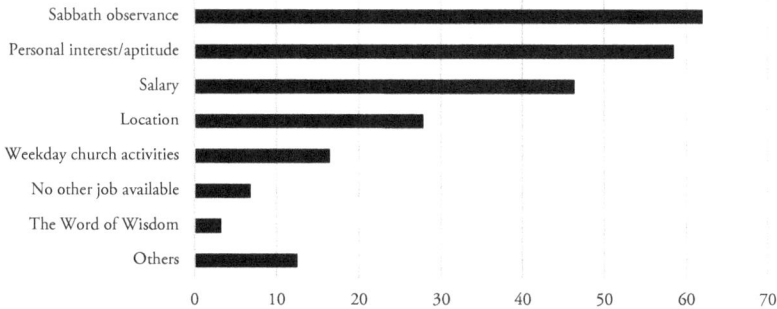

Note: sample size (N)=281.
Source: Japan LDS Survey.

tion from alcoholic drinks, black tea, and coffee.[9] Conflicts occur in any life situation, including in the workplace, where anonymity is involved. If anonymity defines the boundary between the workplace and the larger society, the survey results reported in Figures 5-4 and 5-5 concerning green tea and coffee/black tea are about conflicts that arise in the larger society even when they take place in the context of one's work.

Figuerres (1999, p. 26) observes from his experience as a missionary and mission president in Japan that the Word of Wisdom is not about quitting a particular drink ("integrity to self") but about honoring "social obligation," "maintaining harmony," and "integrity to others." Figuerres further notes that American missionaries, when they see Japanese investigators and converts struggling with the Word of Wisdom, think of them as "wimp[s]," but what they fail to understand is the social implications of refusing to accept what is offered as a gesture of hospitality or social courtesy, and as part of the ritual of relationship building. Identity conflict arises because, in the absence of a personal relationship, the giver does not understand the motive of the Latter-day Saint refusing the offer.

Green Tea

Green tea in Japan is not just a drink to quench one's thirst but is a pervasive cultural institution with a symbolic meaning. Practiced as the

---

9. Harmful health consequences of tobacco use are so well-established that abstention from tobacco is not an issue in Japan. Smokers constituted only 16.7 percent of the adult population (27.1 percent for men; 7.6 percent for women) in 2019 (NCC 2019).

tea ceremony, it is a spiritual ritual and an art form, as beautifully explained in the *Book of Tea*, a celebrated introduction to Japanese aesthetics written by Kakuzo Okakura. In ordinary life, green tea is served by the host as a token of hospitality, and the way the guest drinks it displays his or her cultural refinement and graciousness. It is also an occasion to express one's appreciation for the handcraft of the potter who created the cup in which the tea is being served. Upon arriving, the guest is not asked if he or she would like a cup of tea; it is simply served upon being seated. Occasionally, the host may ask if the guest would like a cup of black tea or coffee. If the answer is negative, a cup of green tea is brought in (this explains why conflict involving black tea or coffee could be just as frequent). Green tea is also routinely served at school lunch. Latter-day Saint children bring their own thermoses, which may invite attention, if not ridicule, from their classmates. Refusing green tea is made doubly difficult by the widespread perception in Japan that green tea is a healthy drink; many members feel the same way and find it difficult to explain the purpose of this religious practice to others.

Conflict can occur in work situations (though not so much in the workplace) where the absence of a personal relationship causes personal interactions to be driven by custom alone. We are acquainted with a faithful Latter-day Saint who represented his large organization at a welcome reception hosted by the chairman of the board of another organization. The tea ceremony was performed in his honor, where, in an expression of ultimate hospitality, a cup of the finest green tea was served and passed, starting with him, from one participant to another. He remarked afterwards that, at that moment, the only reasonable thing he could do was fake drinking the tea and, as expected, say "it was a delicious tea."

We are also acquainted with another faithful Latter-day Saint who worked as a maid with a cleaning service company. Her boss was something of a bully who cared more about not offending the mistress of the house than about protecting her subordinate, and thus she forbade the maid from leaving a cup of tea undrunk when served. This Latter-day Saint woman carried with her a thermos into which she emptied the cup of tea each time it was served. Latter-day Saints in Japan often encounter such situations as salespersons, office visitors, potential buyers at an automobile dealership, or even guests of honor—that is, as anonymous members of Japanese society.

The higher incidence of conflict occurring in society than in the family can be confirmed by comparing the findings reported in Figure 5-1

Table 5-3. Social Acceptance and Conflict in Work and Society,
by Place and Type of Employment

	Conflict score (1=never; 2= seldom; 3=occasionally)[1]			Agreement score[2] (4=somewhat; 5=strongly)
	Average	Word of Wisdom - green tea, black tea, coffee	Sunday and weekday church	
All (N=277/276)[3]	1.79	2.16	1.64	4.37
By place of employment (selective):				
Self-employed (N=82/81)[3]	1.87	2.21	1.71	4.37
Public sector (N=16)	1.35	1.53	1.09	4.63
Foreign-affiliated company (N=13)	1.69	2.00	1.73	4.77
Other private sector (N=143/142)[3]	1.80	2.20	1.63	4.29
By type of work (selective):				
Professionals (N=78/77)[3]	1.69	2.04	1.53	4.35
Corporate sales (N=24)	1.97	2.35	1.79	4.33
Retail/service & entertainment (N=24)	1.86	2.31	1.96	4.17
Management/executive (N=24)	1.74	2.10	1.50	4.46
Education (N=37/36)[3]	1.77	2.03	1.68	4.53
Construction/manufacturing (N=20)	1.91	2.40	1.60	4.25

Notes: [1]average conflict score, on a scale of 1–4, comes from the same source as Figure 5-4; it is the average of individual scores for Sabbath observance, weekday church, social drinking, socializing on weeknights, green tea, and coffee or black tea; a higher score means greater conflict; [2]agreement score comes from Table 5-1, where the respondents were asked to assess their agreement, on a scale of 1–5, with the statement "My peers support my choices as a result of my church membership"; a lower score means greater social acceptance; [3]sample size (N) depends on the area of potential conflict: Word of Wisdom observance and church attendance, respectively. Source: Japan LDS Survey.

with those in Figure 5-4, and by comparing Figure 5-2 with Figure 5-5. While only 2 percent reported "frequent" conflict and another 7.5 percent "occasional" conflict in the family, 13.3 and 19.8 percent, respectively, reported "frequent" and "occasional" conflict in society. Combined, a third of the survey respondents reported either "frequently" or "occasionally" experiencing situations of social awkwardness, if not outright breaches of societal rectitude, with tea drinking. Likewise, the average conflict score for those receiving little family or peer support was 2.0 (on a scale of 1 [never] to 4 [frequent]) in the case of the family, compared to the score of 2.8 in the case of society. Interestingly, nearly identical findings are observed for coffee and black tea. This can be explained by Japan's hospitality culture, where a guest is expected to be served by the host, regardless of what type of liquid is involved.

Conflict involving tea drinking is so pervasive that no deliberate career choice appears to help avoid it (Table 5-3). When the conflict score (on a scale of 1–4) is compared across places or types of employment, the score was, without exception, higher for green tea (as well as coffee/black tea) than for Sunday and weekday church attendance by a half point on average; the difference for those employed in construction and manufacturing was as large as 0.8. Even those who were self-employed or those with managerial or executive positions (with conflict scores of 2.1–2.2)—while being able to minimize conflict with church attendance—faced conflict with tea drinking more than "seldom." These numbers suggest that even though one can minimize conflict with church attendance through deliberate career choices, he or she cannot avoid conflict with tea drinking more than "seldom" (though less than "occasional"). The only exception was public sector jobs. It may be that those in the public sector have fewer obligations to meet "clients" outside their organizations.

This difficulty of avoiding conflict with green tea may explain why so few (about 3 percent) of the respondents stated that the Word of Wisdom was a consideration for their employment decisions (see Figure 5-7). That is, no career choice would help mitigate the incidence of conflict significantly. Moreover, the social pervasiveness of conflict involving green tea may have something to do with the relatively low perception of social acceptance for Latter-day Saints as a group. Only 23 percent of respondents agreed "strongly" with the statement "Latter-day Saints are highly regarded as good neighbors and colleagues" (see Table 5-1), suggesting in this context their perception that the Latter-day Saint practice of abstaining from green tea is not widely respected or understood in society. In contrast, the self-perception of their own social acceptance as individuals was much higher (56.3 percent agreed "strongly" with the statement that "My peers support my choices as a result of my church membership"). It is intimated in these perceptions that conflict tends to occur when the relationship is anonymous.

Extracurricular School Activities

Japanese schools are another source of conflict within the larger society. From preschool and kindergarten on, Japanese schools sponsor several Sunday events every year, including class observation and sports days. These could prevent Latter-day Saint families from attending church several times a year, depending on the number of children and the number of schools involved. But these are annual, one-time issues to cope with. What is perennial and more troubling in terms of keeping the youth in the faith is the extracurricular clubs the schools sponsor, from middle school on, including drama, choir, brass band, and science—not to mention baseball, soccer, judo, Japanese fencing, volleyball, and other sports. In recent surveys, 90.6 percent of middle school students (with 81.7 percent of boys and 58.3 percent of girls in sports), and 85.2 percent of high school students (with 58.9 percent in sports), reported participating in such school-sponsored clubs (Okada 2009; Mizuno et al. 2019). Called *bukatsu* or *bukatsudō*, these activities become all-consuming in the lives of middle and high school students.

Some have observed that these clubs serve a fundamental role in the socialization of Japanese youth into the values and behavioral patterns of adult society, including learning the hierarchy of seniors and juniors (Cave 2004). Students spend a few hours every day after school, all day on Saturdays, Sundays, and national holidays, and most every day during school recesses, including the summer (the Japanese school year goes from April to March of the following year, making the 40-day-long summer recess part of regular school). In practical terms, *bukatsudō* is where students build close and long-lasting friendships, which can contribute to a positive school experience (Shiramatsu 1997; Okada 2009), and those few who do not participate are deprived of opportunities to make friends. These socializing aspects of *bukatsudō*, which give Japanese youth valuable skills (such as cooperation, teamwork, self-discipline, and initiative), appear to be highly valued by employers. There is a wide-spread perception that not participating in *bukatsudō* will adversely impact future employment prospects. At critical moments in their lives, Latter-day Saint adolescents face a choice between remaining faithful to their church (where they find few, if any, friends) and devoting more and more of their time to building friendships outside the church.

In the Japan LDS Survey, we asked the respondents to think about their children or the youth they know in their congregations and to select up to three factors that contribute the most to preventing them from participating in church activities, which included (1) extracurricular school activities; (2) peer pressure from nonmember schoolmates; (3) school events on Sundays; (4) Word of Wisdom observance (green tea); and (5) college

Table 5-4. Obstacles to Youth Remaining Active in the Church
(Top five factors; percent of respondents)

Extracurricular activities	Peer pressure	Sunday school events	Word of Wisdom – green tea	College entrance preparation
69.4	63.6	42.0	20.0	12.4

Notes: sample size (N)=445; respondents were asked to select up to three from among the list as posing the greatest obstacle to youth remaining active in church.
Source: Japan LDS Survey.

entrance preparation.[10] We had 445 individuals who responded to this question (Table 5-4). Not surprisingly, *bukatsudō* received the largest number of responses, with 69.4 percent of respondents choosing this option, followed by peer pressure (63.6 percent) and Sunday events (42.0 percent).

Peer pressure and *bukatsudō* are not the same thing, but they are related in that one builds on and reinforces the other. Except for the Word of Wisdom, these obstacles are all related to Japan's education system. Several respondents voluntarily remarked how burdensome the requirements of attending Seminary (weekday religious education for ninth- to twelfth-grade youth) could become, when they coincide with preparation for entrance exams for high school (in the ninth year) and for college (in the twelfth year), calling for greater flexibility to accommodate their school requirements. A 65-year-old male respondent observed that forcing the youth to give up *bukatsudō* to observe the Sabbath could sometimes be counterproductive, as they feel resentment and stop coming to church altogether. About half the youth in Japan appear to drop out of activity in the church by the time they reach adulthood (see Table 6-2 in chapter 6).

---

10. Japanese universities have historically relied on university-administered entrance examinations (typically held on one or two days in February and March) to select the incoming class of freshmen. In response to a declining population of young people, and under pressure from the ministry of education to diversify the method of selection, universities (especially private universities) have been accepting an increasing number of students based on a variety of criteria, including a score on the annually administered national college admission test. For the 2020–21 academic year, only 51 percent of the incoming freshmen for the country as a whole were selected on the basis of university-administered entrance examinations. Even so, the nation's most prestigious national universities continue to rely on university-administered entrance examinations for more than 80 percent of their new students (MEXT 2021a).

5-7. Conclusion

This chapter has sought evidence of identity conflict that Latter-day Saints experience in Japan as members of a minority religion, including in family relationships, in the workplace, and in the larger society, and investigated how such conflict, especially in the context of Sabbath observance, is mitigated by deliberate career choices. The Japan LDS Survey has found that the overwhelming majority (87–91 percent) of Latter-day Saints in Japan had a relatively high perception of their social acceptance by families and peers and felt comfortable practicing their beliefs. Very few individuals experienced conflict in the family in the context of participation in institutional Buddhism and Shinto rituals (0.2–0.7 percent for "frequent" conflict; another 4.3–7.4 percent for "occasional" conflict), as well as in Sabbath and Word of Wisdom observance (1.4–2.0 percent for "frequent" conflict; another 5.9–7.9 percent for "occasional" conflict).

The incidence of conflict was somewhat greater in the workplace, which is often permeated by endemic long working hours and social drinking. Conflicts were experienced "frequently" and "occasionally" by 6.8–7.1 percent and another 7.2–12.1 percent, respectively, of survey respondents in the observance of Sunday and weekday church attendance. The incident was even higher for social drinking and socializing on weeknights, with 2.5–2.9 and 10.8 percent, respectively, reporting "frequent" and "occasional" conflict. Even so, the average conflict score was relatively low in all areas, ranging between 1.6 and 2.1 (on a scale of 1 through 4); that is, somewhere between "seldom" and "occasionally." Surprisingly, there was little incidence of overtime work among the Latter-day Saint population. A third reported no overtime work, while only 10 percent worked more than 20 hours a week, with the median of 3.8 hours. This explains why so few considered work to be a hindrance to attending weekday church activities.

In terms of Sabbath observance, there was evidence of conflict-avoiding career choices that attempt to minimize room for tension. The shares among Latter-day Saints of the self-employed (18.6 percent) and professionals (28.4–41.7 percent) far exceeded the corresponding national shares (10 percent and 17.5–22.5 percent, respectively), while the share of retail jobs (2.5 percent) fell far short of the corresponding national figure (12.7–15.7 percent). The social pervasiveness of tea drinking, however, precluded room for career choices to eliminate potential conflict. The prevalence of experiencing conflict "frequently" was 13.3 percent (c.f. 2.0 percent in the family), and "occasional" conflict was another 19.8 percent (c.f. 7.5 percent). In terms of the average conflict score, Latter-day Saints experienced conflict more frequently than "seldom" though somewhat less frequently than "occasional."

Identity conflict in the larger society was also contextualized by Japan's education system, which plays a far more critical role than family or church in the socialization of children and their initiation to adulthood. By sponsoring activities on Sundays and other extracurricular activities throughout the week (known as *bukatsudō*), Japanese schools can become all-consuming in the lives of children from middle school on. In the Japan LDS Survey, 69.4 percent of respondents considered *bukatsudō* as the factor contributing the most to keeping Latter-day Saint youth away from church, followed by 63.6 percent for peer pressure and 42.0 percent for school-sponsored Sunday events. In addition, preparation for entrance examinations for high school and college, happening in ninth and twelfth grades in Japan, presented potential conflict with Seminary requirements for Latter-day Saint youth.

In summary, the overwhelming majority of active Latter-day Saints have embraced the Latter-day Saint identity and have taken action to prioritize this identity in the organization of their lives. The incidence of identity conflict occurs rarely in the workplace, and it is even rarer in relationships involving nonmember families and relatives. Latter-day Saints appear to have found accommodation for their unique religious practices through establishing long-term relationships. Conflict does occur when the relationship is anonymous. This type of conflict cannot be entirely eliminated as long as one participates in Japanese society. Even so, frequency appears to be manageable, with the average conflict score, while more than "seldom," being less than "occasional." This means that a foreign religion that does not fully align with cultural norms *can* find acceptance in Japan. Japanese society is sufficiently tolerant of a range of behavior, allowing Latter-day Saints to find a niche for their particular lifestyle. At the same time, the social costs of church membership are by no means small, as indicated by the large share of individuals who have dropped out of activity or who never joined the Church after investigating its teachings.

CHAPTER 6

CHALLENGES AND OPPORTUNITIES IN A CHANGING SOCIETY

6-1. Introduction

This penultimate chapter shifts attention from a narrow focus on the survey results to a broader consideration of the challenges and opportunities facing The Church of Jesus Christ of Latter-day Saints in Japan as it navigates its future. To do so, we must pay attention to those Latter-day Saints who have ceased to participate actively in the church as well as to those who, when presented with the opportunity, chose not to convert. This can be done indirectly. The survey respondents (who are for the most part religiously active Latter-day Saints) identified the obstacles they had faced in conversion and in remaining active. We assume that these are the same obstacles preventing others from adopting or maintaining their religious identity. All religions in Japan face formidable challenges going forward, given Japan's adverse demographic trend and rising religious apathy. The Church of Jesus Christ of Latter-day Saints has fared relatively well compared to others (see Figure 1-4 in chapter 1), but its fortune may change if the adverse societal trend continues.

The rest of this chapter is organized as follows. Section 6-2 reviews the structural changes in Japanese society against which the future of the Church must be assessed, including rising religious apathy and the shrinking, aging, and regional migration of the population. Section 6-3 discusses the obstacles to conversion and retention, including how Japan's religious climate concerning nontraditional religions may have been changing in recent decades. Section 6-4 reviews the tectonic changes in Japan's cultural institutions, including the greater social participation of women, the decline in institutional Buddhism, increasing labor mobility among younger workers, and greater ethnic diversity. Section 6-5 explores possible areas where some institutional acculturation could be attempted in order to reduce the costs of church membership. Section 6-6 considers the challenges of living in Japan as Latter-day Saints and how the Church can manage the trade-off between accommodating cultural tension and maintaining the commitment of members. Finally, section 6-7 presents a conclusion.

Figure 6-1. Japanese Population, 1980–2021
(In thousands; share of Greater Tokyo Region)

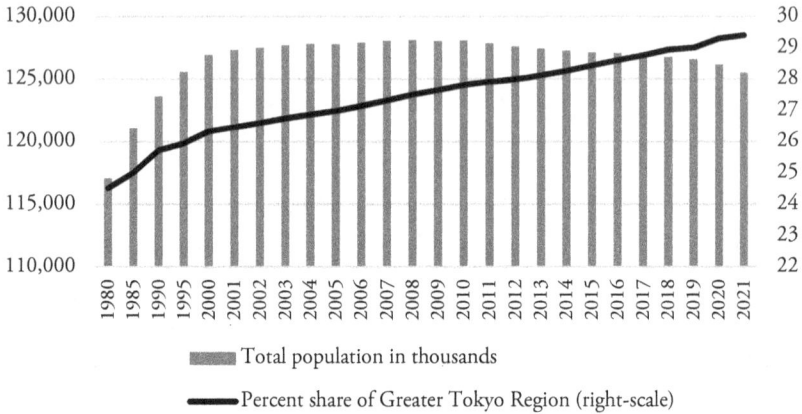

Total population in thousands

Percent share of Greater Tokyo Region (right-scale)

Source: e-stat.

Figure 6-2. Number of Births and Total Fertility Rate in Japan, 1970–2021

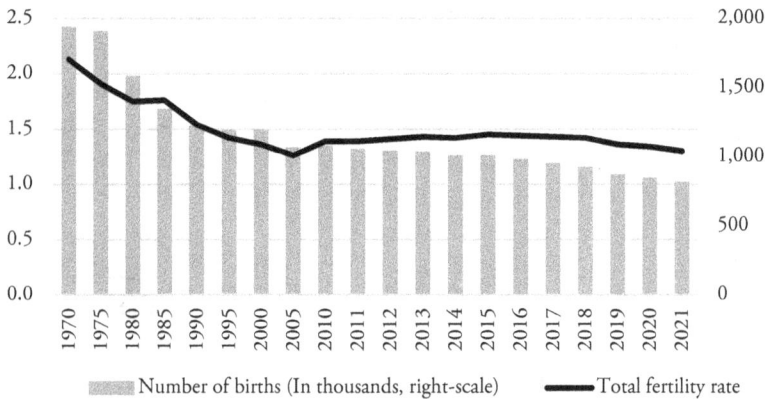

Number of births (In thousands, right-scale)   Total fertility rate

Note: total fertility rate is the number of children a woman is expected to bear during her lifetime, given the current schedule of age-specific fertility rates.
Source: e-stat.

6-2. Structural Changes in Japanese Society

Shrinking and Aging Population

First and foremost, demographics is the most profound change affecting Japanese society. Japan's total population peaked at 128 million in the latter part of the first decade of this century and has since been shrinking by about 0.2 percent per year (Figure 6-1). This has resulted from a steady decline in the number of births, which fell from 1.9 million in 1970 to

Figure 6-3. Age Profile of the Japanese Population, 1970–2021
(Percentage shares of each age group)

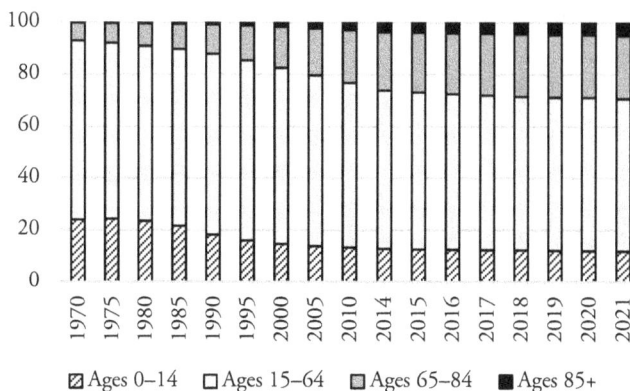

Source: e-stat.

800,000 in 2021 (Figure 6-2). The declining births in turn have reflected the declining total fertility rate (the total number of children a woman is expected to bear during her lifetime), which fell below the replacement rate of 2.1 in the early 1970s. A national government agency projected in 2018 that, if the current trend continued, Japan could lose as much as 30.7 percent of its population (or 39 million people) over 50 years from 2015 to 2065 (NIPSS 2018).

Japan boasts one of the highest life expectancies in the world, which in 2021 was 81.5 years for men and 87.6 years for women (MHLW 2021b).[1] This was the third highest life expectancy for men (after Switzerland and Norway) and the highest in the world for women. Coupled with declining births, this has caused the population to age significantly. The proportion of those ages 0–14 in the total population, for example, declined from 23.9 percent in 1970 to 11.9 percent in 2021, while the proportion of those ages 65 and older rose from 7.1 percent to 29.3 percent (Figure 6-3). The total dependency ratio increased from 44.9 percent to 70.1 percent, and the age dependency ratio from 10.3 percent to 49.9 percent.[2] The strain on the working population is already considerable.

---

1. There was a slight decline from the previous year because of the COVID-19 pandemic.

2. The total dependency ratio is designed to measure the burden on those who are typically in the workforce (ages 15–64) of supporting those typically not in the labor force (ages 0–14 and 65+). The age dependency ratio uses only those over the age of 65 as the numerator.

Figure 6-4. Manufacturing Employment in Japan, 1980–2021

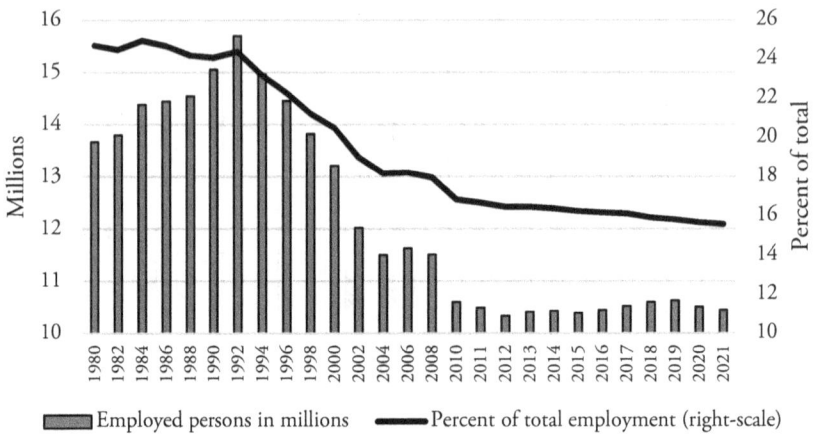

Employed persons in millions   Percent of total employment (right-scale)

Source: e-stat.

The Church of Jesus Christ of Latter-day Saints has not been immune to the social forces underpinning this trend. Even though the fertility rate of the active Latter-day Saint population appears to be somewhat greater than the general population, the average number of children per Latter-day Saint woman in our sample is considerably smaller for women born after 1981 (1.9) than for those born before (2.8) (see Table 2-1 in chapter 2). The age distribution of the Latter-day Saint population appears to mirror the general population. One of the respondents voluntarily expressed her concern that, with the aging of the population, it might become difficult to maintain church activity in the future. Another wrote that his branch already was predominantly made up of elderly members.

Regional Migration of the Population

The population decline is not distributed evenly across regions. An important source of the imbalance comes from the recent developments in the world economy, especially the rise of Asia's newly industrialized countries. To compete in the global market, Japanese firms have been moving manufacturing production offshore through foreign direct investment in search of lower costs. Between 1992 and 2012, Japan lost more than a third (5 million) of its manufacturing jobs (Figure 6-4), many of which were relocated to production sites abroad (Huijie 2018). As many of the plants were located in regions outside Tokyo, Japan's regional economies have suffered serious economic damage, albeit subject to regional variation due to the consolidation of remaining domestic manufacturing capacity in certain areas (Kashima 2019).

Figure 6-5. Geographical Mobility of Latter-day Saints in Japan:
Length of Time in the Current Region
(Percent of respondents)

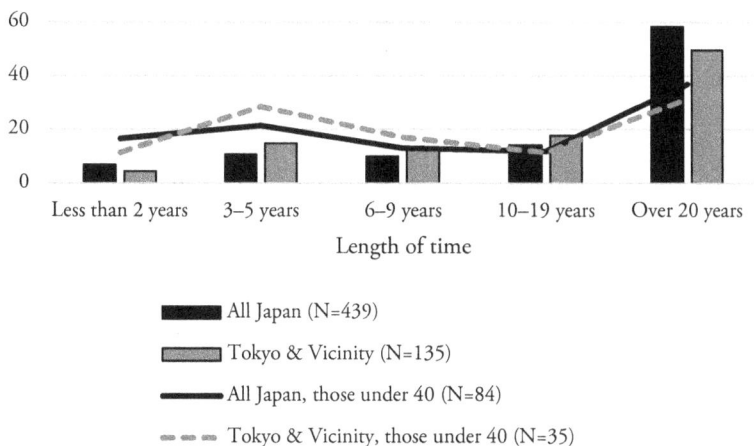

Source: Japan LDS Survey.

In contrast, the capital region around Tokyo, home to many global corporate headquarters, has remained prosperous.[3] Even though Japan's total population has declined, that of the Tokyo metropolitan region (South Kanto) has actually increased moderately, with its share rising from around 25 percent in 1980 to nearly 30 percent more recently (see Figure 6-1). The increasing concentration of the population in South Kanto is evident in the Japan LDS Survey (Figure 6-5). The share of those who had lived in their current regions for 3 to 19 years was larger for the Tokyo region, while the share of those who had lived longer than 20 years was smaller. The share of those under the age of 40 who had lived in their current regions for 3 to 5 years was larger for the Tokyo region (28.6 percent) than for all of Japan (21.4 percent). Since congregations are run entirely through the volunteer efforts of their membership, in a typically small congregation outside of population centers, losing even one family, or seeing one young man not come home after serving a mission, can be a significant blow to maintaining a viable church program. This strain is reflected in the statements of several survey respondents who, when filling out open-ended survey questions, identified disproportionate church service obligations as obstacles to church growth and retention.

---

3. We follow the convention to define the Tokyo metropolitan region as Tokyo and the prefectures of Chiba, Kanagawa, and Saitama. Government statistics refers to the region as South Kanto.

Religious Apathy

Rising religious apathy is another important background against which the future of the Church in Japan needs to be seen. We use the term religious apathy in the specific sense explained below. This idea is related to but is not the same as secularization, which refers to a phenomenon of diminishing religious authority as the level of scientific knowledge and education rises with modernity (Duke 1999). In Japan, it would be more meaningful to apply secularization to the long-established Buddhist or Shinto traditions, as it is done to mainline Christian denominations in the United States. The validity of the secularization thesis, which posits a negative relationship between modernization and the influence of religion in society, has been challenged in the United States, where, as major denominations became "more liberal and less unequivocal" (Duke 1999, p. 15), new churches advocating stricter doctrines emerged to attract dissenters. Likewise, in Japan, the outlet for religious seekers has been nontraditional religious groups, to which Christian denominations, as newcomers to Japan, may be added.

The indigenous religious groups that emerged to fill the spiritual void created by the decline of established religious groups are called "new religions" (*shinkō shūkyō*),[4] some of which may have Buddhist or Shinto roots.[5] In this book, we use the term religious apathy strictly to describe the observed phenomenon of declining membership in these nontraditional religions. There are two reasons. First, we cannot know what people sincerely believe. Apathy, if used in the sense of irreligiosity, cannot be measured in a quantifiable way. Second, membership numbers reported by established religions are dubious. Most Japanese nominally affiliate themselves with Buddhism, Shinto, or both. They make celebratory visits to shrines or participate in Buddhist rituals. These observances, followed by tradition or custom, do not indicate their inner religiosity.[6]

---

4. Earhart (2004) uses the term "new religions" for religious movements that appeared after the late Tokugawa period and became a powerful force after World War II.

5. The most prominent of these are "lay" groups, separate from the temple, that affiliated themselves with the *Nichiren Shōshū* sect of Buddhism, such as *Reiyūkai, Risshō Kōseikai,* and *Sōka Gakkai.* For *Sōka Gakkai,* see Metraux (1994) and Dawson (2001).

6. The combined membership in all established religious groups, as reported by the Japanese government, exceeds the country's total population. At the end of 2021, there were 87.2 million adherents of Shinto and 83.2 million Buddhists,

Table 6-1. Religious Apathy: Annual Percentage Growth,
by Period, of Selected Groups, 1970–2021[1]

	1970–80	1980–90	1990–2000	2000–2010	2010–21
Latter-day Saints	14.1	4.7	2.9	1.1	0.3
Catholics	0.6	1.4	0.6	0.1	-0.4
United Church of Christ	-0.5	0.3	-0.3	-0.8	-1.5
Non-Shinto, non-Buddhist adherents[2]	4.7	-4.1	-0.3	-0.8	-2.6
Total population	1.2	0.5	0.3	0.1	-0.2

Notes: [1]percentage changes are approximated by first differences in natural logarithms; [2]excluding Christians; they are designated as *shokyō* (lit. miscellaneous religions) in the government publication *Shūkyō Nenkan*.
Sources: author's calculations based on Bunkachō, *Shūkyō Nenkan*, annual issues; e-stat, supplemented by Deseret News, *Church Almanac*, annual issues, and www.churchofjesuschrist.org.

Therefore, focusing on membership in nontraditional (non-Shinto, non-Buddhist, but excluding Christian) religions as a better metric of voluntary religious participation, we find that these groups grew rapidly during the 1970s but began to decline in the 1980s (Table 6-1). Because the membership decline preceded the population decline by decades, religious apathy is an independent influence on the growth of religious groups. To the extent that Christianity competes for the same pool of dissenters from established religions, the same forces must have impacted Christian denominations as well (Mullins 2012), possibly including The Church of Jesus Christ of Latter-day Saints more recently. Although the Church, unlike other prominent religious groups, has not experienced an absolute decline in membership, its membership growth has slowed substantially in recent years. The United Church of Christ, Japan's largest Protestant denomination, was already experiencing an outright membership loss in the 1970s.

6-3. Obstacles to Conversion and Retention

Conversion

We saw earlier that a relatively large share (36 percent) of converts named family opposition as the greatest hurdle to their conversion, while about an equal share (37 percent) reported experiencing no obstacle. An interesting pattern emerges when we divide the sample into three groups:

for a combined total of 170.5 million, compared to the total population of 125.5 million (Bunkachō 2022).

Figure 6-6. The Greatest Hurdle to Conversion
(Percent of respondents)

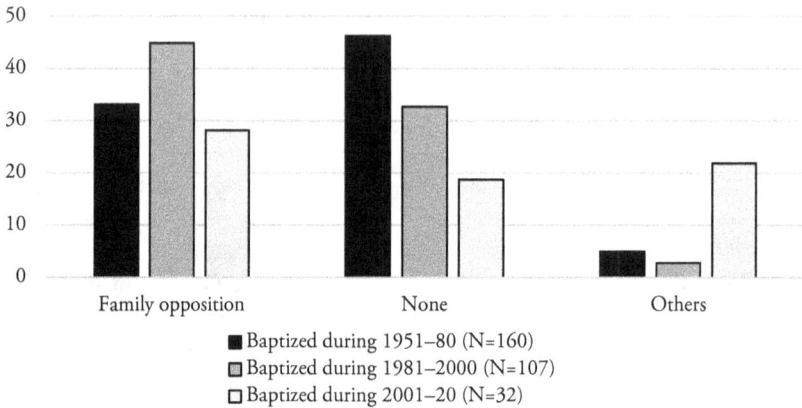

■ Baptized during 1951–80 (N=160)
☐ Baptized during 1981–2000 (N=107)
☐ Baptized during 2001–20 (N=32)

Source: Japan LDS Survey.

those baptized during (1) 1951–80, (2) 1981–2000, and (3) 2001–20 (Figure 6-6). The share of those experiencing family opposition rises from 33.1 percent to 44.9 percent, then falls to 28.1 percent. The initial rise may be due, at least in part, to the rising hostility toward organized religion characteristic of the period, which intensified after the deadly sarin attack on the Tokyo subway that was carried out in 1995 by a doomsday cult known as Aum Shinkikyō. The share of those experiencing no obstacle also declined, from 46.3 to 32.7 percent, and further to 18.8 percent. Offsetting these declines, more individuals reported various kinds of opposition ("others"), which rose from 5.0 percent to 21.9 percent and were not specified.[7]

The fall in family opposition (after a temporary rise) is consistent with the decline of institutional Buddhism and the increase in the average age of converts (to be explored further below). The fall in the share of those experiencing no obstacle could possibly mean that the climate has become

---

7. Those who selected "other" obstacles to conversion were asked to specify what they meant in an open-ended question. Some directly identified religious prejudice or suspicion toward religious organizations. Many respondents also reported that church attendance on Sundays was difficult, given the school, work, and community events that are typically scheduled then. These answers confirm what we have discussed in previous chapters. Others referred to difficulties marrying within the faith, and many emphasized the importance of membership creating a welcoming environment and extending friendship to new attendees. A few expounded on "commandments" to refer specifically to tithing, and one respondent indicated that tithing was not tax-deductible in Japan as it is in the United States.

Figure 6-7. Obstacles to Retention
(Percent of respondents)

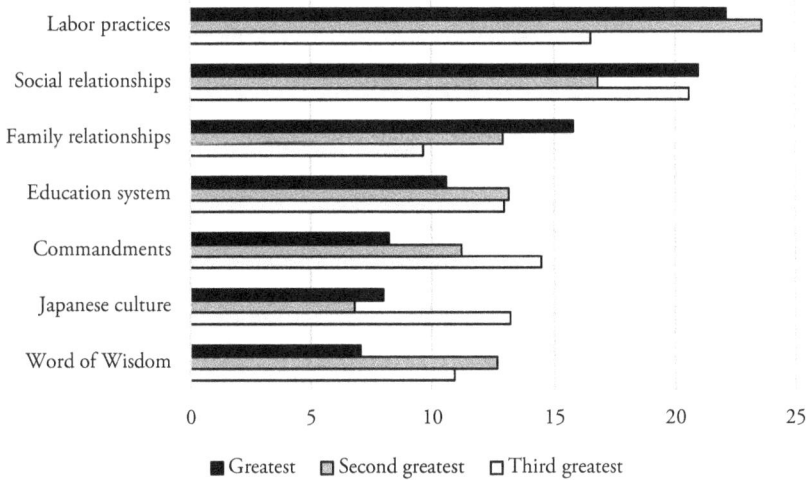

Note: sample (N)=439.
Source: Japan LDS Survey.

less friendly to nontraditional religions. The rising share of those reporting various "other" kinds of opposition possibly suggests an increasingly more complex society, where individuals are subject to pressures from various quarters. Family relationships may no longer be the most dominant pressure, but people are finding Latter-day Saint identity poses conflict with various other identities, such as memberships in sports clubs, volunteer organizations, and hobby groups.

Retention

Concerning member retention, we asked the respondents to rank the three most important obstacles (out of a list of seven) to "keeping Japanese members active." We had 439 individuals who responded to this question (Figure 6-7). The greatest obstacle, in their estimation, was Japan's labor practices, which involve long working hours and social drinking, with 22 percent ranking it the most important and another 23.6 percent ranking it as the second. Close behind were social relationships (e.g., loss of friends), with 20.9 percent ranking it the most important and another 16.8 percent ranking it as the second, followed by family relationships and the education system. Although the overwhelming majority of the respondents considered none of these to be serious enough obstacles to *them*, their perception was that they posed obstacles to *others*, including their

Table 6-2. Status of Children in Latter-day Saint Households
(Percent of respondents in each group)

	No inactive child	At least one inactive child	No member child	Total
Men (N=159)	42.1	55.4	2.5	100
Women (N=187)	46.5	49.2	4.3	100

Source: Japan LDS Survey.

Figure 6-8. Embarrassed to Admit Church Membership
(Percent of respondents in each group)

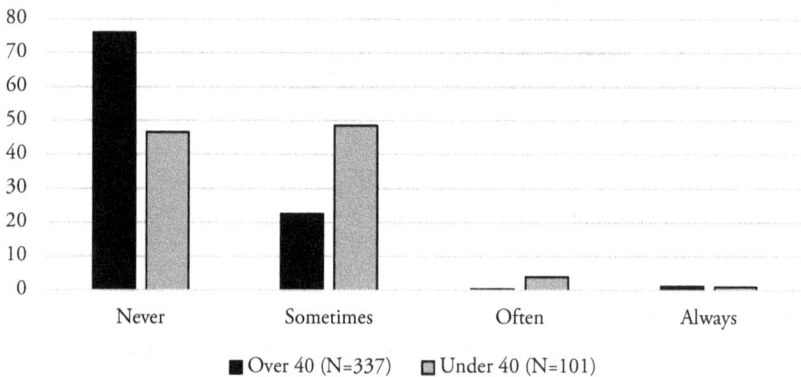

■ Over 40 (N=337)   ▢ Under 40 (N=101)

Source: Japan LDS Survey.

children: 55.4 percent of men and 49.2 percent of women reported that they had at least one member child who was no longer active (Table 6-2).

Changing Religious Climate

The increasingly unfriendly climate for nontraditional religions, intimated above, is confirmed when the respondents are divided into two groups: those born before 1981 ("over 40") and those born in 1981 and after ("under 40"). First, a greater share of younger Latter-day Saints (48.5 percent) than older Latter-day Saints (22.6 percent) "sometimes" felt embarassed to admit their church membership (Figure 6-8). On the flipside, fewer younger members (46.5 percent) than older members (76.0 percent) "never" felt embarassed. Part of the reason may be that younger members tend to have more junior positions in their organizations, giving them less control over finding themselves in uncomfortable life situations.

Second, in the survey, younger Latter-day Saints were more likely to experience conflict in the family, the workplace, and the greater society

Figure 6-9. Identity Conflict: Over Forty vs. Under Forty
(Percent of respondents in each group; sum of "frequent" and "occasional")

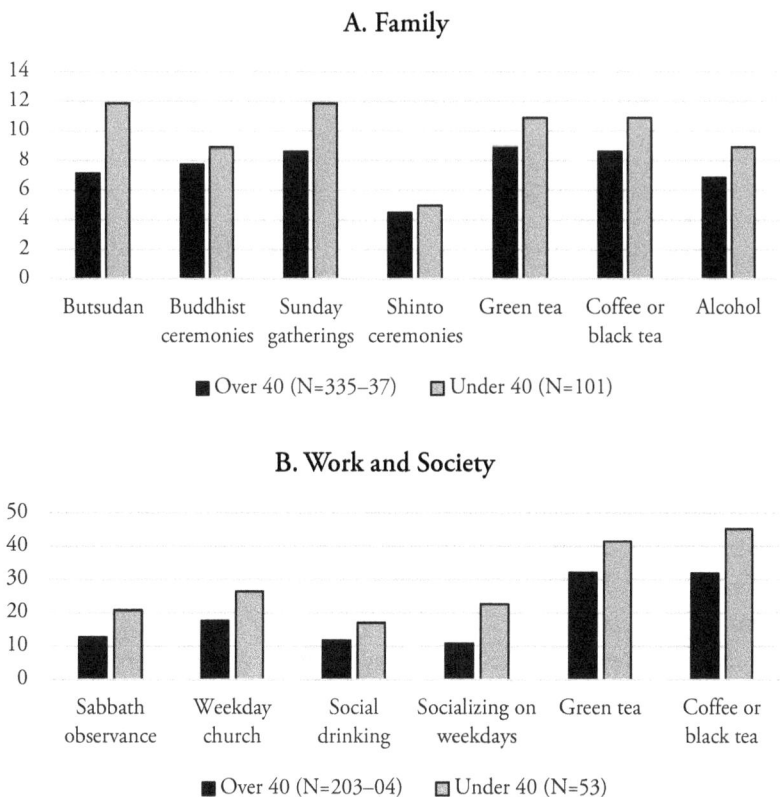

A. Family

■ Over 40 (N=335–37)   □ Under 40 (N=101)

B. Work and Society

■ Over 40 (N=203–04)   □ Under 40 (N=53)

Source: Japan LDS Survey.

in all potential areas (Figure 6-9). For example, when "frequent" conflict and "occasional" conflict are combined, the share of those experiencing conflict rises from 11.8 percent among the older cohort to 17.0 percent among the younger cohort for social drinking, and from 32.0 to 41.5 percent for green tea. The incidence of conflict in the family remained small in absolute value, ranging between 5.0 and 11.9 percent for younger Latter-day Saints and between 4.5 and 8.9 percent for older members. Even so, the share among the younger was a few percentage points higher in each area (e.g., 11.9 percent among the younger cohort vs. 7.2 percent among the older cohort in the case of *butsudan*).

The nature of obstacles to retention may have changed across generations (Figure 6-10). In our earlier survey question about retention (cf. Figure 6-7), we found little generational difference except in two areas: so-

Figure 6-10. Obstacles to Keeping Members: Over Forty vs. Under Forty (Percent of respondents in each group)

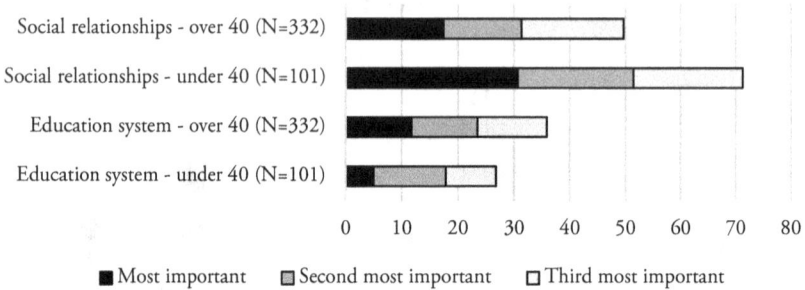

Social relationships - over 40 (N=332)
Social relationships - under 40 (N=101)
Education system - over 40 (N=332)
Education system - under 40 (N=101)

0 10 20 30 40 50 60 70 80

■ Most important   ▨ Second most important   ☐ Third most important

Source: Japan LDS Survey.

cial relationships and the education system (Figure 6-10). A smaller share of younger Latter-day Saints (26.7 percent) than older Latter-day Saints (35.8 percent) considered the education system to be an important factor, while a much larger share (71.3 percent) considered social relationships to be important (cf. 49.7 percent for the older cohort). The importance of social relationships as an obstacle to retention may in part reflect the increasingly adverse impact of negative demographics and religious apathy in more recent years, which has reduced the growth of membership and the number of new converts, making it less likely for younger members to find meaningful relationships at church.

6-4. Japan's Changing Cultural Institutions

Elements of culture, despite their persistence, can change when they cease to make sense for a variety of reasons. Forces for change have never been greater than during the past few decades, with technological progress and a dramatic fall in the costs of communications and air travel that has nearly eliminated national borders. In Japan, a confluence of these global factors, along with the country-specific ones noted earlier, have unleashed a tectonic shift in its decades-old, if not centuries-old, cultural institutions, challenging quintessential, if not caricaturist, features of Japanese society: male-dominance and ethnic homogeneity.

Breakdown in the Foundation of Social Structure

An increasing number of women have entered the labor force in recent decades, amounting to a net increase of 8.9 million from 1980 to 2021 and raising the share of women from 38.7 to 44.6 percent (Figure 6-11). In part to counter the adverse demographic trend, the Japanese government

Figure 6-11. Labor Force in Japan, 1980–2021
(In millions)

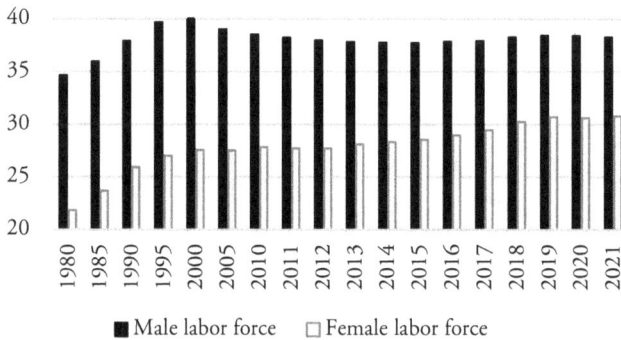

■ Male labor force   □ Female labor force

Source: e-stat.

has been promoting the social participation of women through legislation aimed at ensuring gender equality, including the Equal Employment Opportunity Law of 1985 and the Women's Advancement Promotion Law of 2015. For women to achieve full parity with men may take another generation, but there are visible changes in the professional ranks of the rising generation. For example, women constituted 37 percent of the 2021 cohort of newly recruited national civil servants (Cabinet Office 2022) and 41.1 percent of those admitted to medical schools in 2021 (MEXT 2021b). Prejudice and discrimination against women are deep-seated in Japanese society, but there are signs of a fundamental change in gender stratification.

The erosion of domestic manufacturing and the shrinking labor force to fill positions typically occupied by younger workers have led the Japanese government to adopt policies that, in retrospect, opened up Japanese society. First, the central and local governments have been promoting tourism. Especially beginning around 2003, the central government has targeted tourism as Japan's new export industry. In 2008, it launched a "Visit Japan Campaign," with specific promotional measures aimed at creating a "tourism nation." Coinciding with the rising incomes of neighboring Asian countries, the number of foreign visitors (excluding long-term residents) increased spectacularly, from a mere 2.3 million in 1985 to 31.9 million in 2019, the last year before the COVID-19 global pandemic virtually closed the country's borders to short-term foreign visitors (Figure 6-12, the bar graph).

Second, the government has been actively recruiting international students to Japan's higher education schools. The number of international

Figure 6-12. Foreign Nationals in Japan, 1985–2019

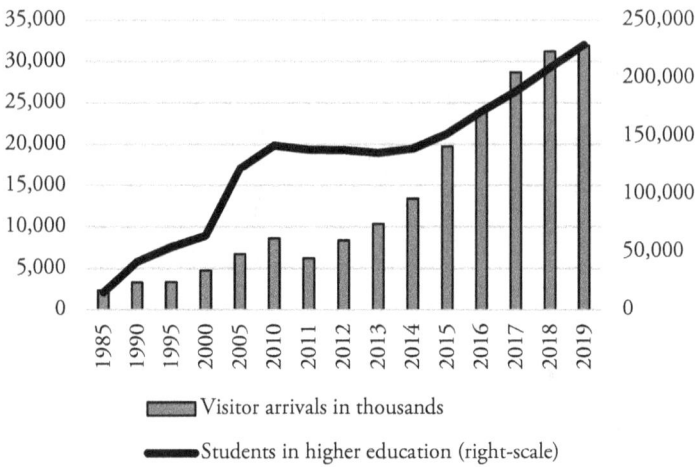

Visitor arrivals in thousands

Students in higher education (right-scale)

Note: data are not extended beyond 2019 because the COVID-19 pandemic drastically reduced the number of foreign visitors from 2020 through 2022.
Sources: Japanese National Tourist Association (JNTO) (2021) and Japanese Student Services Association (JASSO) (2021).

Figure 6-13. Share of Foreign Residents in Japan, by Region, 1980–2021 (Percent of total)

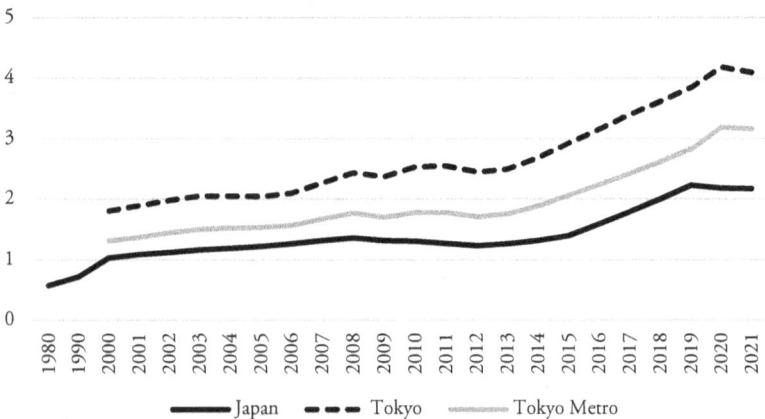

Japan — — Tokyo — Tokyo Metro

Source: e-stat.

students, predominantly from East, Southeast, and South Asia, rose from a mere 15,000 in 1985 to 228,000 in 2019 (Figure 6-12, the line graph). If we include those enrolled in Japanese language schools, the number becomes 312,000, exceeding the goal of 300,000 set in 2008 to achieve by 2020. Even though the majority of the public is opposed to liberalizing

Figure 6-14. Marriages in Japan Involving a Foreign Spouse

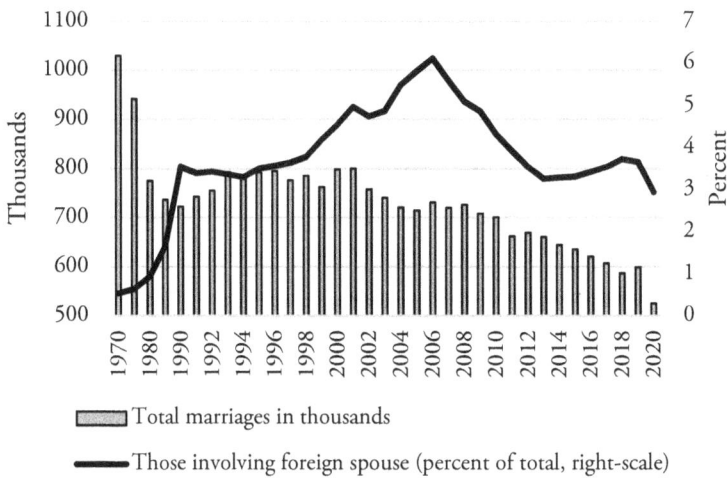

Total marriages in thousands

Those involving foreign spouse (percent of total, right-scale)

Source: e-stat.

immigration (see Figure 2-10 in chapter 2), the government, responding to the needs of the business community to fill mainly retail jobs, has at least in part used higher education as a backdoor way to immigration. A student visa allows the holder to work up to 28 hours a week. Many of those who complete their education, having acquired language proficiency, choose to remain in Japan to work, as is liberally permitted for such individuals.

Coupled with an increasing number of expatriates who come and work in Japan for a period of time, this has increased the number of foreign residents in Japan from a mere 0.6 percent of the total population in 1980 to 2.2 percent in 2021—a net increase of 2.1 million people (Figure 6-13). The share of foreign residents is considerably higher in the Tokyo metropolitan region (3.2 percent in 2021) and even higher in Tokyo proper (4.1 percent). As expected, the share of marriages that involve a foreign spouse has been on the rise, even as the total number of marriages itself has declined (Figure 6-14). The share of such marriages rose from 0.6 percent in 1970 to an average of 3.5 percent during 2011–20 (with a peak of 6.1 percent in 2006).[8]

---

8. The declines from 2019 to 2020 in total marriages and the share of those involving a foreign spouse may have been caused by the COVID-19 pandemic. Reflecting a declining number of marriage-age individuals, the absolute number of such marriages declined from the peak of 45,000 in 2006 to 22,000 in 2019 and further to 15,500 in 2020.

Figure 6-15. Number of Buddhist Temples in Japan, 1980–2021

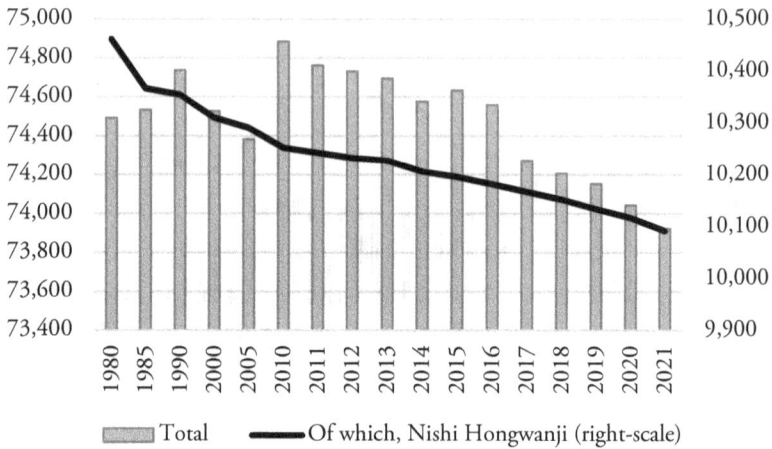

Note: those registered with the minister of education only.
Source: Bunkachō, *Shūkyō Nenkan*, annual issues.

Breakdown of Institutional Buddhism

Consistent with the secularization thesis, the weakening grip of institutional Buddhism on Japanese life has been an on-going process since the turn of the twentieth century. As more people moved from farming communities into cities in the nineteenth and twentieth centuries, the ties that bind them to their family temples have been weakening with each passing generation. Third-generation families may not even know who the head monks are and may even choose to hold a funeral for their immediate family members at a nearby temple, at home, or increasingly, in a commercial funeral hall. If requested by the family, the funeral hall could arrange for a registered monk to perform the ceremony, just for that occasion. Some even dispense with holding a funeral altogether and arrange for a registered monk just to recite the sutras at the crematory (Ukai 2015). In either case, the family will never see the monk again.

Japan is a highly urbanized society, where the proportion of people living in cities currently exceeds 90 percent (World Bank 2023).[9] Along with urbanization, more and more people have migrated out of communities with strong Buddhist traditions, and the number of Buddhist temples

---

9. The rate of urbanization in Japan increased steadily from 63.3 percent in 1960 to exceed 90 percent in 2010, and it reached 91.8 percent in 2020, according to the definition used by the World Bank.

registered with the Japanese government has declined as a result (Figure 6-15).[10] The number of temples for all denominations declined from 74,884 in 2010 to 73,922 in 2021, for a net loss of nearly 1,000 just over a decade. For the Nishi Hongwanji Temple, Japan's largest Buddhist denomination, the number declined steadily from 10,461 in 1980 to 10,092 in 2021, a loss of nine temples per year.

According to Ukai (2015), the official figures are a gross underrepresentation of the disappearance of Buddhist temples in Japan. Of the approximately 77,000 temples, he stated, about 20,000 had no resident monks (they rely on monks from neighboring temples to conduct services when required, with the parishioners maintaining the physical facilities) and more than 2,000 had ceased operation altogether. Each temple is incorporated as a juridical person, making it difficult for the head temple to close or dissolve a non-operating temple. These temples stand empty and abandoned, but their legal entities continue. With a diminished number of dues-paying parishioners, many monks have an employment income from outside the temple. The declining number of Buddhist temples is only symptomatic of the rising secularization of Japanese society, where the proportion of households with *butsudan* was estimated to be about 50 percent at the time of his writing (Ukai 2015).

Breakdown of Japanese Labor Practices

Endemic social drinking in the workplace occurs in the context of a long-term relationship between the worker and the firm. Such an environment creates an incentive to build intra-firm personal relationships by engaging in intimate conversations made possible by drinking. The traditional Japanese employment system, however, has been breaking down in recent decades, with fundamental structural changes in the Japanese economy (including the relocation of manufacturing activity abroad, as noted), as well as a rise in corporate bankruptcies brought about by rapid technological change and increasing global competition. Young people no longer have the expectations that they will be working for the same firm ten years from now, much less twenty years from now.

As a result, they are more concerned with building up their own human capital, for example, by quitting work to go to graduate school. This is evident in official labor statistics, which indicate that an increasing

---

10. Some denominations responded to the population migration by establishing new temples in highly populated areas, especially Tokyo. This explains why the peak was reached in 2010.

Figure 6-16. Labor Mobility Among Prime-Age Male Workers in Japan, 1984–2021
(Percent of total workers in each group)

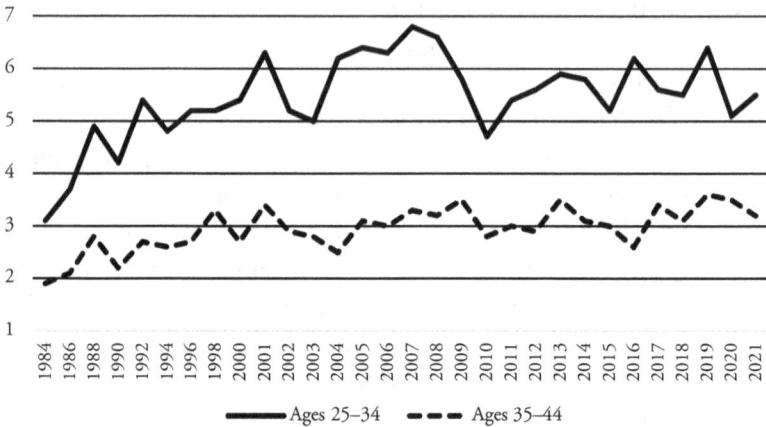

————— Ages 25–34   ▬ ▬ ▬ Ages 35–44

Notes: number of employed persons who changed jobs during the past twelve
months as percent of total; data for February through 2001 and for Q1 thereafter.
Source: e-stat.

number of prime-aged male workers (who had been the stable part of
the traditional employment system) are changing jobs (Figure 6-16). For
example, the share of workers who changed jobs during the past twelve
months rose from 3.1 percent in 1984 to 6.4 percent in 2019 for those
ages 25–34 (the average for 2012–21 was 5.7 percent).[11] Fewer young
workers feel the same sense of loyalty the previous generation of workers
felt to their employers, and fewer feel constrained by the traditional norms
of the workplace. The greater participation of women in the workplace
as equals, moreover, has weakened the expectations for workers to work
longer hours and gather for after-work drinking.

6-5. Room for Institutional Acculturation?

Offsetting the adverse impact of demographics and rising religious
apathy on nontraditional religions are the major shifts in Japan's cultural
institutions, which may offer new opportunities by promoting tolerance
for diversity. Such changes may already be happening. A 39-year-old
male respondent to the survey, for example, was harassed in 2008 by his
boss for not drinking, but he stated that he now found it much easier to

---

11. Women have historically changed employment more often due to marriage or
childbirth, which makes their labor mobility about 2 percentage points higher. The
corresponding ten-year average for women was 7.8 percent for those ages 25–34.

talk freely of his faith, concluding: "society is dramatically changing." A 54-year-old male noted that the hurdle to conversion was diminishing and not being able to drink was no longer a liability at work. A 70-year-old female stated that her associates had become health-conscious and respectful of the rights of others who chose not to drink. This woman no longer experienced the conflict she had previously faced in Word of Wisdom observance at work and among her relatives.

Framed in the language of economics, the success or failure of conversion or retention depends on the benefits relative to the costs of Latter-day Saint identity. To the extent that the doctrines can only remain the same, there is a natural limit to the ability of The Church of Jesus Christ of Latter-day Saints to increase the (perceived) benefits of its membership, except through better advertising or by training more effective leaders. As for the costs, would the changes in the cultural institutions be sufficient to offset the adverse impact of the demographic trend and increasing religious apathy? Again, what the Church can do is rather limited. It has prided itself on its uniformity in organizational structure and programs and has left foreign members to make their own acculturation (cultural adaptation). Even so, one can legitimately ask if there is room for any institutional acculturation. We explored this issue in the Japan LDS Survey.

Views on Institutional Acculturation

We asked the respondents if the Church had done enough to meet their culture-specific needs. Adopting a new religion requires acquiring a vast amount of new religious capital, including a different worldview, a different set of beliefs, and even a different form of cultural capital, such as language. The survey questions related to the way the Church had made adjustments to mitigate the tension that could arise between the traditional religious and cultural capital of Japan and that of its American headquarters. We posed to the respondents five statements on different aspects of institutional acculturation, asking them to assess their agreement with each on a scale of 1 (strongly disagree) to 5 (strongly agree) (Table 6-3).

To triangulate their responses, there were two types of statements, each eliciting a differentiated response. The first three statements (A, B, C) were worded in such a way that agreement meant endorsement of the status quo, an acknowledgement that the Church had either already made sufficient adaptation or had no need to make adaptation. With the last two statements (D and E), agreement meant that the respondent saw a need for more institutional acculturation, an indictment of the status quo.

Table 6-3. Views on Local Institutional Acculturation
(Percent of respondents in each group)

		1 Strongly disagree	2 Somewhat disagree	3 Neither agree nor disagree	4 Somewhat agree	5 Strongly agree	Total	Average score
A. The Church in Japan should adhere strictly to the *General Handbook* prepared at church headquarters in America without cultural adaptations	All (N=429)	5.6	14.5	19.3	35.7	24.9	100	3.6
	Men (N=191)	8.4	14.1	13.1	36.1	28.3	100	3.6
	Women (N=235)	3.4	14.9	24.3	35.3	22.1	100	3.6
B. The Church in Japan has made sufficient adjustments for differences in the culture in Japan in terms of its social practices	All (N=423)	9.2	14.2	32.2	30.3	14.2	100	3.3
	Men (N=187)	12.8	11.8	32.1	31.0	12.3	100	3.2
	Women (N=233)	6.4	15.9	32.2	29.6	15.9	100	3.3
C. The Church curriculum materials for Sunday school, Primary, YM/YW, EQ/RS are well suited for the needs and interests of Japanese members	All (N=424)	2.8	13.0	30.7	36.6	17.0	100	3.5
	Men (N=188)	4.8	16.5	29.3	35.6	13.8	100	3.4
	Women (N=233)	1.3	9.9	32.2	37.8	18.9	100	3.6
D. The Church in Japan uses too many foreign/imported words that are not part of colloquial Japanese	All (N=425)	9.9	16.9	34.6	24.9	13.6	100	3.2
	Men (N=187)	8.6	16.0	37.4	23.0	15.0	100	3.2
	Women (N=235)	11.1	17.0	32.8	26.4	12.8	100	3.1
E. The Church in Japan tries too much to follow the practices of American members and should make more adjustments for the culture in Japan	All (N=428)	18.2	16.6	36.4	20.1	8.6	100	2.8
	Men (N=189)	19.6	15.3	32.3	20.1	12.7	100	2.9
	Women (N=236)	17.4	16.9	40.3	19.9	5.5	100	2.8

Source: Japan LDS Survey.

A remarkable finding is that, regardless of how the statement was worded, the average response broadly fell in the middle range, that is, "neither agree nor disagree." In terms of distribution, however, more people tended to disagree "strongly" with negative questions (D and E) and agree "strongly" with positive questions (A, B, C). From this we can see the conservative tendency of active Japanese Latter-day Saints, who have accepted approvingly what their church has offered.

Potential Areas for Institutional Acculturation

The fact that active Japanese Latter-day Saints approve the status quo on average does not mean that institutional acculturation is necessarily at an optimum level. Our sample predominantly includes religiously active Latter-day Saints. In thinking about prospective opportunities for the Church, the perspectives of those who have not converted or remained active are important. From this standpoint, the views of those who do not approve of the status quo should be given due regard. Moreover, not all statements are of the same nature for thinking about acculturation. For instance, the question of whether the *General Handbook* should be adhered to strictly may be more of a theological issue,[12] upon which the Church may not have a lot of discretion. At the other extreme is the question of whether the Church in Japan uses too many foreign or imported words. This is strictly an administrative issue, which can be fixed if found problematic.

In Japanese Latter-day Saint parlance, for example, English transliterated words abound, even more so than in other Christian denominations, including *wādo* (ward), *sutēku* (stake), *yangu adaruto* (young adult), and *minisutaringu* (ministering). In 2009, the Church introduced the transliterated word for bishop (*bishoppu*) to replace the century-old biblical term *kantoku*, ostensibly because Japanese generally associate *kantoku* with the general manager of a baseball team (for which the same word is used). On the same occasion, the Church introduced a new set of terms for ecclesiastical offices to correspond more closely with the English originals, thereby creating a strange vocabulary totally out of line with conventional Japanese colloquial usage.

---

12. More than 60 percent (64.4 for men and 57.6 for women) either "strongly" or "somewhat" agreed that the *General Handbook* should be adhered to strictly. This could mean that the handbook has become increasingly less prescriptive in recent years, so that Japanese Latter-day Saints find sufficient room for local adaptation where necessary. Since 2020, the handbook has been formally called *General Handbook: Serving in The Church of Jesus Christ of Latter-day Saints*.

Nearly 39 percent of the respondents "somewhat" and "strongly" agreed that the Church in Japan uses too many foreign or transliterated words that are not part of colloquial Japanese usage. Thirteen respondents noted the unusual vocabulary as an obstacle to conversion. A 63-year-old female respondent considered transliterated words difficult to understand, especially for new members and those who did not understand English, and stated that this contributed to their sense of isolation and uneasiness. A 32-year-old female noted how uneasy her nonmember friends felt with the proliferation of transliterated words when they came to church. A 61-year-old male said the translation of ecclesiastical offices introduced in 2009 was not part of the Japanese language, while another 61-year-old male thought that the use of natural Japanese words would diminish the "distance" with nonmembers.

About 29 percent of the respondents "somewhat" and "strongly" agreed that the Church in Japan tried too much to follow the practices of American members, while more than 23 percent "somewhat" and "strongly" disagreed that the Church had made sufficient adjustments for differences in social practices. A 60-year-old male respondent stated that even the Japanese leaders were too "Americanized," while a 43-year-old female observed that Japanese members took themselves too seriously in trying to follow "an American manual" and were being burned out. A 26-year-old female said that the manuals produced in Salt Lake City, being targeted mainly at a readership with a Christian background, were difficult to understand. A 26-year-old male questioned the wisdom of translating materials produced in English word-for-word and imposing the content on Japanese members, hoping that they would understand.

6-6. Challenges and Opportunities

Living in Japan as Latter-day Saints

A surprisingly large number (261) of individuals responded to the survey's open-ended invitation to provide "any additional or clarifying thoughts" regarding (1) living in Japan as a Latter-day Saint (147 comments given), (2) the obstacles to the growth and acceptance of the Church in Japan (202 comments), and (3) how the Church can help them better with the challenges of being Latter-day Saints in Japan (113 comments). Some comments were as brief as a few words, while others were as long as a paragraph. About a third of these were articulated opinions about which the individuals must have felt strongly enough to express (we have already reported some of them throughout the book as qualitative evidence). The views voluntarily expressed under the safety of anonymity may be taken as an intimation of potential areas where the costs of church membership (identity conflict) might be reduced and the benefits (positive church experience) might be increased.

First, close to twenty respondents mentioned aspects of Japan's conformist culture as an obstacle to retention. Anyone who does not conform with group norms feels uncomfortable, and some of them may decide to drop out. This is sometimes reflected in the style of leadership as well. A 41-year-old male respondent thought that a whole generation of members had left the church because of the well-meaning leaders who "take a stern look" at others. Several referred to a dominant thinking among the members that there was only one right way to do things. A 31-year-old female and a 36-year-old male thought that greater inclusivity and tolerance for diversity would help the Church meet the needs of a greater number of individuals by allowing more of them to feel welcome. According to another respondent, every person who did not keep the Word of Wisdom had ceased attending church. This confirms our earlier explanation of the finding that compliance with the Word of Wisdom among active Latter-day Saints was much higher in Japan (94–98 percent) than in the United States (67–88 percent; see Figure 4-12 in chapter 4).

Building group consciousness is one of the implicit aims of Japanese education from preschool through high school. Japanese children are taught from earliest childhood to obey authority and to cooperate with others. This was demonstrated during the COVID-19 pandemic of 2020–22 when virtually every Japanese wore a mask in public without being "mandated" by the government (they did so because everyone else was doing so). The Church's emphasis on obedience to authority reinforces this aspect of Japanese culture. Japan's local leaders attempt strictly to follow the letter of the *General Handbook* and of any other directive that may come from Salt Lake City or the Area Presidency in Tokyo.

This extreme culture of obedience can create a stifling climate for both leaders and members, and can take joy out of church service and worship. A 58-year-old male respondent pointed out the need for the authorities to recognize the potential of their well-meaning encouragement creating an additional burden and driving more members out of activity. There were too many meetings, many observed, not because they were needed but because the handbook prescribed them. As most of them are held on Sunday, those with leadership responsibilities could be away from home all day.

Second, several respondents mentioned, as an example of lack of sensitivity to Japanese customs, the authorities' seeming disregard for the importance of New Year's celebrations in Japanese cultural life, when family and relatives typically gather. There was a directive some years ago from the Area Presidency not to abbreviate meetings on a Sunday when it falls on New Year's Day. It appears that most Japanese leaders are still faithfully adhering to this directive from many years ago. A 66-year-old female respondent "always feels sick" whenever she sees Japanese leaders accepting the foreign tradition of Christmas celebration in preference to Japanese tradition.

We mention these comments, not because we are necessarily advocating an abbreviated meeting schedule when a Sunday falls on New Year's Day, but because these remarks illustrate well the nature of this cultural climate. For one thing, Japanese leaders typically follow their superiors without questioning (at least in public). We saw in chapter 4 that a greater share of Latter-day Saints in Japan than in the United States gave precedence to church leaders over personal revelation as the source of spiritual authority (67.6 vs. 62.0 percent for men; 79.3 vs. 68.7 percent for women). Yet, enough members in Japan (32.4 percent for men and 20.7 percent for women) were seen to give precedence to personal revelation. These individuals may complain in private when they disagree, may quietly and perhaps grudgingly comply, and may cease attending church when the limit of endurance is reached.

Finally, fifteen individuals provided a set of eighteen comments referring to the Word of Wisdom (especially regarding green tea) as an obstacle to conversion and retention. Given the prominent role green tea plays in Japanese society, this comes as no surprise. A 69-year-old male respondent stated that serving green tea was an expression of hospitality and it would be impolite not to accept it, wishing it would not be considered a violation of the Word of Wisdom. Many thought the social aspect of the Word of Wisdom was limiting the Church's acceptance in Japan, with an 82-year-old male respondent (who had joined the church in 1959) pointing out the incongruence of allowing a member to consume a large chunk of red meat while refusing him admission to the temple for taking a little sip of green tea (adding that only 10 percent of those who had joined the Church with him in the 1950s remained active). These opinions were often justified by stating that green tea is not damaging to health.

The Role of Tension

The consideration of how much institutional acculturation might be feasible must be tempered by the need to maintain what Stark (1998) calls "a medium level tension" with the host society (see also Duke 1998). In a series of papers inspired by the growth of The Church of Jesus Christ of Latter-day Saints since the nineteenth century, Rodney Stark has argued that its success can be explained by its cultural continuity with the host society (i.e., the United States) combined with a moderate tension that sets it apart from other groups in terms of strictness; a religious movement must be "strict, but not too strict" to succeed (Stark 1998). Some degree of strictness is needed to minimize the "free-rider" problem that can dilute resources and commitment by filtering out the non-committed members who participate for the purposes of receiving social or economic resources without paying their dues (Wallis 1991).

Rainock and Takagi (2020) discuss this issue in the context of two indigenous Christian denominations in Japan, the Spirit of Jesus Church (*Iesu no Mitama Kyōkai*, founded in 1941) and the Holy Ecclesia of Jesus (*Sei Iesu Kai*, 1946). These two denominations have pushed the cultural adaptation of Christianity to the limit and thereby virtually eliminated the social costs of being Christians in a non-Christian society (Mullins 1998).[13] While the activity rates of these churches far exceed that among Japanese Latter-day Saints,[14] they appear to be heading toward institutional extinction:[15] their membership had declined to a mere 12,852 and 4,442, respectively, in 2021.[16] Based on the experiences of indigenous Christian

---

13. The Christian Canaan Church (*Kirisutokyō Kanan Kyōdan*, founded in 1940) may also be added to the list. The Holy Ecclesia of Jesus provides Christian alternatives to a number of rituals traditionally observed at Shinto shrines and, as in Japanese Buddhism, memorial services for the dead; the Christian Canaan Church observes memorials for the dead according to the Japanese calendar and custom. Interestingly, the Spirit of Jesus Church practices the New Testament rituals of foot-washing and baptism for the dead.

14. In 2018, it was 43.0 and 52.7 percent, respectively (Rainock and Takagi 2020).

15. The experience of the Spirit of Jesus Church, by far the most successful of all indigenous Christian movements, is particularly instructive. By 1960, it had grown to become the third largest Protestant denomination in Japan; by the mid-1980s, it had claimed a membership of over 300,000. The momentum, however, could not be sustained long after the death, in 1970, of its charismatic founder.

16. Membership in the Christian Canaan Church was 390 at the end of 2021 (Bunkachō 2022).

movements in Japan, Mullins (1998, pp. 167, 169) concludes that while Christianity is "too deviant for widespread acceptance by Japanese," churches could "dig their own graves through 'over-indigenization.'"

It is difficult to know what it means to have a moderate amount of tension with the host society when cultural continuity is weak, as might be the case with The Church of Jesus Christ of Latter-day Saints in Japan (how much cultural overlap there is between the Church and the host society can be a matter of debate).[17] Religion must meet a variety of needs, including financial and emotional support, social interaction, and even the positive emotions of what eminent French sociologist Émile Durkheim termed "collective effervescence," when one feels at home within a strong religious community (Durkheim 1917). One should not drive away those truly seeking solace, comfort, and meaning in a community of believers by making the costs of entry too high. Achieving the delicate balance of moderate tension—just enough to reward commitment but not so excessive as to discourage growth—in the context of Japan remains a challenging question.

6-7. Conclusion

This penultimate chapter has considered the challenges and opportunities facing The Church of Jesus Christ of Latter-day Saints in Japan as it navigates its future. The overarching structural changes in Japanese society—the shrinking and aging of the population and the rising religious apathy—pose serious challenges to all nontraditional religious groups. At the same time, counterbalances to these forces are the ongoing changes in Japan's cultural institutions, which are expanding the range of socially acceptable behavior by promoting tolerance for diversity. Several respondents in the Japan LDS Survey stated that some positive changes were already happening in the direction of reducing the costs of church membership. The fact that membership in nontraditional religious groups, including almost all Christian denominations, has been declining in recent decades does not mean that The Church of Jesus Christ of Latter-day Saints cannot continue to attract religious seekers in Japan by meeting their ever-present spiritual needs.

---

17. Even though some religious practices, such as Sabbath and Word of Wisdom observance, clearly represent a significant cultural gap with the host society, the teachings of The Church of Jesus Christ of Latter-day Saints resonate well with some aspects of Japanese culture, including: reverence for ancestors; inculcation of kindness, humility, honesty, thrift, and hard work as virtues; and emphasis on education. There is much cultural continuity in some areas.

We have devoted some space to considering the opinions expressed by a large number of survey respondents, who responded to the survey's open-ended invitations, to explore any institutional acculturation and the potential areas where the costs of church membership could be reduced and the benefits raised. As outside observers, and as social scientists, we are not in a position to offer our own personal views that are not backed by evidence collected from the survey. How to balance the need to reduce identity conflict through institutional acculturation, and the need to meet the spiritual needs of religious seekers by offering what only The Church of Jesus Christ of Latter-day Saints can offer through its unique teachings, requires careful thought. There are no easy solutions to questions of culture that satisfy everyone. It appears to us that any cultural adaptation, to be widely accepted and sustained, can only be made on the basis of extensive consultation with a wide range of stakeholders.

CHAPTER 7

A SUMMARY OF MAJOR FINDINGS

7-1. Introduction

This concluding chapter summarizes the major findings from the Japan LDS Survey, viewed from various groups of stakeholders: scholars and researchers of religion, the general public, Latter-day Saint missionaries and mission leaders, Latter-day Saint leaders (including those based outside Japan), and Japanese Latter-day Saints. The Church of Jesus Christ of Latter-day Saints is a rare modern phenomenon. From a relatively small membership base largely confined to the Great Basin in the western United States at the turn of the twentieth century, it has grown to become a global religion of nearly seventeen million members with more than 31,000 congregations scattered across the world within a short span of time.[1] As such, the survey provides scholars and researchers with microdata on an aspect of that global growth in a particular location. Ours is the first comprehensive and systematic survey of Japanese Latter-day Saints designed to identify what they believe and how they practice their religion. It offers Latter-day Saint leaders and missionaries valuable tools with which to understand the cultural background of the people to whom they minister. Japanese Latter-day Saints will discover from the survey who their fellow Saints are and what they think.

The following summary of major findings is presented as a set of bullet points, organized in terms of what we think might be the takeaways for different groups of stakeholders. Unlike the preceding chapters where we based our views strictly on the quantitative evidence from the survey, in this chapter we take the liberty of expressing our personal views more freely in some instances, extrapolating from the survey findings as well as the voluntary comments of respondents. Because similar messages are relevant to different stakeholders, the takeaways are necessarily overlapping in some cases though they may be worded differently (e.g., the ideological inclinations of Japanese Latter-day Saints are of interest both to the general public and to fellow Latter-day Saints). The summary is intended to help the reader digest the various strands of data presented in the book in order to draw a manageable conclusion. It is also intended to motivate the reader to read the rest of the book if he or she is starting with this summary.

---

1. The numbers are from the "Church Newsroom," accessed March 24, 2023.

7-2. Takeaways for Scholars and Researchers

- Culture exerts a powerful influence on individual religious choices. There is no other way to explain why so few in Japan are Christians, much less members of The Church of Jesus Christ of Latter-day Saints. Yet, culture allows choice and variation, providing not a single choice, but a menu of possible actions in a given situation. Even with little institutional acculturation, the Church can find converts in a small segment of the population with the strength of its message. The survey provides prima facie evidence that it is possible to be both Japanese and a Latter-day Saint.

- Religious conversion most often takes place at a young age. More than 90 percent of Latter-day Saint converts in our sample (almost all of whom are active practitioners) joined The Church of Jesus Christ of Latter-day Saints before the age of 30, with the average age being 22.1. Moreover, around 30 percent of them identified knowledge of or familiarity with Christianity prior to their conversion. These findings are consistent with the predictions of the large literature on the sociology and economics of religion.

- The overwhelming majority of active Latter-day Saints in Japan have fully embraced a new religious identity. Around 90 percent (depending on the metric used) of them feel socially accepted by their peers and families, feel comfortable practicing their beliefs, hold strong religious convictions in different doctrinal areas, and fully comply with outward religious practices (such as Sabbath observance and the Word of Wisdom) that are expected of Latter-day Saints.[2]

- The Church, as a highly centralized organization, provides little room for institutional acculturation, making it necessary that acculturation, if any, takes place at the individual level. The most visible manifestation of individual acculturation is seen in the career choices of Latter-day Saints in Japan. In our sample, the share of Latter-day Saints in the professional occupations (estimated to be between 28 and 42 percent, depending on the definition) was considerably higher than the general population share of 18 percent. More than 60 percent of

---

2. The Word of Wisdom refers to the Latter-day Saint practice of abstaining from the consumption of alcohol, tea, coffee, tobacco, and addictive drugs. Because tobacco is no longer widely consumed in Japan, the survey did not inquire about the respondent's observance of this aspect of the Word of Wisdom.

the survey respondents stated that Sabbath observance had been an important consideration for their career decisions.

• Another method of individual acculturation is building long-term relationships, by which the overwhelming majority of Latter-day Saints seem able to avoid conflict in the workplace, for example, as regards the pervasive practice of social drinking. Anonymity creates conflict in the wider society. Whereas the share of Latter-day Saints who encountered frequent conflict with family in various areas never exceeded 2 percent, 13 percent experienced conflict with the custom of serving green tea "frequently" (another 20 percent "occasionally"). When they are anonymous members of society, there is little they can do to reduce the incidence of conflict with such a pervasive social institution.

• The survey dispels any notion that the Church, as a minority religion, predominantly attracts social misfits. Only 12 percent reported that they had felt they fit in poorly with their peers while they were in secondary school. Moreover, the ideological spectrum of Latter-day Saints in Japan closely mirrors that of Japanese society, from the most conservative to the most progressive. They are a diverse group of individuals, with a large percentage of career professionals, who do not constitute a subculture of Japanese society.

• The joint influence of culture and foreign religion is evident in reproductive decisions. In line with the national trend, the average number of children a woman bears during her lifetime has been declining among the Latter-day Saint population: the average for those under the age of 40 was 1.9, whereas the average for those over the age of 40 was 2.8. Yet, the average number of children has consistently exceeded the national average (now about 1.3), undoubtedly influenced by the pronatalist theology of the Latter-day Saint faith.

7-3. Takeaways for the General Public

• The age profile of the Latter-day Saint population in Japan broadly mirrors the country's aging population. Based on our sample, we estimate that more than 40 percent of active Latter-day Saints are over the age of 60.

• Japanese Latter-day Saints, despite their commitment to the same religious beliefs, are a diverse group of people. They represent a good cross section of Japanese society, from the most conservative to the most progressive, in terms of their political and social views. In our sample, the average self-assessment of their place on the ideological spectrum was about right in the middle.

- On political issues, the views of Latter-day Saints differ little from those of the general population: 65 percent supported a strong Japan–U.S. alliance (cf. the national share of 50–70 percent), and 36 percent supported amending the constitution in favor of explicitly recognizing the right of self-defense (cf. the national share of about 30 percent). The share of those with no political party support (54 percent) was larger than the national share of around 43 percent, which translates to a smaller share of those who supported the ruling Liberal Democratic Party, given similar shares of support to the opposition parties.

- On contemporary social issues, Latter-day Saints tend to be more conservative than the general population, except for immigration, for which 41 percent expressed support (cf. the national share of 33–40 percent). Latter-day Saints in our sample expressed particular opposition to legalizing same-sex marriage (even though the question was phrased, not as a moral issue, but strictly as a citizenship right), with only 24 percent expressing support (cf. the national share of 65 percent). Likewise, support for allowing separate surnames for husband and wife was particularly weak among the Latter-day Saints, with only 36 percent expressing support (cf. the national share of 67 percent).

- Latter-day Saints tend to have somewhat larger families than the national average, reflecting the pronatalist theology of the Latter-day Saint faith: 72.0 percent of men and 57.2 percent of women in the survey had three or more children. Even so, in line with the national trend, the average number of children Latter-day Saint women bear during their lifetimes has been declining, though the average number has remained higher than the national average (i.e., about 1.9 vs. the national average of 1.3 in 2021).

- Religiously active Latter-day Saints in Japan tend to marry within the faith: 97 percent of men and 88 percent of women, who were either married or divorced, reported that their current or former spouse was also a Latter-day Saint.

- Japanese Latter-day Saints are on average somewhat more educated than the general population, with 72 percent of both men and women having received postsecondary education (the share increases to more than 80 percent for those under the age of 40). However, the educational advantage of Latter-day Saints may be diminishing as 80 percent of high school graduates in Japan currently go on to receive postsecondary education.

- Japanese Latter-day Saints, compared to the general population, have far more experience living in foreign countries (even excluding their experience as missionaries), with 22 percent having lived abroad for more than a year for work or school in 2021 (the share increases to 35 percent for women under the age of 40). In contrast, the estimated national population share, at most, was 6–9 percent.

- The share of Latter-day Saints in professional occupations (estimated to be between 28 and 42 percent, depending on the definition, in 2021) is considerably higher than the general population share of 18 percent. This has allowed them to practice their religion more freely without experiencing frequent conflict in the workplace.

7-4. Takeaways for Latter-day Saint Missionaries and Mission Leaders

- Conversion to The Church of Jesus Christ of Latter-day Saints most frequently takes place at a young age. More than 90 percent of the Latter-day Saint converts in our sample (the overwhelming majority of whom were active members) joined the Church before the age of 30, with the average age of 22.1. The average age of conversion, however, has been increasing in recent years for reasons we cannot fully explain. It may be that parents have become more protective of their children than in the past and do not readily grant permission to be baptized. Also, the Church is better known now than in the past, making it more acceptable to older adults. It may also be that mission leaders are placing more emphasis on finding adults with families than in the past. These remain our speculations.

- The largest share (37 percent) of religiously active Latter-day Saint converts experienced no opposition of any kind to their conversion, possibly because our sample included only those who had actually joined the Church (therefore, this may not be the average experience of all Japanese who investigated the Church). A smaller but almost equal share (36 percent) reported family opposition to have been the biggest obstacle to their conversion. In our view, this reflects the fact that most of the converts joined the Church before the age of 30. No male convert who joined the Church after the age of 30 reported experiencing family opposition. Some women, however, continue to experience family opposition into their forties and fifties. When only women are considered, the share of those who experienced family opposition increases from 36 to 44 percent.

- This is the conundrum the Church's missionary work faces going forward: whereas individuals are more receptive when they are young, they are also more likely to face family opposition. The Church can only grow by welcoming young people into membership if it effectively helps their parents understand the positive aspects of church membership. Chapter 3 notes in some detail how one of the missions in Japan used a novel type of parental consent form that contained two parts: (1) the child promised, among other things, that by learning the teachings of Jesus Christ, he/she would "respect parents, cherish our home, encourage education," and (2) the parent or guardian in turn signed the form and expressed their hope that the child would live by such a promise. We were told by the mission president that the rate of parental consent had increased substantially as a result.

- Cultural continuity (for example, in the form of prior familiarity with Christianity) is important as a facilitator of conversion. About 30 percent of Latter-day Saint converts in our sample reported having knowledge of Christianity (e.g., the Bible, Jesus Christ, and other Christian denominations) prior to their conversion. When teaching someone with no Christian background, missionary work may benefit from highlighting the areas of cultural continuity; for example, the Church's family history work (given the Japanese culture of reverence for ancestors). The role of members, the press, or social media, while not very important in the conversion of older Latter-day Saints, has become increasingly more important as the Church has grown in membership. This trend is likely to continue.

- The missionaries play an important role in the conversion process, with 87 percent of Latter-day Saint converts identifying missionaries' role as the most consequential. Open-ended comments from respondents indicate that it was not just the teaching of the lessons that had an impact, but the missionaries' love, example, brightness, energy, smile, character, and other intangible attributes that they project. In other words, acquiring the Christ-like attributes of missionary conduct as advocated by *Preach My Gospel: A Guide to Sharing the Gospel of Jesus*

Christ, the standard reference for missionary work, perhaps plays a larger role than simply mastering the Japanese language.

- By far the most consequential doctrine of the Church that contributed to conversion was the plan of salvation, identified by 52 percent of Latter-day Saint converts, followed by the Joseph Smith story (33 percent). The experience of one mission president suggests that the Joseph Smith story could be effectively told in less than one minute when first contacting someone, highlighting the Church's unique perspective on the Godhead. The Book of Mormon could be introduced with a few additional sentences.

- Although less than 20 percent of converts identified a Church member (who was not a member of the family) as having played a role in their conversion, the voluntary comments of respondents suggest that members whom they met at church did play a significant role. For example, one member simply said, "Please come again." This visitor said it was the key to his conversion. Most of the comments highlight the importance of the feeling that the visitor was welcome in this new group. Training members on this simple type of outreach can be a significant factor in bringing new friends into the Church.

7-5. Takeaways for Latter-day Saint Leaders

- The age profile of the Latter-day Saint population broadly mirrors Japan's aging population. We estimate from our sample that more than 40 percent of active Latter-day Saints are over the age of 60. Some units are already made up almost entirely of elderly members.

- The overwhelming majority of religiously active Latter-day Saints in Japan have fully embraced the Latter-day Saint identity. In our sample, about 85 percent of them lived within 30 minutes of their meetinghouses (48 percent within 15 minutes). Around 90 percent held no or little doubt about the existence of God and fully accepted all or most of Latter-day Saint doctrines and teachings. Their compliance with outward religious practices (such as the Word of Wisdom and the law of chastity) was extremely high, with more than 93 percent reporting full compliance in some cases.

- The strength of religious conviction, as well as the compliance of religious practices, was higher among Japanese Latter-day Saints than among their American counterparts who attended church at least weekly. The share in Japan of highly committed or observant members could be as much as 10 percentage points higher. This likely reflects the lower activity rate of Japanese Latter-day Saints. Whereas an estimated less than 20 percent attend church regularly in Japan, the share in the United States is much larger, perhaps 40 to 60 percent, depending on the area. This means that the active church membership in the United States includes a more diverse group of people with varying degrees of commitment.

- The lower activity rate of Latter-day Saints in Japan may to some extent reflect the difficulty of reconciling the Latter-day Saint identity with other identities in Japanese society. Not everyone is adept at individual acculturation. Open-ended responses to the survey indicate that, in Japan, there is strong peer pressure for conformity with the Word of Wisdom. The high compliance of those who attend church can even be an indictment of the Church in Japan as an inhospitable place for those who are trying to keep the Word of Wisdom but for various reasons find it difficult.

- Japanese Latter-day Saints are more likely than their American counterparts to give precedence to priesthood leaders over personal revelation as a source of spiritual authority. Adjusted for church activity status, 68 percent of men (cf. 62 percent in the United States) and 79 percent of women (cf. 69 percent in the United States) expressed such a view. While the majority gave precedence to priesthood leaders in both countries, the higher shares for both men and women in Japan are consistent with the stereotypical Japanese cultural trait of deference to higher authority.

- While both Japanese and American Latter-day Saints broadly endorse the status of women in the Church, the support for the status quo is greater among Japanese Latter-day Saints, especially Japanese women. Remarkably, less than 1 percent of Japanese women (cf. 18 percent of American women) reported that they were bothered by women not being given the priesthood, and only 6 percent (cf. 18 percent) agreed with the statement "women do not have enough voice in the Church." This differing endorsement of the status quo between Japan and the United States possibly reflects cross-cultural differences in the expectation of gender parity in organizational leadership. It is also possible that, in the case of Japanese women, those who could develop a strong Latter-day Saint identity were precisely those individuals whose existing worldview embraced traditional gender roles.

- Without a significant degree of acculturation, no foreign religion can expect to appeal to a large segment of the population. Whether or not the Church should aim for greater institutional acculturation is a matter of debate. The average views of Latter-day Saints in Japan, when asked whether the Church has done enough to meet culture-specific needs in different areas of church administration, fall about right in the middle (the average score in our sample was around 3.6 on a scale of 1 through 5). This should not be taken to mean that the average Latter-day Saint in Japan approves the status quo. Rather, it should be taken to mean that a large share, though not the majority, of active Latter-day Saints consider that room exists for cultural adaptation in church administration. Our sample predominantly includes religiously active Latter-day Saints who have learned to live their religion as it is currently administered. In thinking about prospective opportunities for the Church, the perspectives of those who have dropped out of activity should also be given due regard. The voluntary comments made by many respondents to the survey express a strong desire for more adaptation to the Japanese culture and for consideration of the local circumstances of the members.

- Members can play an important role in the conversion of friends whom missionaries bring to church. Leaders can do more to teach members how important it is to extend a simple hand of fellowship.

7-6. Takeaways for Japanese Latter-day Saints

- Japanese Latter-day Saints represent a good cross section of Japanese society, from the most conservative to the most progressive, in terms of their political and social views. In our sample, the average self-assessment of their place on the ideological spectrum was about right in the middle. Japanese members should not feel they are on the fringes of Japanese society, nor should they expect their fellow members to share similar ideological views just because they belong to the same church.

- On political issues, the views of Latter-day Saints differ little from the general population: 65 percent supported a strong Japan–U.S. alliance (cf. the national share of 50–70 percent), and 36 percent supported amending the constitution in favor of explicitly recognizing the right of self-defense (cf. the national share of about 30 percent). The share of those with no political party support (54 percent) was larger than the national share of around 43 percent, which translates to a smaller share of those who supported the ruling Liberal Democratic Party, given similar shares of support to the opposition parties.

- On contemporary social issues, Latter-day Saints tend to be more conservative than the general population, except for immigration, for which 41 percent expressed support (cf. the national share of 33–40 percent). Latter-day Saints expressed particular aversion to legalizing same-sex marriage, with only 24 percent expressing support (cf. the national share of 65 percent). Likewise, support for allowing separate surnames for husband and wife was particularly weak among Latter-day Saints, with only 36 percent expressing support (cf. the national share of 67 percent).

- The Church professes both a belief in religious authority and a belief in personal revelation. When members were pressed to compare these two beliefs, 73 percent of Japanese Latter-day Saints (68 percent for men and 79 percent for women) gave precedence to their priesthood leaders over personal revelation as a source of spiritual authority.

- The overwhelming majority of active Japanese Latter-day Saints, especially the women, endorse the status of women in the Church. In our sample, less than 1 percent of women were bothered by women not being given the priesthood, and only 7 percent strongly agreed with the statement "women do not have enough voice in the Church."

- The average views of Latter-day Saints in Japan, when asked whether the Church has done enough to meet culture-specific needs in different areas of church administration, fall about right in the middle (the average score in our sample was around 3.6 on a scale of 1 through 5). This means that, while many are happy with the way the church is administered, an equal number feel that there is more the Church could do to accommodate the culture-specific needs of Japanese members. In particular, many members felt that green tea should not be part of the Word of Wisdom and that there should be less use of English (Romanized) terminology in church vocabulary.

- While members in Japan have not played a significant role in introducing friends to the Church, they have played an important part in welcoming friends brought to church by the missionaries.

7-7. Challenges for the Future

- The Church of Jesus Christ of Latter-day Saints faces the challenges of an adverse demographic trend and rising religious apathy. Japan's population peaked in 2008 at 128 million and has been declining since. Most nontraditional religions, including major Christian denominations, have already been experiencing absolute declines in membership. The Church has not yet experienced an absolute decline in membership because the relative success of its missionary program has largely offset the attrition of membership. If these trends continue, however, the Church may also begin to experience declining membership in the future, especially as no dramatic increase can be expected in the number of missionaries assigned to Japan.

- The declining and aging population has already increased the share of elderly members in many Japanese congregations. Aggravating this demographic headwind is the migration of the population into the capital region around Tokyo, as manufacturing employment has collapsed in many regions. It may become increasingly difficult to maintain congregations across the country, at least in the form of branches and wards organized within a stake structure. Innovative thinking may be needed to meet the spiritual needs of a widely dispersed population. Some comments by members in outlying districts expressed a feeling that they are not given adequate ministering by leaders from headquarters.

- Counterbalancing such a pessimistic scenario are positive developments that are increasing society's tolerance for diversity, including the greater participation of women in the workplace and the greater presence of foreigners. There is no reason to doubt that the Church can take advantage of these societal changes to appeal to a larger segment of the population by offering what no other institution can offer to religious seekers. One key is to reduce the costs in terms of identity conflict of church membership through greater institutional acculturation, but any acculturation should not be allowed to dilute the unique doctrines and ordinances of the Church. How to balance the two requires careful thought. There are no easy solutions to questions related to culture that satisfy everyone. Any cultural adaptation, to be widely accepted and sustained, can only be made on the basis of extensive consultation with a wide range of stakeholders.

References

Aoki, Masahiko. 1990. "Toward an Economic Model of the Japanese Firm." *Journal of Economic Literature* 28: 1–27.

Asahi Shinbun. 2017. "Yoron Chōsa." *Asahi Shinbun.* February 21, 2017. Tokyo.

———. 2018. "Yoron Chōsa." Accessed March 24, 2023. https://www.asahi.com/articles/ASM1965D4M19UZPS008.html.

———. 2019. "Yoron Chōsa." Accessed March 24, 2023. https://www.asahi.com/articles/ASM4L5WQJM4HUZPS00R.html.

———. 2021a. "Yoron Chōsa." Accessed March 24, 2023. https://www.asahi.com/articles/ASP3P7DSCP3MUZPS003.html.

———. 2021b. "Yoron Chōsa." Accessed March 24, 2023. https://www.asahi.com/politics/yoron/kenpo2021/?iref=com_yorontop.

———. 2021c. "Yoron Chōsa." Accessed March 24, 2023. https://www.asahi.com/articles/ASP4F43DFP4CUZPS004.html.

Becker, Sascha O., and Ludger Woessmann. 2013. "Not the Opium of the People: Income and Secularization in a Panel of Prussian Counties." *American Economic Review* 103: 539–44.

Bourdieu, Pierre. 1986. "The Forms of Capital." In *Handbook of Theory of Research for the Sociology of Education*, edited by John G. Richardson, 241–58. Westport, CT: Greenwood.

Brenner, Philip S., Richard T. Serpe, and Sheldon Stryker. 2014. "The Causal Ordering of Prominence and Salience in Identity Theory: An Empirical Examination." *Social Psychology Quarterly* 77: 231–52.

Bunkachō (Agency for Cultural Affairs). Government of Japan. *Shūkyō Nenkan.* Tokyo. Annual issues.

Bureau of Statistics, Government of Japan. 2023a. "Rōdōryoku Chōsa 2022 nen Heikin Kekka no Yōyaku." Accessed March 24, 2023. www.stat.go.jp/data/roudou/sokuhou/nen/ft/pdf/index1.pdf.

———. 2023b. *Nihon no Tōkei.* Accessed March 24, 2023. www.stat.go.jp/data/nihon/19.html.

Cabinet Office, Government of Japan. 2022. "Danjo Kyōdō Sankaku Hakusho." Accessed March 24, 2023. https://www.gender.go.jp/about_danjo/whitepaper/r04/zentai/pdf/r04_print.pdf.

———. 2023. "Josei Katsuyaku Danjo Kyōdō Sankaku no Genjō to Kadai." Accessed March 24, 2023. https://www.gender.go.jp/research/pdf/joseikatsuyaku_kadai.pdf.

Cave, Peter. 2004. "'Bukatsudō': The Educational Role of Japanese School Clubs." *Journal of Japanese Studies* 30: 383–415.

Dawson, Lorne L. 2001. "The Cultural Significance of New Religious Movements: The Case of Soka Gakkai." *Sociology of Religion* 62: 337–64.

Deseret News. 1995–2001. *Church Almanac of The Church of Jesus Christ of Latter-day Saints*. Salt Lake City. Annual issues.

DiMaggio, Paul. 1997. "Culture and Cognition." *Annual Review of Sociology* 23: 263–87.

Duke, James T. 1998. "Cultural Continuity and Tension: A Test of Stark's Theory of Church Growth." In *Latter-day Saint Social Life: Social Research on the LDS Church and its Members*, edited by James T. Duke, 71–104. Provo, UT: Religious Studies Center, Brigham Young University.

———. 1999. "Secularization in American Society: Contemporary Religious Trends." In the Proceedings of the International Society 10th Annual Conference, "The Challenges of Sharing Religious Beliefs in a Global Setting." August 16, 1999. Provo, UT: David M. Kennedy Center for International Studies, Brigham Young University, 11–24.

Durkheim, Émile. 1917. *The Elementary Forms of the Religious Life: A Study in Religious Sociology*. London: G. Allen & Unwin.

Earhart, H. Byron. 2004. *Japanese Religion: Unity and Diversity*, 4th ed. Belmont, CA: Wadsworth/Thomson.

Figuerres, Cyril I. A. 1999. "Challenges of Establishing the Church in Japan." In the Proceedings of the International Society 10th Annual Conference, "The Challenges of Sharing Religious Beliefs in a Global Setting," August 16, 1999. Provo, UT: David M. Kennedy Center for International Studies, Brigham Young University, 25–31.

Genron NPO. 2019. "Nihon no Seiji Minshu-shugi ni kansuru Yoron Chōsa." Accessed March 24, 2023. http://www.genron-npo.net/future/archives/7410.html.

Glaeser, Edward L., and Bruce I. Sacerdote. 2008. "Education and Religion." *Journal of Human Capital* 2: 188–215.

Global Firepower. 2021. "GlobalFirepower.com Ranks (2005–Present)." Accessed March 24, 2023. https://www.globalfirepower.com/global-ranks-previous.php.

Government of Japan. "E-stat." Accessed March 24, 2023. https://www.e-stat.go.jp.

Hammersley, Martyn. 2019. *The Concept of Culture: A History and Reappraisal*. London: Palgrave Macmillan.

Heaton, Tim B. 1998a. "Vital Statistics." In *Latter-day Saint Social Life: Social Research on the LDS Church and its Members*, edited by James T. Duke, 105–32. Provo, UT: Religious Studies Center, Brigham Young University.

———. 1998b. "Religious Influences on Mormon Fertility: Cross-National Comparisons." In *Latter-day Saint Social Life: Social Research on the LDS Church and its Members*, edited by James T. Duke, 425–40. Provo, UT: Religious Studies Center, Brigham Young University.

Hoffman, John P. 2007. *Japanese Saints: Mormons in the Land of the Rising Sun*. Lanham, MD: Lexington.

Hungerman, Daniel M. 2014. "The Effect of Education on Religion: Evidence from Compulsory Schooling Laws." *Journal of Economic Behavior and Organization* 104: 52–63.

Iannaccone, Laurence R. 1990. "Religious Practice: A Human Capital Approach." *Journal for the Scientific Study of Religion* 29: 297–314.

———. 1998. "Introduction to the Economics of Religion." *Journal of Economic Literature* 36: 1479–82.

Ikezoe, Hirokuni. 2018. "Japan's Employment System and Public Policy, 2017–2022." *Japan Labor Issues* 2: 25–28.

Jidōsha Kensa Tōroku Jōhō Kyōkai (Japan Automobile Inspection and Registration Information Association, JAIRIA). 2021. "Todōfukenbetsu no Jikayō Jōyōsha no Fukyū Jōkyō." Accessed March 24, 2023. https://airia.or.jp /publish/file/r5c6pv000000wkrb-att/r5c6pv000000wkrq.pdf.

Kokuritsu Gan Kenkyū Sentā (National Cancer Center, NCC). 2019. "Kitsuenritsu." Accessed March 24, 2023. https://ganjoho.jp/reg_stat/statistics/stat/smoking /index.html.

Kokuritsu Shakai Hoshō Jinkō Mondai Kenkyūsho (National Institute of Population and Social Security Research, NIPSS). 2018. "Nihon no Shōrai Suikei Jinkō." Tokyo.

Kokusai Kankō Shinkō Kikō (Japan National Tourism Organization, JNTO). 2021. "Hōnichi Gaikyaku Sū." Accessed March 24, 2023. www.jnto.go.jp/jpn /statistics/marketingdata_outbound.pdf.

Lebra, Takie Sugiyama. 1976. *Japanese Pattern of Behavior*. Honolulu: University of Hawaii Press.

Lipset, Seymour Martin. 1992. "The Work Ethic, Then and Now." *Journal of Labor Research* 13: 45–54.

Metraux, Daniel A. 1994. *The Soka Gakkai Revolution*. Lanham, MD: University Press of America.

Miller, Alan S. 1995. "A Rational Choice Model of Religious Behavior in Japan." *Journal of the Scientific Study of Religion* 34: 234–43.

Ministry of Defense (MOD), Government of Japan. 2021. "Zainichi Beigun Kankei Keihi." Accessed March 24, 2023. https://www.mod.go.jp/j/approach /zaibeigun/us_keihi/zainitibeigun_kankeikeihi_r02.pdf.

Ministry of Education, Culture, Sports, Science and Technology (MEXT), Government of Japan. 2021a. "Daigaku Nyūgakusha Senbatsu Kanren Kiso Shiryō Shū." Accessed March 24, 2023. https://www.mext.go.jp/content /20210330-mxt_daigakuc02-000013827_9.pdf.

———. 2021b. "Reiwa 3 nendo Igakubu (Igakuka) no Nyūgaku Senbatsu ni okeru Danjobetsu Gōkakuritsu ni tsuite." Accessed March 24, 2023. https:// www.mext.go.jp/content/2021930-mxt_daigakuc02-100001375_1_2.pdf.

———. 2022. "Reiwa 2 nendo Gakkō Kihon Chōsa no Kōhyō nitsuite." Accessed March 24, 2023. www.mext.go.jp/content/20200825-mxt_chousa01 -1419591_8.pdf.

Ministry of Foreign Affairs (MOFA), Government of Japan. 2022. "Kaigai Zairyū Hōjinsū Chōsa Tōkei." Accessed March 24, 2023. www.mofa.go.jp/mofaj /toko/tokei/hojin/index.html.

Ministry of Health, Labour and Welfare (MHLW), Government of Japan. 2019. "Jikangai Rōdō no Jōgen Kisei." Accessed March 24, 2023. www.mhlw .go.jp/content/000463185.pdf.

———. 2021a. "Reiwa 3 nen Jinkō Dōtai Tōkei no Gaikyō." Accessed March 24, 2023. www.mhlw.go.jp/toukei/saikin/hw/jinkou/kakutei21/dl/09_h5.pdf.

———. 2021b. "Reiwa 3 nen Kan-i Seimei Hyō no Gaikyō." Accessed March 24, 2023. https://www.mhlw.go.jp/toukei/saikin/hw/life/life21/index.html.

Minkov, Michael. 2013. *Cross-Cultural Analysis: Comparing the World's Modern Societies and Their Cultures.* Los Angeles: Sage Publications.

Mitchell, Travis. 2017. "In America, Does More Education Equal Less Religion?" *Pew Research Center.*

Mizuno, Koh, Kazue Okamoto-Mizuno, and Kazuki Iwata. 2019. "Napping Behaviors and Extracurricular Club Activities in Japanese High School Students: Associations with Daytime Sleep Problems." *Clocks and Sleep* 1: 367–84.

Morris, Michael A. 2012. *Concise Dictionary of Social and Cultural Anthropology.* Oxford: Blackwell.

Mullins, Mark R. 1998. *Christianity Made in Japan: A Study of Indigenous Movements.* Honolulu: University of Hawaii Press.

———. 2012. "Secularization, Deprivatization, and the Reappearance of 'Public Religion' in Japanese Society." *Journal of Religion in Japan* 1: 61–82.

Nakane, Chie. 1970. *Japanese Society.* Berkeley and Los Angeles: University of California Press.

Nanmin Shien Kyōkai (Japan Association for Refugees, JAR). 2020. "Nanmin wo Shiru." Accessed March 24, 2023. www.refugee.or.jp/refugee/#section04.

Nihon Gakusei Shien Kikō (Japan Student Services Organization, JASSO). 2021. "2020 nendo Gaikokujin Ryūgakusei Zaiseki Jōkyō Chōsa Kekka." Accessed March 24, 2023. https://www.studyingjapan.go.jp/ja/_mt/2021/04/date2020z.pdf.

Nihon Hōsō Kyōkai (NHK). 2019. "Kōshitsu ni kansuru Ishiki Chōsa." Accessed March 24, 2023. https://www3.nhk.or.jp/news/special/japans-emperor6/opinion_poll/.

———. 2020. "Gaikokujin to no Kyōsei Shakai ni kansuru Yoron Chōsa." Accessed March 24, 2023. https://www.nhk.or.jp/bunken/research/yoron/pdf/20200401_11.pdf.

———. 2021a. "Yoron Chōsa." Accessed March 24, 2023. https://www.nhk.or.jp/senkyo/shijiritsu/archive/2021_04.html.

———. 2021b. "Yoron Chōsa." Accessed March 24, 2023. https://www.nhk.or.jp/politics/articles/lastweek/59584.html.

———. 2021c. "Seiji Ishiki Getsurei Denwa Chōsa." Accessed March 24, 2023. https://www.nhk.or.jp/senkyo/shijiritsu/pdf/aggregate/2021/y202108.pdf.

Numano, Jiro. 2000. "Toshika to Shinshūkyō no Kōryū." *Gendai Shakaigaku* 2: 85–96.

Okada, Yuji. 2009. "Bukatsudō e no Sanka ga Chūgakusei no Gakkō e no Shinri-shakai-teki Tekiō ni Ataeru Eikyō." *Kyōiku Shinri Gaku Kenkyū* 57: 419–31.

Okakura, Kakuzo. 1906. *The Book of Tea.* New York: Fox, Duffield & Company.

Partanen, Juha. 2006. "Spectacles of Sociability and Drunkenness: On Alcohol and Drinking in Japan." *Contemporary Drug Problems* 33: 177–204.

Pew Research Center. 2017. "In America, Does More Education Equal Less Religion?" Accessed March 24, 2023. https://www.pewresearch.org/religion /2017/04/26/in-america-does-more-education-equal-less-religion/.

Prime Minister's Office, Government of Japan. "The Constitution of Japan," official translation. Accessed March 24, 2023. https://japan.kantei.go.jp/constitution _and_government_of_japan/constitution_e.html.

Rainock, Meagan, and Shinji Takagi. 2020. "The LDS Church in Contemporary Japan: Failure or Success?" In *The Palgrave Handbook of Global Mormonism*, edited by R. Gordon Shepherd, A. Gary Shepherd, and Ryan T. Cragun, 635–54. Cham, Switzerland: Palgrave Macmillan.

Riess, Jana. 2019. *The Next Mormons: How Millennials Are Changing the LDS Church*. New York: Oxford University Press.

Sam, David L. 2006. "Acculturation: Conceptual Background and Core Components." In *The Cambridge Handbook of Acculturation Psychology*, edited by David L. Sam and John W. Perry, 11–26. Cambridge: Cambridge University Press.

Schwadel, Philip. 2011. "The Effects of Education on Americans' Religious Practices, Beliefs, and Affiliations." *Review of Religious Research* 53: 161–82.

Schwartz, Seth J., Jennifer B. Unger, Byron L. Zamboanga, and José Szapocznik. 2010. "Rethinking the Concept of Acculturation: Implications for Theory and Research." *American Psychologist* 65: 237–51.

Serpe, R. T. 1987. "Stability and Change in Self: A Structural Symbolic Interactionist Explanation." *Social Psychology Quarterly* 50: 44–55.

Shimizu, Shinji. 1990. "An Alcoholic Social System: Drinking Culture and Drinking Behaviors in Japan." *Seishin Hoken Kenkyū* 36: 85–100.

Shiramatsu, Satoshi. 1997. "Kōtō Gakkō ni okeru Bukatsudō no Kōka ni kansuru Kenkyū." *Nihon Kyōiku Keiei Gakkai Kiyō* 39: 74–88.

Stark, Rodney. 1998. "The Basis of Mormon Success: A Theoretical Application." In *Latter-day Saint Social Life: Social Research on the LDS Church and its Members*, edited by James T. Duke, 29–70. Provo, UT: Religious Studies Center, Brigham Young University.

Stark, Rodney, and Roger Finke. 2000. *Acts of Faith: Explaining the Human Side of Religion*. Berkeley and Los Angeles: University of California Press.

Stolzenberg, Ross M., Mary Blair-Loy, and Linda J. Waite. 1995. "Religious Participation in Early Adulthood: Age and Family Life Cycle Effects on Church Membership." *American Sociological Review* 60: 84–103.

Stryker, Sheldon, and Peter J. Burke. 2000. "The Past, Present, and Future of an Identity Theory." *Social Psychology Quarterly* 63: 284–97.

Sugiyama, Sachiko. 1997. "Gairai Shūkyō to Minzoku Shūkyō to no Dainamikusu." *Shūkyō Kenkyū* 71: 93–118.

Swidler, Ann. 1986. "Culture in Action: Symbols and Strategies." *American Sociological Review* 51: 273–86.

Takagi, Shinji. 2016. *The Trek East: Mormonism Meets Japan, 1901–1968*. Salt Lake City: Greg Kofford.

Takahashi, Yoko. 2018. "Nichibei ni okeru Jieigyōshusū no Keisoku." Discussion Paper DP18-07. Tokyo: Japan Institute for Labor Policy and Training.

The Church of Jesus Christ of Latter-day Saints. "Facts and Statistics." Newsroom. Accessed March 24, 2023. https://newsroom.churchofjesuschrist.org /facts-and-statistics.

Tōkyō Shōkō Risāchi (TSR). 2017. "Chōjikan Rōdō ni kansuru Ankēto Chōsa." Accessed March 24, 2023. https://www.tsr-net.co.jp/news/analysis /20170310_01.html.

United States Census Bureau. 2020. "Educational Attainment in the United States: 2019." Accessed March 24, 2023. https://www.census.gov/content/census /en/data/tables/2019/demo/educational-attainment/cps-detailed-tables .html.

Verter, Bradford. 2003. "Spiritual Capital: Theorizing Religion with Bourdieu against Bordieu." *Sociological Theory* 21: 150–74.

Vivanco, Luis A. 2018. *A Dictionary of Cultural Anthropology*. Oxford: Oxford University Press.

Wallis, Joe L. 1991. "Church Ministry and the Free Rider Problem: Religious Liberty and Disestablishment." *The American Journal of Economics and Sociology* 50: 183–96.

Watch Tower Bible and Tract Society of Pennsylvania. 2021. "2021 Service Year Report of Jehovah's Witnesses Worldwide." Accessed March 24, 2023. https://www .jw.org/en/library/books/2021-service-year-report/2021-country-territory/.

World Bank. 2023. "Population Estimates and Projections." Accessed March 24, 2023. https://datacatalog.worldbank.org/dataset/population-estimates-and -projections.

World Economic Forum (WEF). 2022. *Global Gender Gap Report 2022*. Geneva: World Economic Forum.

Young, Lawrence A. 1994. "Confronting Turbulent Environments: Issues in the Organizational Growth and Globalization of Mormonism." In *Contemporary Mormonism: Social Science Perspectives*, edited by M. Cornwall, T. Heaton, and L. A. Young, 43–63. Urbana: University of Illinois Press.

日本語要旨

本研究の動機とあらすじ

　本書は、2021年10月から11月にかけて実施した、日本における末日聖徒イエス・キリスト教会の会員を対象としたサーベイ（アンケート）調査に基づいて執筆された。おもにソーシャルネットワークを通して実施されたサーベイの性格上、回答者は、ほぼ例外なく、末日聖徒として強いアイデンティティを持つ、いわゆる「活発」会員である。したがって、なぜより多くの日本人が教会に入会しないのかという改宗の問題、なぜ改宗した者の一部が教会にとどまらないのかという定着の問題は、本研究の対象外である。本研究の焦点は、末日聖徒が宗教的少数派として、何を信じ、どのようにホスト社会との軋轢を管理しているのかという宗教実践の問題に置かれる。

　本書の表題「*Unique But Not Different*」は、「個性的、されど特異にあらず」とでも翻訳されうるのであろうか。そこには、本研究で明らかにされた知見が秘められている。すなわち、日本の末日聖徒は、社会の下位文化集団ではなく、政治観や社会観の面で、両極を含む社会の広範囲な立場を代表する多様な構成員の集団であるという、新鮮な発見である。大多数は、末日聖徒としてのアイデンティティを心から受け入れ、そのアイデンティティを優先すべく日常生活を営んでいる。社会学や社会心理学の文献で「アイデンティティの衝突」と呼ばれる現象は、末日聖徒の間では、職場においてさえも、稀である。このように、本研究は、日本人のアイデンティティと末日聖徒のアイデンティティを合わせ持つことが可能だという、一応の証拠を提供する。

　上記のように、本書では、複雑な現代社会における個人による社会行動の分析に適した「アイデンティティ理論」の枠組みで議論を進める。現代社会において、個人は複数の集団に属している。各個人は、親や子として家族に所属する一方、学生として学校、雇用主や従業員として職場にも所属している。中には、信者として教会、ボランティアとして非営利団体に所属する者もいる。ここで、アイデンティティとは、所属する集団や組織によって求められる役割が象徴する「意味」や「意義」を指す。時として、個人は、合わせ持つ異なるアイデンティティが衝突する場面を経験する。そのような衝突があるとき、優先されるアイデンティティには「顕著性」があると言われる。「アイデンティティ

の顕著性」という概念が、ホスト社会における少数派宗教行動を分析するため、容易に適用されうることは明らかであろう。

　日本人としてのアイデンティティに付随するのは、言うまでもなく、日本文化が求める一定の行動様式である。「文化」の普遍的な定義はないが、「集団によって広く共有される信条、世界観、価値、意味、制度、行動様式の集合」と考えられよう。文化の特徴として、それが「社会化」と呼ばれる過程を通じて学習されることにより、一世代から次世代に継承されること、その結果、持続性があることが言える。同時に、技術革新や社会環境の変化により、時代にそぐわなくなった側面は変革を迫られる。日本文化は、今まさに、こうした変革の時代に置かれているのである。日本の末日聖徒が社会で経験する衝突が稀だという事実は、この文脈で理解することもできよう。

　以下、本研究から得られた結論の要点を、掻い摘んでまとめてみよう。

日本の末日聖徒

- 大多数の回答者は、末日聖徒のアイデンティティを優先すべく生活を営んでいる。およそ84％（48％）は、教会堂から30分（15分）以内に居住していると回答した。既婚者、離婚者、寡婦・寡夫に質問したところ、男性の97％、女性の88％が、配偶者は教会員である（あった）と回答した。

- ファミリーサイズは、宗教、文化、それぞれの影響を受けている。社会全体の傾向に対応して、末日聖徒女性が生む子供の数は、40歳以上の平均2.8人から、40歳未満の平均1.9人に減っているが、それでも社会平均（1.3人）より0.6人ほど多い。男性の72％、女性の57％は、3人以上の子供がいると回答した。

- 社会の高齢化は、末日聖徒にも影響を与えている。回答者の41.5％が60歳以上の高齢者であった。これは、おおむね、日本における高齢者の割合に相当する。

- 回答者の72％（40歳未満に限ると83％）は、13年以上の教育を受けており、日本社会の平均修業年数を上回ると推測される。ただし、現在、大学や専門学校に進む高校卒業生の割合は80％を超えており、今後、末日聖徒が有する教育上の優越性は縮小するであろう。

- 伝道経験を除外しても、末日聖徒の22％（40歳未満女性に限ると35％）は、外国に1年以上居住した経験があると回答した。日本全体について同様な統計は存在しないが、大きく見積もっても、6〜9％程度だと推測される。平均的末日聖徒は、平均的日本人よりも、国際経験が豊かである。

- 少数派宗教として、末日聖徒イエス・キリスト教会が、社会的不適合者をひきつけるという考えは支持されない。中学高校時代に「自分は学友とあまり打ち解けられなかった」と回答した者は、全体の12％に過ぎなかった。どちらかと言えば、末日聖徒になる者は社交性に富んでいる。

改宗

- 改宗者のおよそ90％は、30歳前に入会している（平均年齢は22.1歳）。さらに、30％前後は、改宗前、キリスト教について何らかの知識を有していた。改宗の平均年齢と文化的連続性に関するこれらの結果は、宗教社会学、経済学の文献と整合的である。ただし、改宗年齢は、近年、われわれが理解しない理由によって上昇傾向にある。文化的連続性の観点からは、今後、家族歴史を含め、日本文化と共有する側面を重視することが、教会発展の鍵となるであろう。

- 末日聖徒の87％は、宣教師が改宗過程で重要な役割を果たしたと回答した。一方、親族を除く教会員が重要な役割を果たしたと回答したのは、学友や同僚など合わせても、20％に満たなかった（複数回答可）。意見欄を読むと、改宗者の心を動かしたのは、特別な能力や技量ではなく、宣教師の「模範」や会員の「歓迎の言葉」であったことが察せられる。

- 改宗に影響した最重要教義として、末日聖徒の52％が「救いの計画」を挙げた。「ジョセフ・スミスの経験談」を挙げたのは33％であった。

- 末日聖徒の37％は、改宗の際、何も反対を経験しなかったと回答したが、ほぼ同数の36％は、家族の反対が最大の障壁であったと回答した。これは、大多数が若くして改宗したことに関係している。30歳以上で改宗した男性の場合、家族の反対を経験した者はいない。しかし、女性では、40歳、50歳代で改宗した場合でも、家族の反対を経験した者が少なからずいた。

政治社会観

- 主義、主張として、末日聖徒の標榜する立場は社会の両極端を含み、多様性に富んでいる。回答者に、思想的傾向を自己評価してもらったところ、平均は、保守・革新（進歩）のほぼ中間であった。末日聖徒は、日本社会の下部集団では決してなく、その縮図なのである。

- 特定の政治問題では、末日聖徒の65％は強い日米同盟を支持し、36％は憲法第9条の改正（自衛権の成文化）を支持した。全国世論調査によって

得られる割合とさほど異ならない。ただし、無党派の割合（54％）は全国調査のそれ（43％）よりも大きく、その分、自民党支持者の割合は小さい。

- 直近の社会問題では、全国平均よりも保守的な傾向がみられる。同性婚の合法化は、あくまでも市民権の問題として提起したにもかかわらず、全国世論調査の65％に対し、末日聖徒の間では、支持者の割合は24％に過ぎなかった。同様に、選択的夫婦別姓制度を支持する割合は、全国調査の67％に対し、36％であった。しかしながら、例外として、積極的な移民政策を支持する割合は、全国調査の33～40％に対し、末日聖徒の間では41％であった。

信仰と宗教実践

- 回答者のほぼ100％は、神の存在に対し大きな疑問を抱かず、末日聖徒の教えのほぼすべてを受け入れている。およそ90％は、自分が宗教の実践において家族や同僚に容認されていると感じており、信仰を実践することに何ら抵抗を感じていない。さらに、90％前後が、末日聖徒に求められる外形的な宗教規範（「安息日」「知恵の言葉」「純潔の律法」など）を厳格に順守している。

- 末日聖徒イエス・キリスト教会は、中央集権的な組織であり、地元に認められた文化適応の余地は限定的である。これは、必要な文化適応が、たとえば職業選択など、個人レベルで起こることを意味する。定義いかんで、末日聖徒の28～42％が専門職についていると推測されるが、これは日本社会における割合（18％）と比べてきわめて高い。60％以上は、安息日の教会に出席できるかどうかが、職業選択の決め手の一つであったと述べている。

- 長期的な人間関係の構築も、広義の文化適応である。軋轢の背後には、往々にして、人間関係の匿名性があるからである。たとえば、飲酒や喫茶に関しては、家族において軋轢を頻繁に経験する者は全体の2％程度であるが、家族外では13％まで上昇する。職場においても軋轢が比較的稀なのは、長期的関係を築くことで、人間関係から匿名性を取り除くことが影響していると考えられる。

- 霊的な権威の源をどこに置くかについて、日本の末日聖徒の73％（男性68％、女性79％）は、個人の啓示よりも、神権指導者に優先順位を与えた。同様な傾向は、米国の末日聖徒でも見られるが、日本よりも個人の啓示に重きを置く傾向が強い。米国で神権指導者に優先順位を与える末日聖徒

の割合は、男性で62％（日本では68％）、女性で69％（日本では79％）であった。[1]

- 回答者の大多数は、教会における女性の地位を是認した。この傾向は、とくに女性で顕著である。神権が与えられていないことに抵抗を感じる女性は、全体の1％未満であり、教会で女性の声が十分に反映されていないと考える女性は、全体の7％に過ぎなかった。同様な傾向は、米国の末日聖徒の間でも見られるが、日本ほど極端ではない。教会における女性の地位に抵抗を感じる米国女性の割合は、最低週1回教会に出席する者に限ってみると、日本の1％未満に対し、18％であった。同様に、女性の声が反映されていないと感じる女性も、日本の6％に対し、18％であった。

- 宗教的確信や献身の強さにおいて、日本の末日聖徒は米国の末日聖徒に勝っているようにも思える。平均的な実践度や献身度を数値化すると、日本の方がおおむね10％ほど高い。この事実の解釈には注意を要する。日米差は、おそらく、活発率の差を反映しているのであろう。仮に日本の活発率を20％だとすると、米国では、地域によって、40〜60％程度だと想定される。日本の2〜3倍もする出席率の中には、多様な人々が含まれる。日本では、高度に献身的な会員以外、そもそも教会に出席していないのである。

組織的文化適応と教会の将来

- 十分な文化適応なくして、外来宗教がホスト社会に広く受け入れられることはない。末日聖徒イエス・キリスト教会が、組織的な文化適応を目指すべきかについては、様々な意見がある。本調査では、教会運営が日本文化に十分な配慮をしているかどうか問うた。平均的な回答は、イエスとノーのほぼ中間であった（5項目の平均値は、1〜5の尺度で3.6）。これをもって、日本の平均的末日聖徒が教会運営の現状を是認していると解釈するのは不適切だろう。教会の使命や将来の成長を考えるとき、活発会員の半数が現状を否認していることに重きを置かなければならない。活発会員の半数が否認しているのであれば、改宗しながら、教会を欠席している80％の人々は、どう考えているのだろうか。

- 日本において、末日聖徒イエス・キリスト教会は、少子高齢化および無宗教化というチャレンジに直面している。日本の総人口は2008年ピークに

---

1. 本研究では、日米比較にあたり、相互比較性を確保するため、週1回以上教会に出席する末日聖徒のみを、男女別に比較した。

達した後、年率0.2％ほどの速度で縮小している。主要キリスト教諸派を含む、非伝統的宗教団体の信者数も絶対的な減少を経験している。末日聖徒イエス・キリスト教会が目に見える会員数の減少を経験していないのは、現存会員の自然減を伝道活動によって得られる新会員が埋め合わせしてきたからである。今後、日本に割り当てられる宣教師数に大きな増加が見込まれないとすれば、会員の絶対数が今後減少する可能性も否定できない。そうなれば、全国津々浦々、複数ユニットから成るステークという形態で教会を運営していくことは困難になる。

- そうした事態は、不可避ではない。世俗化された社会においても、宗教の道を求める者は一定数いるはずである。そのような求道者にいかに訴え、改宗者をいかに定着させるかは、教会の選択の範囲にある。日本社会においては、より多様性を尊重する文化が形成されつつある。若者が働き方に対して持つ意識も変化しつつある。日本社会は、末日聖徒イエス・キリスト教会に対して、チャレンジと同時に、飛躍するチャンスも提供しているのである。

- このチャンスに応じるため、教会には、思慮分別のある組織的な文化適応が求められよう。経済学用語で表現すれば、より多くの日本人が教会活動に参加できるよう、改宗と定着の費用を下げる取り組みが求められるのである。われわれは、社会科学者として、具体的な提言をする立場にない。一つだけ言えることは、文化適応の問題に関しては、自然進化的な側面もあり、「解答」は集団の構成員に広く分散されていることである。一握りの人間が、トップダウンで決める類の問題ではない。文化適応が、広く支持され、長く持続するには、あらゆる利害関係者と幅広く協議した結果に基づくものでなければならない。

図表のタイトルおよび凡例項目

（断りのない限り、凡例は、上から下、左から右に表示）

第1章

表1-1. エンダウメントを受けた回答者（全回答者に対する割合、％）

受けている、受けていない、合計

表1-2. 回答者の専任伝道経験（各集団別全回答者に対する割合、％）

（左から）有経験（うち外国伝道）、無経験、合計
（上から）全回答者、40歳未満全員、全男性、40歳未満男性、全女性、40歳未満女性

表1-3. 婚姻状況の日米比較（各集団別全回答者に対する割合、％）

（左から）日本全回答者、日本男性、日本女性、米国全回答者、米国男性、米国女性
（上から）既婚者、離婚者、寡婦・寡夫、未婚者、その他（米国のみ）、合計
（注）以下、日米比較は、相互比較性を確保するため、両国とも、最低週1回教会に出席する末日聖徒に限り、加えて男女別に比較する。

図1-1. 日本における主要キリスト教派信者数（2021年、千人）

カトリック教会、エホバの証人、末日聖徒、日本基督教団、聖公会、バプテスト教会、ルーテル教会

図1-2. 末日聖徒イエス・キリスト教会の会員および伝道部数（1973〜2021年）

棒グラフ：会員数（千人）、線グラフ：伝道部数（右縦軸）

図1-3. 末日聖徒イエス・キリスト教会のユニットおよびステーク数（1973〜2021 年）

棒グラフ：ユニット数、線グラフ：ステーク数（右縦軸）

図1-4. 日本における非伝統的宗教信者数（1971〜2021年、千人）

黒線：正統派キリスト教信者、灰色線：非仏教・非神道信者（右縦軸）
（注）ここでは、「正統派キリスト教」とは、戦前にルーツを有する教派で、カトリック中央協議会、日本聖公会、日本基督教団、日本福音ルーテル教会、日本バプテスト連盟の5宗教法人、「非仏教・非神道」とは、文化庁『宗教年鑑』において「諸教」と位置付けられている宗教法人を意味する。

図1-5. 回答者の男女別構成比（%）

黒：男性、灰色：女性

図1-6. 回答者の年齢別構成比（対各集団別全回答者、%）

（それぞれ、左から）全回答者、男性、女性

図1-7. 回答者の地域別構成比（%）

北海道、東北、北関東、東京、南関東、東海、北陸、近畿、中国、四国、九州、沖縄

図1-8. 回答者の教会出席頻度（全回答者に対する各集団の割合、%）

週2回以上、週1回程度、月1〜2回、年数回、稀に出席、出席せず

図1-9. 回答者の会員歴（各集団別全回答者に対する割合、%）

全回答者、40歳未満全員、全男性、40歳未満男性、全女性、40歳未満女性
（それぞれ、上から）改宗者、2世会員、3世会員

図1-10. 会員歴の日米比較（各集団別全回答者に対する改宗者の割合、%）

全回答者、男性、女性
黒：日本、灰色：米国

図1-11. 回答者の婚姻状況（各集団別全回答者に対する割合、%）

既婚者、寡婦・寡夫、離婚者、未婚者
（それぞれ、上から）全回答者、男性、女性

図1-12. 回答者の雇用状況（各集団別全回答者に対する割合、%）

常勤、専業主婦、定時制、退職者、失業者、学生
（それぞれ、上から）全回答者、全男性、全女性、40歳未満女性

第2章

表2-1. 日本女性が生む子供数、1980年代と2021年の比較（各集団別全回答者に対する割合、%）

（左から）子供数、全女性（1981〜84年）、末日聖徒女性（1981〜84年）、末日聖徒女性（本調査、2021年）
（上から）なし、1人、2人、3人以上、平均数（括弧内、40歳以上、40歳未満）

表2-2. 回答者の社交性：「中学高校時代の友人関係を思い出すとき、学友たちとどれほど打ち解けられましたか」（各集団別の全回答者に対する割合、%）

（左から）1.あまりできず、2.多少、3.かなり、4.非常によく、合計、平均値
（上から）全回答者、男性、女性、全改宗者、2世・3世会員

表2-3. 回答者の政治観（各集団別全回答者に対する割合、%）

（左から）1.賛成しない、2．どちらかというと賛成しない、3．どちらとも言えない、4．どちらかというと賛成する、5．賛成する、合計、平均値
（上から）
「末日聖徒は、福音にそった価値観を社会で実現するため、政治に積極的に関与すべきだ」
「わたしは、自衛のための武力保持を成文化するため、日本国憲法第9条の改定を支持する」
「わたしは、東アジアにおける平和を確保する手段として、強い日米安保同盟を支持する」
（それぞれ、上から）全回答者、男性、女性

表2-4. 回答者の社会観（各集団別全回答者に対する割合、%）

（左から）1.賛成しない、2．どちらかというと賛成しない、3．どちらとも言えない、4．どちらかというと賛成する、5．賛成する、合計、平均値
（上から）
「わたしは女性が天皇になるのを支持する」
「わたしは、基本的人権として、男女平等を支持する」
「わたしは、教義的には抵抗があるが、人権としての同性婚を支持する」
「わたしは、選択制夫婦別姓制度を支持する」
（それぞれ、上から）全回答者、男性、女性

表2-5.　回答者の移民および難民政策に関する見解（各集団別全回答者に対する割合、％）

（左から）1.賛成しない、2.　どちらかというと賛成しない、3.　どちらとも言えない、4.どちらかというと賛成する、5.賛成する、合計、平均値
（上から）
「わたしは、日本社会がより多くの移民を受け入れることを支持する」
「日本はより多くの難民を受け入れるべきである」
（それぞれ、上から）全回答者、男性、女性

図2-1.　現在および以前の配偶者の教会籍（各集団別全回答者に対する割合、％）

全回答者、男性、女性
黒：末日聖徒、灰色：非末日聖徒

図2-2.回答者の子供数（各集団別全回答者に対する割合、％）

なし、1人、2人、3人、4人、5人、6人以上
黒：男性、灰色：女性

図2-3.回答者の修学年数（各集団別全回答者に対する13年以上修業者の割合、％）

全男性、全女性、40歳未満男性、40歳未満女性、40〜59歳男性、40〜59歳女性
灰色：学部・専門学校、黒：大学院

図2-4.修学年数の日米比較（各集団別全回答者に対する割合、％）

日本男性、米国男性、日本女性、米国女性
灰色：学部・専門学校、黒：大学院

図2-5.海外に1年以上居住した回答者（各集団別全回答者に対する居住経験者の割合、％）

全回答者、40歳未満全員、男性、40歳未満男性、女性、40歳未満女性
黒：米国、灰色：その他外国

図2-6.教会における友人関係（各集団別全回答者に対する割合、％）

教会外より教会内で友人多し、教会で友人多くあり、教会で親しい友人あり、教会の友人に教会外で会わず、教会で友人なし
白：全員、黒：男性、灰色：女性

図2-7. 回答者の政治社会観（各集団別全回答者に対する割合、％）

1.保守的、2.　どちらかというと保守的、3.　保守的でも進歩（革新）的でもない、4. どちらかというと進歩（革新）的、5. 進歩（革新）的、その他
（それぞれ、上から）全回答者、男性、女性

図2-8. 回答者の政党支持率、対全国比較（対各調査別全回答者、％）

無党派、自由民主党、立憲民主党、維新の会
（それぞれ、左から）末日聖徒（本調査）、朝日全国調査、NHK全国調査

図2-9. 回答者の安全保障に関する見解、対全国比較（各調査別全回答者に対する支持者の割合、％）

憲法第9条の改正、堅固な日米同盟
（それぞれ、左から）末日聖徒（本調査）、朝日全国調査、NHK全国調査

図2-10. 回答者の直近社会問題に関する見解、対全国比較（各調査別全回答者に対する支持者の割合、％）

女性天皇、同性婚、選択的夫婦別姓制度、積極的な移民政策
（それぞれ、左から）末日聖徒（本調査）、朝日全国調査、NHK全国調査

第3章

表3-1. 改宗者構成比の推移

（左から）1951〜80年の改宗者、1981〜2020年の改宗者、うち1981〜2000年の改宗者、うち2001〜20年の改宗者
（上から）男女比（％男性）、平均改宗年齢、13年以上教育修業者の割合（％）、思想傾向平均値、社交性平均値
（注）思考傾向平均値とは、図2-7において、「1＝保守的〜5＝進歩（革新）的」の尺度で自己評価を平均値化したもの。社交性平均値とは、表2-2において、「1＝あまりできず〜5＝非常によく」の尺度で「中学高校時代、学友たちとどれほど打ち解けられたか」への回答を平均値化したもの。

図3-1. 回答者の改宗暦年（各集団別全回答者に対する各時代の割合、％）

1951〜60年、1961〜70年、1971〜80年、1981〜90年、1991〜2000年、2001〜10年、2011〜20年
（それぞれ、上から）全回答者、男性、女性

図3-2. 回答者の改宗年齢（各集団別全回答者に対する各年齢層の割合、％）

20歳未満、20〜29歳、30〜39歳、40〜49歳、50〜59歳、60歳以上
（それぞれ、上から）全回答者、男性、女性

図3-3. 改宗前の知識と経験（各集団別全回答者に対する割合、％）

聖書の知識、イエス・キリストの知識、他キリスト教派、末日聖徒の友人・同僚、マスコミ等メディアを通した認識
（それぞれ、上から）全回答者、男性、女性

図3-4. 改宗の助けとなった教義や教え（各集団別全回答者に対する割合、％）

救いの計画、ジョセフ・スミス、家族・永遠の家族、祈り・個人の啓示、モルモン書、イエス・キリストと贖い、教会の社交活動、生ける預言者、その他
（それぞれ、上から）全回答者、男性、女性

図3-5. 改宗に特別な役割を果たした人物（各集団別全回答者に対する割合、％）

宣教師、学友、配偶者・家族、職場の同僚、隣人、その他
（それぞれ、上から）全回答者、男性、女性

図3-6. 日本における末日聖徒宣教師数（1974〜2021年）

黒：日本人数、灰色：外国人数、線グラフ：日本人比率（％、右縦軸）

図3-7. 改宗時に経験した最大の障壁（各集団別全回答者に対する経験者の割合、％）

家族の反対、知恵の言葉、安息日、什分の一、友人の反対、なし、その他
（それぞれ、上から）全回答者、男性、女性

図3-8. 性別および年齢別でみた「家族の反対」（各集団別全回答者に対する経験者の割合、％）

全回答者、20歳未満、20〜29歳、30〜39歳、40歳以上
（それぞれ、左から）全回答者、男性、女性

> 図3-9. 改宗以前の知識と経験の変遷（各集団別全回答者に対する該当者の割合、%）

聖書の知識、イエス・キリストの知識、他キリスト教派、末日聖徒の友人・同僚、マスコミ等メディアを通した認識

（それぞれ、左から）1951〜80年の改宗者、1981〜2000年の改宗者、2001〜20年の改宗者

第4章

> 表4-1. 自分が末日聖徒であることについて一番喜びを感じる部分（該当項目を3つまで選択、各集団別全回答者に対する割合、%）

（左から）全回答者、40歳未満全員、全男性、40歳未満男性、全女性、40歳未満女性

（上から）

A.救い主イエス・キリストに焦点を置いた生活

B.家族は永遠でありえるという知識

C.今日、預言者が地上にいるという安心

D.教会によって提供される隣人に奉仕する機会

E.知恵の言葉を守ることによって依存症を避けられること

F.互いを支え合う共同体を教会で肌に感じること

G.困難な時に信仰によってもたらされる平安

H.教会が子供たちや若者に重点を置くこと

I.神殿での礼拝

合計

> 表4-2. 回答者が神に抱く信仰（各集団別全回答者に対する割合、%）

（左から）全回答者、男性、女性

（上から）

A.わたしは神が存在することを知っている。まったく疑いはない。

B.わたしは多少の疑いはあるが、神の存在を心から信じる。

C.わたしは神の存在を信じるときもあれば、信じないときもある。

D.わたしは人格を持った神は信じないが、ある種の崇高な力としての神を信じる。

E.わたしは神が存在するかどうか知らないし、それを知る方法があるとも信じない。

F.わたしは神の存在を信じない。

合計

表4-3. 末日聖徒教義の受容度（各集団別全回答者に対する割合、%）

（左から）全回答者、男性、女性
（上から）
A.わたしは、末日聖徒イエス・キリスト教会の教えをすべて、心から信じる。
B.わたしは、末日聖徒イエス・キリスト教会のほとんど（多く）の教えを信じる。
C.末日聖徒イエス・キリスト教会の教えのいくつかは、信じるのが難しい。
D.末日聖徒イエス・キリスト教会の教えのほとんど（多く）は、信じるのが難しい。
E.わたしは、末日聖徒イエス・キリスト教会の教えを信じない。
合計

表4-4. 霊的権威の優越性に関する信条（各集団別全回答者に対する割合、%）

（左から）全回答者、40歳未満全員、全男性、40歳未満男性、全女性、40歳未満女性
（上から）
A.末日聖徒は、理由を理解できなくても、神権指導者の勧告に従うべきである。
B.末日聖徒は、結果的に神権指導者の勧告に反することになっても、祈りを通して個人の啓示を求め、個人の啓示に従って行動すべきである。
合計

表4-5. 回答者の宗教実践度（各集団別全回答者に対する割合、%）

（左から）1.ほとんどせず、2.多少、3.かなり、4.ほぼ完全、合計、平均値
（上から）毎日の祈り、聖典の勉強、神殿参入、会員伝道、教会奉仕
（それぞれ、上から）全回答者、男性、女性

表4-6. 回答者の「知恵の言葉」実践度（各集団別全回答者に対する割合、%）

（左から）1.ほとんどせず、2.多少、3.かなり、4.ほぼ完全、合計、平均値
（上から）緑茶、コーヒー・紅茶、タバコ、アルコール飲料
（それぞれ、上から）全回答者、男性、女性

表4-7. 回答者の「純潔の律法」「什分の一」実践度（各集団別全回答者に対する割合、%）

（左から）1.ほとんどせず、2.多少、3.かなり、4.ほぼ完全、合計、平均値
（上から）純潔の律法、什分の一
（それぞれ、上から）全回答者、男性、女性

表4-8. 回答者の女性と神権に関する見解（各集団別の全回答者に対する割合、％）

（左から）1.賛成しない、2.どちらかというと賛成しない、3.どちらとも言えない、4.どちらかというと賛成する、5.賛成する、合計、平均値
（上から）
A.日本では堕胎は合法的で広く行われているが、わたしは、教会が認める場合（近親相姦や強姦等）を除き、堕胎が神の教えに反すると信じる。
B.末日聖徒イエス・キリスト教会では、女性の声が十分に反映されているとは言えない。
C.時々、女性に神権が与えられていないことに、抵抗を感じることがある。
（それぞれ、上から）全回答者、男性、女性

図4-1. 回答者が集うユニットの出席者数（全回答者の割合、％）

25人未満、25〜49人、50〜74人、75〜99人、100〜149人、150人以上

図4-2. 教会堂までの交通手段（全回答者の割合、％）

自家用車、自転車、鉄道、徒歩、バス・路面電車、その他

図4-3. 性別、地域別、年齢別でみた自家用車使用者（全回答者に対する割合、％）

男性、女性、北海道、東北、北関東、東京、南関東、東海、北陸、近畿、中国、四国、九州、沖縄、70歳以上、60歳以上、50歳以上、40歳以上、30歳以上、30歳未満

図4-4. 回答者が集う教会堂までの所要時間（全回答者の割合、％）

15分以下、16〜30分、31〜60分、1時間以上

図4-5. 地域別でみた教会堂までの平均所要時間（各集団別全回答者に対する割合、％）

北海道、東北、北関東、東京、南関東、東海、北陸、近畿、中国、四国、九州、沖縄
（注）「1=1〜15分、2=16〜30分、3=31〜45分、4=46〜60分、5=61分以上」を尺度とした地域別平均値。

図4-6. 自分が末日聖徒であることについて一番喜びを感じる部分―日米比較（各集団別全回答者に対する割合、%）

B.永遠の家族、A.イエス・キリストに置かれた焦点、G.信仰による平安、C.生ける預言者、F.強い共同体
（それぞれ、上から）日本男性、米国男性、日本女性、米国女性

図4-7. 神に抱く信仰―日米比較（各集団別全回答者に対する割合、%）

日本男性、米国男性、日本女性、米国女性
灰色：わたしは多少の疑いはあるが、神の存在を心から信じる。
黒：わたしは神が存在することを知っている。まったく疑いはない。

図4-8. 末日聖徒教義の受容度―日米比較（各集団別全回答者に対する割合、%）

日本男性、米国男性、日本女性、米国女性
（それぞれ、下から）
その他
「わたしは、末日聖徒イエス・キリスト教会の教えをすべて、心から信じる」
「わたしは、末日聖徒イエス・キリスト教会のほとんど（または多く）の教えを信じる」

図4-9. 個人の啓示よりも神権指導者に優越性を与える末日聖徒（各集団別全回答者に対する割合、%）

全回答者、改宗者、2・3世会員、週最低1回教会に集わない者、専任宣教師経験のない者、70歳以上の者、大学院教育を受けた者

図4-10. 霊的権威の優越性に関する信条―日米比較（各集団別全回答者に対する割合、%）

A.神権指導者、B.個人の啓示
（それぞれ、上から）日本男性、米国男性、日本女性、米国女性

図4-11. 個人の宗教実践度―日米比較（各集団別全回答者に対する実践者の割合、%）

毎日の祈り、聖典の勉強、会員伝道、教会奉仕
（それぞれ、上から）日本男性、米国男性、日本女性、米国女性
（注）実践者とは、日本の場合、「かなり」「ほぼ完全」と答えた者、米国の場合、「毎日」あるいは「最低週1回」と答えた者を意味する。

図4-12.「知恵の言葉」実践度―日米比較（各集団別全回答者に対する実践者の割合、%）

緑茶、コーヒー・紅茶、タバコ、アルコール飲料
（それぞれ、上から）日本男性、米国男性、日本女性、米国女性
（注）実践者とは、日本の場合、「かなり」「ほぼ完全」と答えた者、米国の場合、過去6カ月間当該物質の消費を控えた者を意味する。

図4-13.「什分の一」実践度―日米比較（各集団別全回答者に対する実践者の割合、%）

日本男性、米国男性、日本女性、米国女性
（注）実践者とは、日本の場合、「かなり」「ほぼ完全」と答えた者、米国の場合、税後・税前を問わず、所得に対して10%を「定期的に」納めた者を意味する。

図4-14. 堕胎の否認―日米比較（各集団別全回答者に対する否認者の割合、%）

日本男性、米国男性、日本女性、米国女性
（注）否認者とは、日本の場合、「神の教えに反する」と考えた者、米国では、「不道徳的」と考えた者を意味する。

図4-15. 教会における女性と神権に関する見解―日米比較（各集団別全回答者に対する割合、%）

A（上の図）：末日聖徒イエス・キリスト教会では、女性の声が十分に反映されてない。
B（下の図）：時々、女性に神権が与えられていないことに、抵抗を感じることがある。
（それぞれの図について、左から）日本男性、米国男性、日本女性、米国女性
黒：賛成する、灰色：賛成しない

第5章

表5-1. 日本社会と末日聖徒（全回答者に対する割合、%）

（左から）1.賛成しない、2. どちらかというと賛成しない、3.どちらとも言えない、4. どちらかというと賛成する、5.賛成する、合計、平均値
（上から）
A.末日聖徒は、良き隣人、同僚として、好意的に思われている。
B.末日聖徒は、日本ではあまり知られていない。人々は末日聖徒に関心を払わない。
C.わたしの友人や同僚は、わたしが末日聖徒として選ぶ選択を尊重してくれる。
D.わたしの家族や親族は、わたしが末日聖徒として選ぶ選択を尊重してくれる。
E.わたしは、周りの人と異なることがあっても、気兼ねなく自分の信仰を実践している。

表5-2.「あなたは、自分が末日聖徒イエス・キリスト教会の会員であると認めるとき、気まずく思うことはありますか」（各集団別全回答者に対する割合、%）

（左から）全回答者、活発回答者、全男性、活発男性、全女性、活発女性
（上から）まったくない、時々、頻繁に、常に、合計
（注）ここでは、便宜上、「活発」とは「週1回以上教会に出席する者」を意味する。

表5-3. 職業・職種別にみた軋轢—個人の持つ家族や社会との関係

（左から）「1=なし、2=稀、3=時々、4=常に」の尺度で数値化した軋轢値：平均値、知恵の言葉、教会出席、（右端）自己社会的受容感
（上から）全回答者、自営業、公共部門、外資系、他民間部門、専門職、営業、小売およびサービス・娯楽、経営・管理職、教育、建設・製造
（注）自己社会的受容感とは、表5-1において、「1=賛成しない〜5=賛成する」の尺度により、「わたしの友人や同僚は、わたしが末日聖徒として選ぶ選択を尊重してくれる」に対する同意度を数値化したもの。

表5-4. 青少年定着の5大障壁（3つまで選択可能、全回答者に対する各障壁を選んだ者の割合、%）

部活動、友人関係、日曜日の学校行事、緑茶、大学受験

図5-1. 家族内で経験する軋轢（全回答者に対する経験者の割合、%）

仏壇、法事、日曜日の行事、神道関係、緑茶、コーヒー・紅茶、アルコール
黒：頻繁、灰色：時々

図5-2. 家族内で経験する軋轢—個人が持つ家族・社会との関係（「1＝なし、2＝稀、3＝時々、4＝常に」の尺度で数値化した軋轢度）

仏壇、法事、日曜日の行事、神道関係、緑茶、コーヒー・紅茶、アルコール
棒グラフ（濃灰色）：表5-1において「D.　わたしの家族や親族は、わたしが末日聖徒として選ぶ選択を尊重してくれる」に（どちらかというと）賛成しなかった者
棒グラフ（薄灰色）：表5-1において「E.　わたしは、周りの人と異なることがあっても、気兼ねなく自分の信仰を実践している」に（どちらかというと）賛成しなかった者
線グラフ：全回答者の平均軋轢値

図5-3. 1週間当たり平均的残業時間（それぞれの回答者数）

なし、5時間まで、10時間まで、20時間まで、30時間まで、30時間以上
黒：給与所得者、灰色：自営業者

図5-4. 職場や社会で経験する軋轢（全回答者に対する経験者の割合、％）

安息日の順守、週日の教会活動、酒の提供される場での接待等、週日夜の付き合い、緑茶、コーヒー・紅茶
黒：頻繁、灰色：時々

図5-5. 職場や社会で経験する軋轢—個人が持つ家族や社会との関係
（「1＝なし、2＝稀、3＝時々、4＝常に」の尺度で数値化した軋轢度）

安息日の順守、週日の教会活動、酒の提供される場での接待等、週日夜の付き合い、緑茶、コーヒー・紅茶
棒グラフ（濃灰色）：表5-1において「C.　わたしの友人や同僚は、わたしが末日聖徒として選ぶ選択を尊重してくれる」に（どちらかというと）賛成しなかった者
棒グラフ（薄灰色）：表5-1において「E.　わたしは、周りの人と異なることがあっても、気兼ねなく自分の信仰を実践している」に（どちらかというと）賛成しなかった者
線グラフ：全回答者の平均軋轢値

図5-6. 職業と職種（失業者と退職者を含む全回答者に対する割合、％）

A（上の図）：職業・雇用形態（左から）公共部門、自営業（無従業員）、会社役員、自営業（経営者）、外資系、教会職員、いずれにも該当せず
B（下の図）：職種（左から）専門職、事務職、教育、経営・管理職、営業、サービス・娯楽、建設・製造、小売、その他
（注）失業・退職者の場合、失業・退職前の職業と職種について質問。

図5-7. 就職の際、一番の決め手となった理由（該当項目3つまで選択可能、全回答者に対する割合、%）

安息日、関心や能力、給料・待遇、勤務地、教会の週日活動、他に選択肢なし、知恵の言葉、その他

第6章

表6-1. 期間別でみた各人口集団の増加率（年率%）

（左から）1970～80年、1980～90年、1990～2000年、2000～10年、2010～21年
（上から）末日聖徒、カトリック教徒、日本基督教団、非仏教・非神道信者（除キリスト教徒）、日本総人口

表6-2. 末日聖徒家庭の子弟教会出席状況（各集団別全回答者に対する割合、%）

（左から）全員出席、少なくとも1人不出席、教会員子弟なし、合計
（上から）男性、女性

表6-3. 教会運営の文化適応度に関する見解（各集団別全回答者に対する割合、%）

（左から）1. 賛成しない、2. どちらかというと賛成しない、3. どちらとも言えない、4. どちらかというと賛成する、5. 賛成する、合計、平均値
（上から）
A.日本の教会は、文化的な違いにもかかわらず、米国の教会本部が作成した「手引き」に厳格に従うべきである。
B.日本の教会は、すでに教会の運営（活動、青少年プログラム、音楽等）を日本の実情に十分適応させている。
C.日曜学校や初等協会、若い男性や若い女性、神権会や扶助協会のテキストは、日本人会員の関心やニーズをよく満たしている。
D.日本の教会は、自然な日本語ではない英語用語（カタカナ表記）を過度に使用している。
E.日本の教会は、米国の教会文化を取り入れすぎている。もっと日本の文化に溶け込ませる努力をすべきである。
（それぞれ、上から）全回答者、男性、女性

図6-1. 日本の人口（1980〜2021年）

棒グラフ：総人口（千人）、線グラフ：首都圏の割合（％、右縦軸）

図6-2. 日本の出生数と合計特殊出生率（1970〜2021年）

棒グラフ：出生数（千人、右縦軸）、線グラフ：合計特殊出生率（人）

図6-3. 日本人口の年齢層別構成比（1970〜2021年、％）

（下から）0〜14歳、15〜64歳、65〜84歳、85歳以上

図6-4. 日本の製造業雇用（1980〜2021年）

棒グラフ：被雇用者数（百万人）、線グラフ：対総被雇用者比（％、右縦軸）

図6-5. 日本末日聖徒の地域間移動性（現地域での居住期間、各集団別全回答者に対する割合、％）

2年未満、3〜5年、6〜9年、10〜19年、20年以上
（それぞれ、左から）
棒グラフ：日本全国、東京および近郊
線グラフ：日本全国（40歳未満）、東京および近郊（40歳未満）

図6-6. 改宗の最大障壁（各集団別全回答者に対する割合、％）

家族の反対、なし、その他
（それぞれ、左から）1951〜80年の改宗者、1981〜2000年の改宗者、2001〜20年の改宗者

図6-7. 教会定着の障壁（全回答者に対する割合、％）

労働慣行、友人関係、家族関係、教育制度、教会の戒め、日本文化、知恵の言葉
（それぞれ、上から）最大の障壁、2番目の障壁、3番目の障壁

図6-8.「自分が末日聖徒イエス・キリスト教会の会員であると認めるとき、気まずく思うことがある」（各集団別全回答者に対する割合、％）

まったくない、時々、頻繁に、常に
黒：40歳以上、灰色：40歳未満

図6-9. 年代別でみた家族および職場や社会で経験する軋轢(各集団別全回答者に対する「時々、頻繁」経験者の割合、%)

黒:40歳以上、灰色:40歳未満
A(上の図):家族(左から)仏壇、法事、日曜日の行事、神道関係、緑茶、コーヒー・紅茶、アルコール
B(下の図):職場や社会(左から)安息日の順守、週日の教会活動、酒の提供される場での接待等、週日夜の付き合い、緑茶、コーヒー・紅茶

図6-10. 年代別でみた教会定着の障壁(各集団別全回答者に対する割合、%)

(上から)友人関係(40歳以上)、友人関係(40歳未満)、教育制度(40歳以上)、教育制度(40歳未満)
(それぞれ、左から)最重要、2番目に重要、3番目に重要

図6-11. 日本の労働力人口(1980〜2021年、百万人)

黒:男性、灰色:女性

図6-12. 日本における外国人(1985〜2019年)

棒グラフ:短期訪問者(千人)、線グラフ:高等教育機関在籍学生(人、右縦軸)

図6-13. 地域別にみた日本の外国籍住民(1980〜2021年、全人口に対する割合、%)

黒線:日本全国、点線:東京、灰色線:首都圏

図6-14. 日本における国際結婚(1970〜2020年)

棒グラフ:全結婚数(千人)、線グラフ:うち国際結婚(%、右縦軸)
(注)ここでは、国際結婚とは、配偶者のいずれかが外国籍である婚姻関係を意味する。

図6-15. 日本の仏教寺院数(1980〜2021年)

棒グラフ:総数、線グラフ:うち浄土真宗西本願寺系(右縦軸)

図6-16. 働き盛り世代の男性転職率(1984〜2021年、過去12か月に転職した者が全体に占める割合、%)

実線:25〜34歳、点線:35〜44歳

日本語あとがき

　本書「*Unique But Not Different*」は、日本の末日聖徒が、何を信じ、いかに宗教を実践しているのかを理解する試みである。本研究は日本を対象にしているが、その手法や結論は、末日聖徒が宗教的少数派として、新たなアイデンティティ（自我同一性）を身につけることを求められるいかなる社会にも適応されうる。本研究は、少数派宗教行動に接近するための、一般的分析方法を提供するからである。社会科学的接近を用いて、米国外（それも非キリスト教国家）に住む末日聖徒が、いかに新たな宗教的アイデンティティを受け入れ、いかにホスト社会との間に生じうる軋轢を管理するに至るかを理解することが、われわれの目的である。

　われわれは、以前、メリサ・イノウエとロリー・マフリー＝キップが指揮する「アジア地域における末日聖徒の宗教行動に関する研究プロジェクト」に参加したが、本書は、当プロジェクトのために実施したサーベイ（アンケート）調査から派生したものである。質問を作成する過程で、このような調査がいかに時間および労働集約的であり、同様な調査を再度実施することが非現実であることが明白になった。すなわち、このような機会は一度しかないのである。そこで、プロジェクトが要求する以上の質問を問うことにより、与えられた一度の機会を最大限活用することにした。サーベイ調査では、質問の数があまり多くなると、回答率が低下することが知られている。われわれは、敢えて、そのリスクを負うことにしたのである。本書は、この決断の果実である。

　サーベイは、メーガン・レイノックの責任で、2021年10月から11月にかけて実施された。レイノックが責任を負ったのは、日本との関係が限定的であるため、サーベイ自体に確保されている匿名性に、さらなる信頼を与えるためである。おもにソーシャルネットワークを通して実施したのであるが、あまり多くの方は参加して下さらないのではないかという当初の危惧に反して、（質問次第で）440から530ばかりの回答を得ることができた。これは統計の信憑性の観点から、きわめて良い結果である。本書は、レイノックのみがアクセスを有する原データの集計結果に基づいて執筆された。第3章はコナン・グレームスが、残りは高木信二が草稿したが、その後、共同で推敲したので、最終稿には共著者すべての見解が正確に反映されている。われわれは、サーベイの内容および本書にて表した意見、解釈、ありうべき誤りに対して連帯責任を負う。

　この研究は、多くの方々の協力なくして完成させることはできなかった。まず、過剰なほどの質問に答えてくださった回答者の方々に感謝を申し上げなければならない。意見欄では、何人かの方が、サーベイを通して日本の末日聖徒を理解しようとする、われわれの試みに感謝してくださった。多くの友人は、サーベイを一人でも多くの方に届けるため、時間と協力を惜しみなく提供してくださった。すべての名前を挙げることは不可能であるが、ここではとくに、天野昭、井上龍一、折戸亜希子、坂田浩美、高岩亜輝子、田中宏二、中村晴兆、沼野治郎、水野祐司、望月孝則、守谷歓二、山田隆司、渡壁愛弓諸氏のお名前を挙げて、謝辞を申し上げる。最後に、ジャナ・リース、ベンジャミン・ノールには、米国の末日聖徒を対象としたサーベイの未公表データを提供していただいた。この場を借りて、両氏に謝辞を申し上げる。

2023年1月

高木信二
コナン・グレームス
メーガン・レイノック

Index

About the Authors

Shinji Takagi (MTS, Mediterranean and Near Eastern Studies, Vanderbilt Divinity School; PhD, Economics, University of Rochester) is professor emeritus of economics at Osaka University, Osaka, Japan. A specialist in international economics, Professor Takagi has also held senior positions at the International Monetary Fund in Washington, DC and visiting professorships at Brigham Young and Yale Universities, among other places. The author of nearly two hundred publications in economics, he has also published more than a dozen publications in Mormon history and biblical studies, including in the *Journal of Mormon History*, B*YU Studies Quarterly*, *Biblical Theology Bulletin*, *Journal of the Bible and Its Reception*, and *Christianity & Literature*, and currently serves on the editorial advisory board of the *Mormon Studies Review*. His previous book on Japan, *The Trek East: Mormonism Meets Japan, 1902–1968* (Greg Kofford, 2016), won the Mormon History Association's biennial Best Book on International Mormonism award. He divides his time between two homes in Ashburn, Virginia, and Fukuoka, Japan, where he holds an honorary position as Distinguished Research Professor at the Asian Growth Research Institute in Kitakyushu.

Conan P. Grames is an international lawyer who has lived and worked in Boston, New York, San Francisco, Princeton (NJ), Washington, DC, and Tokyo. His twenty years' experience living in Japan was divided almost equally between his legal career and his time as a missionary for The Church of Jesus Christ of Latter-day Saints, serving as a young missionary in the Northern Far East Mission, then as president of the Japan Sendai Mission, public affairs director of the Asia North Area, and executive secretary to the Asia North Area Presidency. He is a graduate of the University of Utah and Harvard Law School. Conan is fluent in Japanese and has written and spoken extensively on the history of the Church in Japan. He and his wife, Cindy, are the parents of six married children and currently live in Draper, Utah.

Meagan Rainock (PhD, Sociology, Vanderbilt University) is a researcher versed in both qualitative and quantitative methodologies, and who focuses on the experiences of marginalized communities as they navigate social institutions. Past research projects span the topics of health and well-being, race and ethnicity, social control, and social psychology. She currently performs research and teaches college courses as a Vanderbilt-Fisk Postdoctoral Scholar in Nashville, Tennessee.

Also available from
GREG KOFFORD BOOKS

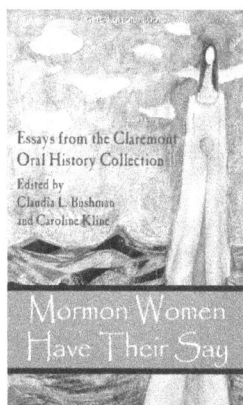

Mormon Women Have Their Say: Essays from the Claremont Oral History Collection

Edited by Claudia L. Bushman and Caroline Kline

Paperback, ISBN: 978-1-58958-494-5

The Claremont Women's Oral History Project has collected hundreds of interviews with Mormon women of various ages, experiences, and levels of activity. These interviews record the experiences of these women in their homes and family life, their church life, and their work life, in their roles as homemakers, students, missionaries, career women, single women, converts, and disaffected members. Their stories feed into and illuminate the broader narrative of LDS history and belief, filling in a large gap in Mormon history that has often neglected the lived experiences of women. This project preserves and perpetuates their voices and memories, allowing them to say share what has too often been left unspoken. The silent majority speaks in these records.

This volume is the first to explore the riches of the collection in print. A group of young scholars and others have used the interviews to better understand what Mormonism means to these women and what women mean for Mormonism. They explore those interviews through the lenses of history, doctrine, mythology, feminist theory, personal experience, and current events to help us understand what these women have to say about their own faith and lives.

Praise for *Mormon Women Have Their Say*:

"Using a variety of analytical techniques and their own savvy, the authors connect ordinary lives with enduring themes in Latter-day Saint faith and history." --Laurel Thatcher Ulrich, author of *Well-Behaved Women Seldom Make History*

"Essential. . . . In these pages, Mormon women will find *ourselves*." --Joanna Brooks, author of *The Book of Mormon Girl: A Memoir of an American Faith*

"The varieties of women's responses to the major issues in their lives will provide many surprises for the reader, who will be struck by how many different ways there are to be a thoughtful and faithful Latter-day Saint woman." --Armand Mauss, author of *All Abraham's Children: Changing Mormon Conceptions of Race and Lineage*

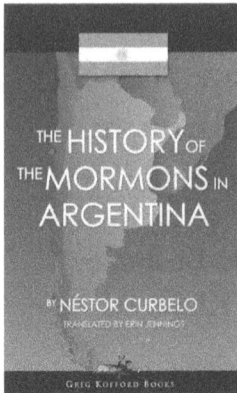

The History of Mormons in Argentina

Néstor Curbelo

English, ISBN: 978-1-58958-052-7

Originally published in Spanish, Curbelo's The History of the Mormons in Argentina is a groundbreaking book detailing the growth of the Church in this Latin American country.

Through numerous interviews and access to other primary resources, Curbelo has constructed a timeline, and then documents the story of the Church's growth. Starting with a brief discussion of Parley P. Pratt's assignment to preside over the Pacific and South American regions, continuing on with the translation of the scriptures into Spanish, the opening of the first missions in South America, and the building of temples, the book provides a survey history of the Church in Argentina. This book will be of interest not only to history buffs but also to thousands of past, present, and future missionaries.

Translated by Erin Jennings

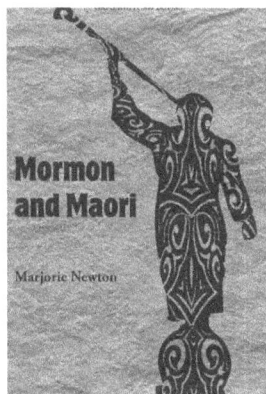

Mormon and Maori

Marjorie Newton

Paperback, ISBN: 978-1-58958-639-0

**2015 Best International Book Award,
Mormon History Association**

Praise for *The Liberal Soul*:

"*Mormon and Maori* is the result of a labor of love that reflects not years but decades of diligent research. Indeed, in combination with Newton's earlier *Tiki and Temple*, it constitutes the most detailed discussion in print of the fascinating 160-year saga of accommodation and adjustment between Maori culture and Mormonism. Unflinchingly honest yet unfailingly compassionate, *Mormon and Maori* is a must-read for anyone interested in the extraordinary history of the LDS experience in New Zealand."
— Grant Underwood, Professor of History, Brigham Young University

"*Mormon and Maori* offers a substantial historical account that structures and organizes *te iwi* Māori's (The Māori people's) often complex relationship and attachment to an American religion. In this respect Newton's work should be considered groundbreaking."
— Gina Colvin, *Journal of Mormon History*

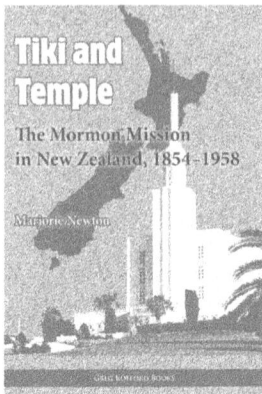

Tiki and Temple: The Mormon Mission in New Zealand, 1854–1958

Marjorie Newton

Paperback, ISBN: 978-1-58958-121-0

**2013 Best International Book Award,
Mormon History Association**

From the arrival of the first Mormon missionaries in New Zealand in 1854 until stakehood and the dedication of the Hamilton New Zealand Temple in 1958, Tiki and Temple tells the enthralling story of Mormonism's encounter with the genuinely different but surprisingly harmonious Maori culture.

Mormon interest in the Maori can be documented to 1832, soon after Joseph Smith organized the Church of Jesus Christ of Latter-day Saints in America. Under his successor Brigham Young, Mormon missionaries arrived in New Zealand in 1854, but another three decades passed before they began sustained proselytising among the Maori people—living in Maori pa, eating eels and potatoes with their fingers from communal dishes, learning to speak the language, and establishing schools. They grew to love—and were loved by—their Maori converts, whose numbers mushroomed until by 1898, when the Australasian Mission was divided, the New Zealand Mission was ten times larger than the parent Australian Mission.

The New Zealand Mission of the Mormon Church was virtually two missions—one to the English-speaking immigrants and their descendants, and one to the tangata whenua—"people of the land." The difficulties this dichotomy caused, as both leaders and converts struggled with cultural differences and their isolation from Church headquarters, make a fascinating story. Drawing on hitherto untapped sources, including missionary journals and letters and government documents, this absorbing book is the fullest narrative available of Mormonism's flourishing in New Zealand.

Although written primarily for a Latter-day Saint audience, this book fills a gap for anyone interested in an accurate and coherent account of the growth of Mormonism in New Zealand.

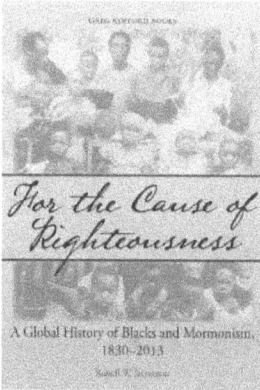

For the Cause of Righteousness: A Global History of Blacks and Mormonism, 1830-2013

Russell W. Stevenson

Paperback, ISBN: 978-1-58958-529-4

**2015 Best Book Award,
Mormon History Association**

"In Russell Stevenson's *For the Cause of Righteousness: A Global History of Blacks and Mormonism*, he extends the story of Mormonism's long-standing priesthood ban to the broader history of the Church's interaction with blacks. In so doing he introduces both relevant atmospherics and important new context. These should inform all future discussions of this surprisingly enduring subject."
— Lester E. Bush, author of "Mormonism's Negro Doctrine: An Historical Overview"

"Russell Stevenson has produced a terrific compilation. Invaluable as a historical resource, and as a troubling morality tale. The array of documents compellingly reveals the tragedy and inconsistency of racial attitudes, policies, and doctrines in the LDS tradition, and the need for eternal vigilance in negotiating a faith that must never be unmoored from humaneness."
— Terryl L. Givens, author of *Parley P. Pratt: The Apostle Paul of Mormonism* and *By the Hand of Mormon: The American Scripture that Launched a New World Religion*

"You might wonder what a White man could possibly say to two Black women about Black Mormon history. Surprisingly a whole lot! As people who consider ourselves well informed in African-American Mormon History, we found a wealth of new information in *For the Cause of Righteousness*. Russell Stevenson's well-researched exploration of Blacks and Mormonism is an informative read, not just for those interested in Black history, but American history as well."
— Tamu Smith and Zandra Vranes (a.k.a. Sistas in Zion), authors, Diary of Two Mad Black Mormons

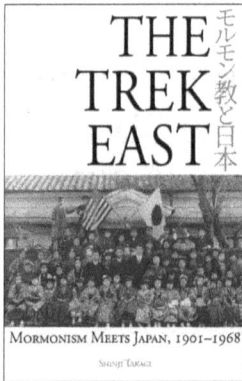

The Trek East: Mormonism Meets Japan, 1901–1968

Shinji Takagi

Paperback, ISBN: 978-1-58958-560-7
Hardcover, ISBN: 978-1-58958-561-4

2017 Best International Book Award, Mormon History Association

Praise for *The Trek East*:

"In *The Trek East*, Dr. Shinji Takagi has produced a masterful treatment of Mormonism's foundation in Japan. Takagi takes an approach that informs us of Mormonism in Japan in a manner that focuses on inputs and results, environmental conditions in Japan and cultural biases of a Mormonism informed by western assumptions."
— Meg Stout, *The Millennial Star*

"This is a wonderful book, full of historical knowledge on a lesser-known subject in LDS history. The author, who is Japanese, LDS and lives in Virginia, is deeply invested in the subject and carefully includes all sides of the history."
— Mike Whitmer, *Deseret News*

"A monumental work of scholarship. . . . I can't imagine that any future study of this period could hope to provide a more thorough and engrossing analytical study of the origins and growth of the Church in Japan. This remarkable contribution is unlikely ever to be supplanted."
— Van C. Gessel, *Journal of Mormon History*

www.ingramcontent.com/pod-product-compliance
Lightning Source LLC
Chambersburg PA
CBHW070303290326
41930CB00040B/1887